Innovation in Audio Description Research

This state-of-the-art volume covers recent developments in research on audio description, the professional practice dedicated to making audiovisual products, artistic artefacts and performances accessible to those with supplementary visual and cognitive needs. Harnessing the power of the spoken word, the projects covered in this book illustrate the value of audiovisual content descriptions not only in relation to the role of breaking down physical, cognitive and emotional barriers to entertainment, but also in informing broader media practices such as video archive retrieval, video gaming development and application software creation.

The first section maps out the field, discusses key concepts in relation to new developments and illustrates their application; the second part focuses on new audiences for AD, whilst the third part covers the impact of new technologies. Throughout this book contributors focus on methodological innovation, regarding audio description as an opportunity to engage in multi-dimensional linguistic and user-experience analysis, as it intersects with and contributes to a range of other research disciplines.

This book is key reading for researchers, advanced students and practitioners of audiovisual translation, media, film and performance studies, as well as those in related fields including cognition, narratology, computer vision and artificial intelligence.

Sabine Braun is Professor of Translation Studies and Director of the Centre for Translation Studies at the University of Surrey (UK).

Kim Starr is a Research Fellow at the Centre for Translation Studies, University of Surrey.

The IATIS Yearbook

Series editor: Sabine Braun

The International Association for Translation and Intercultural Studies (IATIS) is a worldwide forum designed to enable scholars from different regional and disciplinary backgrounds to debate issues pertinent to translation and other forms of intercultural communication.

The series aims to promote and disseminate innovative research, rigorous scholarship and critical thinking in all areas of translation studies and intercultural communication.

Authorizing Translation
Edited by Michelle Woods

Human Issues in Translation Technology
Edited by Dorothy Kenny

Interpreting and the Politics of Recognition
Edited by Christopher Stone and Lorraine Leeson

Innovation in Audio Description Research
Edited by Sabine Braun and Kim Starr

Multilingual Mediated Communication and Cognition
Edited by Ricardo Muñoz Martín and Sandra L. Halverson

For more information or to order, please go to https://www.routledge.com/The-IATIS-Yearbook/book-series/IATIS

Innovation in Audio Description Research

Edited by Sabine Braun and Kim Starr

Routledge
Taylor & Francis Group

LONDON AND NEW YORK

First published 2021
by Routledge
2 Park Square, Milton Park, Abingdon, Oxon OX14 4RN

and by Routledge
52 Vanderbilt Avenue, New York, NY 10017

Routledge is an imprint of the Taylor & Francis Group, an Informa business

British Library Cataloguing-in-Publication Data
A catalogue record for this book is available from the British Library

Library of Congress Cataloging-in-Publication Data
Names: Braun, Sabine, 1961– editor. | Starr, Kim, editor.
Title: Innovation in audio description research / edited by Sabine Braun and Kim Starr.
Description: London; New York: Routledge, 2020. |
Series: The IATIS yearbook |
Includes bibliographical references and index.
Identifiers: LCCN 2020008339 | ISBN 9781138356672 (hardback) |
ISBN 9781003052968 (ebook)
Subjects: LCSH: Audiodescription–Research. |
People with visual disabilities–Services for. | Assistive computer technology. |
Self-help devices for people with disabilities.
Classification: LCC HV1779 .I56 2020 | DDC 362.4/18–dc23
LC record available at https://lccn.loc.gov/2020008339

ISBN: 978-1-138-35667-2 (hbk)
ISBN: 978-0-367-51244-6 (pbk)
ISBN: 978-1-003-05296-8 (ebk)

Typeset in Times New Roman
by Newgen Publishing UK

In memory of our colleague David Vialard

Contents

List of contributors   ix

Introduction: Mapping new horizons in audio description research   1
SABINE BRAUN AND KIM STARR

1   Immersion, presence and engagement in audio described material   13
    LOUISE FRYER AND AGNIESZKA WALCZAK

2   New approaches to accessibility and audio description
    in museum environments   33
    CHRISTOPHER TAYLOR AND ELISA PEREGO

3   Easier audio description: exploring the potential of
    Easy-to-Read principles in simplifying AD   55
    ROCÍO BERNABÉ AND PILAR ORERO

4   Film language, film experience and film interpretation in a
    reception study comparing conventional and interpretative
    audio description styles   76
    FLORIANE BARDINI

5   Audio description 2.0: re-versioning audiovisual accessibility to
    assist emotion recognition   97
    KIM STARR AND SABINE BRAUN

6   Towards a user specification for immersive audio description   121
    CHRIS HUGHES, PILAR ORERO AND SONALI RAI

7   Mainstreaming audio description through technology   135
    ANNA JANKOWSKA

8   Comparing human and automated approaches to
    visual storytelling   159
    SABINE BRAUN, KIM STARR AND JORMA LAAKSONEN

    Index   197

Contributors

Floriane Bardini is a translator and doctoral researcher. She completed her Master's in Specialized Translation at the University of Vic – Central University of Catalonia, where she now conducts research in the field of audiovisual translation and media accessibility. She is currently writing her dissertation on film language, audio description and user experience under the supervision of Dr Eva Espasa.

Rocío Bernabé, a PhD research student in easy-to-understand media services, is Deputy Head of the Professional College of Translation and Interpreting of the SDI in Munich (Germany). She holds an MA in Translation (UGR) and an MA in Accessible Documents, Technologies and Applications (UNIR). She is also an external collaborator of the research group TransMedia Catalonia. She is the project leader of the EU co-funded project Live Text Access that aims to create certified learning materials for real-time intralingual subtitlers by respeaking and velo-typing. She is also project partner and accessibility manager of the EU co-funded project EASIT (Easy Access for Social Inclusion Training).

Sabine Braun is Professor of Translation Studies and Director of the Centre for Translation Studies at the University of Surrey (UK). Her research focuses on technology-assisted translation/interpreting and multimodality. She has led, and contributed to, many EU projects on video-mediated interpreting (e.g. AVIDICUS 1–3; SHIFT) and use of technologies in interpreter education (IVY, EVIVA). She is also currently partner in the H2020 project MeMAD, which combines computer vision, machine learning and human input to create semi-automatic descriptions of audiovisual content as a way to improve media access.

Louise Fryer works as an audio describer, trainer and Ux researcher. She has a doctorate in psychology and was Senior Teaching Fellow (2017–2020) in the Centre for Translation Studies at University College London. She was a partner in the research project ADLAB PRO (2016–2019). She is an advocate of integrated access methods, collaborating with theatre companies and film directors to help AD more closely reflect their artistic vision. Her research interests include immersion in audiovisual media.

Chris Hughes is a lecturer in Computer Science at Salford University, UK. He has worked as a researcher in the fields of data visualisation, simulation and broadcast engineering. His work has developed the concept of responsive subtitles and produced several methods for automatically recovering and phonetically realigning subtitles. He has a particular interest in accessible services and is currently focused on developing new methods for providing accessibility services within an immersive context, such as virtual reality and 360-degree video.

Anna Jankowska, PhD, works at the Chair for Translation Studies at the Jagiellonian University in Kraków and is president of the Seventh Sense Foundation – an NGO providing access services. She has participated in many research projects on audio description and supervised access services provision for many events and sites. Anna is editor-in-chief of the Journal of Audiovisual Translation, a member of the European Association for Studies in Screen Translation (ESIST) and a member of the Polish Audiovisual Translators Association.

Jorma Laaksonen received his Doctor of Science in Technology degree in 1997 from Helsinki University of Technology, Finland, and is presently a senior university lecturer at the Department of Computer Science of the Aalto University School of Science. He is an author of 30 journal and 160 conference papers on media content analysis, computer vision, pattern recognition, statistical classification, machine learning and neural networks.

Pilar Orero teaches at the Universitat Autònoma de Barcelona (Spain). She is a member of the TransMedia Catalonia research group. She participates in ITU IRG-AVA and is a member of ISO/IEC JTC1/SC35 and the Spanish UNE working group on accessibility. She is a leader of EU projects HBB4ALL, ACT and UMAQ, partner in EasyTV and ImAC (2017–2021), an active external evaluator for many worldwide national agencies, and co-founder of MAP (Media Accessibility Platform).

Elisa Perego is Associate Professor at the University of Trieste, Italy, where she teaches English linguistics and translation, translation theory, and research methodology in translation studies. Her research interests and publications mainly focus on audiovisual translation accessibility and reception; subtitling and audio description, which are studied mainly from a cognitive perspective; and empirical and cross-national research methodology. Elisa coordinated the European project ADLAB PRO (2016–2019) on audio description, and she is currently a partner in the European project EASIT (2018–2021) on easy-to-understand language in audiovisual translation.

Sonali Rai leads the Media and Broadcast Innovation Team at the Royal National Institute of Blind People. She works with stakeholders to drive policy, regulation and technical innovations on accessibility in the media, arts and culture sector in the UK. Sonali has a Master's degree in

Media and Communication (Research) and her recent work includes user assessment of immersive environments, synthetic speech for audio description and exploring viewer experience and benefits of personalisation of access services in the broadcast environment.

Kim Starr is a Research Fellow at the Centre for Translation Studies, University of Surrey. She previously worked in the financial and broadcast television sectors, finding time along the way to pursue a Bachelor's degree in politics and law (Queen Mary, University of London), and Master's degrees in journalism (Westminster) and audiovisual translation (Surrey). She was awarded a doctoral scholarship by the AHRC/TECHNE, and completed her PhD in audio description for cognitively diverse audiences in 2017. Kim currently works on the EU-funded 'Methods for Managing Audiovisual Data' (MeMAD) project.

Christopher Taylor is a full professor (retired) of English Language and Translation at the University of Trieste. He has worked in the field of film translation for many years with significant publications including, most recently, 'The Multimodal Approach in Audiovisual Translation' in a special issue of *Target* (2016) and 'Reading Images' (including moving ones) in the *Routledge Handbook of Systemic Functional Linguistics* (2017). He recently coordinated a European Union project ADLAB (Audio Description: Lifelong Access for the Blind) which achieved 'Success Story' status.

Agnieszka Walczak holds a PhD from the Universitat Autònoma de Barcelona. She is a member of the TransMedia Catalonia research group and AVT Lab research group. The main area of her research interests concerns audio description with special focus on its quality aspects and its use in educational contexts. Agnieszka professionally works as a subtitler and audio describer. She also teaches audiovisual translation at the University of Warsaw and at the Maria Curie-Skłodowska University in Lublin, Poland.

Introduction

Mapping new horizons in audio description research

Sabine Braun and Kim Starr

This volume is dedicated to recent developments in research on audio description (AD), the practice of translating images into words that is closely associated with the crucial role audiovisual content and media, and digital technologies, play in today's world. Starting as a volunteer practice to help blind and partially sighted people enjoy theatre productions (Pfanstiehl & Pfanstiehl, 1985; Described and Captioned Media Program, 2012), AD has gradually developed into a professional practice dedicated to making visual content and audiovisual products as well as artistic artefacts and performances accessible to those with visual impairment. Commercially produced AD is available in many countries now and broadcast quotas for programmes offering AD are rising due to legislative efforts aimed at meeting internationally recognised accessibility standards (United Nations, 2006) in relation to media access.

As an academic discipline, the study of AD is mostly situated within the field of translation studies, where—following Jakobson's (1959) distinction between *interlingual, intralingual* and *intersemiotic* translation—AD is conceptualised as a modality of intersemiotic translation in which images or visual elements of audiovisual material (and occasionally sounds that are incomprehensible without seeing the associated visuals) are translated into verbal descriptions (Figure 0.1). In order to make sense of the audiovisual source, audio describers use their ability to combine the different elements of the audiovisual narrative (e.g. visuals, dialogue and/or narration, sound effects, song lyrics, musical scores) into a coherent story in their mind (Braun, 2011, 2016; Vandaele, 2012). Subsequently, they decide which of the visual elements and non-identifiable sound effects are crucial for understanding the story, before verbalising the information conveyed by these elements with the aim of enabling blind audiences to create a similarly coherent story.

Some of the previous AD research has focused specifically on the intermodal nature of AD and has highlighted how the richness of the visual mode and—in relation to audiovisual material—the time restrictions imposed by the need for the descriptions to fit into hiatuses in the soundtrack make information selection and verbalisation in AD highly complex (Braun, 2011, 2016; Fresno *et al.*, 2016; Vandaele, 2012). Other AD research has centred on the linguistic realisation of different aspects of the description (e.g. Jiménez Hurtado, 2007

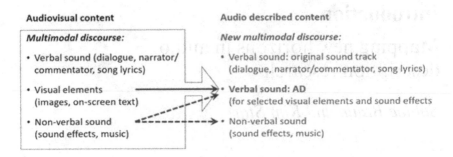

Figure 0.1 AD of audiovisual content as intersemiotic translation.

and Salway, 2007 on lexical choices; Zabrocka and Jankoswka, 2016 on co-speech gestures; Hirvonen, 2012 and Hirvonen and Tiittula, 2012 on visual and verbal representations of space in audio description; Hirvonen, 2013a on linguistic perspectivation strategies for filmic point of view; Hirvonen 2013b on similarities between visual and linguistic representations). A related area that has received attention more recently is AD style. In contrast to the classic position of AD practice, which was to 'describe just what you see', research suggests that narrative approaches which focus more holistically on the story that is told are more effective (Bardini, 2016, 2017; Kruger, 2010; Mälzer-Semlinger, 2012; Ramos Caro, 2016). A case in point in this discussion are emotions, where the traditional practice is to avoid describing emotions while reception research has shown positive effects of conveying emotions in AD (Bardini, 2017; Ramos Caro, 2016). Other research has focused on adapting the AD style and strategies to a given audiovisual genre (Davila-Montess and Orero, 2016 for adverts; Udo and Fels, 2009 for theatre; Orero, 2011 for children; Mangiron and Zhang, 2016 and Walczak and Fryer 2017 for games and other virtual reality environments).

The translation studies approach to AD has thus drawn on and extended key notions traditionally applied to the interlingual (and intralingual) mediation of verbal or multimodal text, including 'interpretation', 'equivalence' and 'rewriting', and has foregrounded the interpretive elements present in all mediation activities. An ongoing conundrum in this research is the 'objectivity' debate, i.e. the question to what extent AD can and should be objective, given that visual content often leaves much room for interpretation, with meaning being in the eye of the beholder (Fryer, 2016; Mazur and Chmiel, 2012; Remael *et al.*, 2014). Whilst this debate has at times taken a prescriptive stance, arguing that subjectivity in AD should be minimised, several points in relation to this debate are noteworthy.

On one hand, audiences often demand 'objective' AD (e.g. Lopez *et al.*, 2018). However, they may know little about how AD is created and about the difficulties associated with achieving objectivity. Televisual AD is part of the post-production process; the audio describer does not normally have access to the director and his/her artistic intentions. Like any other recipient, the describer is therefore left to his/her interpretation of the audiovisual content in question. The nature of human meaning-making is such that a degree of subjectivity in the interpretation process is inevitable in AD and other mediation/transfer activities. Thus, there will always be more than one acceptable solution, and this is further complicated by the fact that blindness is not a homogeneous condition and hence there is a demand for personalisation of audiovisual content within this community. On the other hand, recent studies suggest that an element of subjectivity may, in fact, be desirable, for example, to convey emotions (Ramos Caro, 2016), to aid character identification (Wilken and Kruger, 2016), and to increase the recipients' feeling of 'presence' or immersion (Walczak and Fryer, 2017).

However, whilst AD reception research has sought to understand the preferences of the visually impaired community as a whole, the social context of consuming films and TV programmes, i.e. the interaction between sighted and visually impaired (VI) audiences, has only recently received attention in the research community (Jankowska, 2017). Research investigating the personalisation of AD delivery reveals a variety of approaches, including individual and multiple natural voices to represent different speakers (Braun and Orero, 2010), and experiments with synthetic voices. With regard to using speech synthesis, reception research suggests that synthetic voices are acceptable to visually impaired audiences although natural voices are generally preferred (Fernández-Torné and Matamala 2015; Szarkowska 2011; Szarkowska and Jankowska, 2012; Walczak and Szarkowska, 2012).

Although complemented by other perspectives, notably universal design (Story *et al.*, 1998; Udo and Fels, 2009, 2010) and accessibility (EDeAN, 2009; Greco, 2016), the translation studies lens has largely remained the dominant paradigm for research into AD. Along with the growing body of individual papers cited above, the two most recent edited volumes on AD, Maszerowska *et al.* (2014) and Matamala and Orero (2016), testify to this, whilst also demonstrating how research in AD has gradually broadened to encompass the areas outlined above as well as novel perspectives.

The volume edited by Maszerowska *et al.* (2014) originated in the European ADLAB project. It takes a bottom-up approach to reflecting on AD practice by using one film – *Inglourious Basterds* (2009) – to illustrate a number of issues from the perspective of an international team of audio description experts. The volume has a multidisciplinary outlook, drawing from film studies, translation studies, psychology, cultural studies, linguistics and semiotics, and focuses on addressing typical AD issues from a fresh perspective. Chapter topics include audio introductions; film structure and cohesive narrative; spatio-temporal settings of narrative fiction (narratological approach) and audience mental modelling; describing cinematographic features; text on screen; AD within the context of integrating intra- and extra-diegetic sound; character naming; cultural referencing and AD; facial expressions and gestures. The volume presented by Matamala and Orero combines political overview with emerging areas of research, and exploration of AD production methods and applications. Its topics include human rights and media accessibility; research on cognitive accessibility, prioritisation of information, and description of gestures cutting across different audiovisual genres; and an update on major AD research projects such as ADLAB, DTV4ALL, ALST, AD Press Illustrations Project and the Open Art Project.

At the same time, audiovisual technologies have evolved as part of the rapid digital transformation of society, considerably reshaping not only the broadcasting and media landscape but also the offerings of museums and art exhibitions, and the nature of many live performances. Concurrent developments in broadband technology and media platforms led to the arrival of 'Web 2.0' with the advent of user-generated content and the seemingly relentless proliferation of social media.

Whilst AD has established itself as a practice and service which facilitates access to audiovisual content and art, the production and delivery of AD, which involves the preparation of an AD script, its voicing and the integration of the voiced descriptions into the original audiovisual material (or its live delivery to an audience), relies heavily on human resource. As a result, AD is currently expensive to produce. At the same time, applications of AD which engage new audiences (e.g. language learners, individuals with additional cognitive needs, multi-taskers, educators) and increase exploitation of audio described material would make commercial sense. Apart from financial considerations, the recent increase in user-generated AV content creates an additional challenge for media access, which is still to be fully embraced. Thus, the investigation of novel methods of creating AD that can reduce costs and broaden access without compromising quality is an economically and socially important area for research (Braun and Starr, 2019).

The growing demand for AD and the increasing opportunities for its production and delivery through the use of different technologies but also the emergence of technologies such as 3D video, which require novel approaches to AD, raise new questions about how AD can be efficiently produced and distributed, and who could benefit from such a service. In response to this, different technologies have emerged to support both the creation of AD and its delivery to the end user, and AD has begun to embrace newcomers in the media landscape such as virtual and immersive environments. In a similar vein, AD has been used as a tool to engage different types of audiences in audiovisual material. As a result of these developments, and facilitated by the very same digital transformation, we are witnessing the dawn of a new era in AD research: 'Audio Description 2.0'.

Concomitant with the burgeoning of digital media platforms, institutional funders are increasingly underwriting research projects which challenge the boundaries of audio description in a digital world. Recent examples of this nature include projects employing AD for applications as varied as video retrieval, immersive technological experiences and enhanced cognitive accessibility. Innovative methodologies and technological solutions, which far exceed the ambitions of AD's earliest proponents, sit at the heart of this pioneering work, offering stakeholders the opportunity to reimagine AD for the digital age. Such a seismic shift in the advancement of AD promises to pave the way for a proliferation of new platforms and services, offering groundbreaking solutions for content delivery and retrieval to different audiences.

Technological and methodological innovations and the pace of AD research generally, particularly in light of a growing trend towards inter- and transdisciplinarity, suggest that there is scope for a more contemporary survey of the AD research landscape. In this volume, which draws on research currently conducted in different countries, we aim to offer a fresh perspective and commentary on the work currently being undertaken internationally in the growing field of AD, focusing on research that is situated at the forefront of the developments outlined above.

The current volume consists of three sections. The first part discusses key concepts in relation to new developments in AD such as immersion, presence and engagement, and provides an example of their application to creating AD in a museum or heritage environment. As is the case with all chapters in this volume, both of the above chapters also make reference to methodological innovation. Taking Braun's pledge for more research into 'audience expectations with regard to type and amount of information in the descriptions' (2008: 8–9) as their point of departure, Fryer and Walczak argue in Chapter 1 that such audience research requires a measure of AD experience that can address the diversity of blind and partially sighted audiences. They show how quantitative measures of audience experience and immersion such as the ITC Sense of Presence Inventory (ITC-SOPI) (Lessiter *et al.*, 2001), which were developed and validated for the online gaming industry and virtual reality environments, can be adopted for use in AD research with only minor modification. Furthermore, drawing on the 'perceptual illusion of non-mediation' (Lombard and Ditton, 1997: 7), a classic definition of 'presence' and a multi-construct concept embracing the psychological sense of immersion in any mediated environment, the authors outline presence measures for use with AD audiences and discuss their pros and cons, including overlaps and differentiation between concepts of engagement, immersion and enjoyment. In addition, presence measures are discussed in relation to concepts in mainstream translation studies such as *skopos* and the invisibility of the translator. The chapter concludes by discussing future uses of the presence concept in AD research, highlighting that new audience experiences require adaptive AD approaches in order to make these experiences accessible to blind and partially sighted audiences.

Chapter 2, by Taylor and Perego, considers AD applied to museum contexts, architectural structures and famous landmarks in order to discuss new approaches to accessibility for blind and partially sighted audiences, based on research currently conducted in the European ADLAB PRO (2016) project. Their point of departure is the observation that modern museum environments differ greatly from their precursors, and that AD has to be shaped to accommodate the hands-on approach and the hybrid nature of many contemporary exhibition spaces. One focal point in Taylor and Perego's chapter is the use of digital technology, especially the introduction of digital end-user devices to engage audiences with a museum's offerings. The research draws on museum research and visitor studies frameworks to discuss not only how museums can facilitate access to artefacts through AD but also how this can be supported by consideration of mobility needs within and outside museum buildings. The chapter thus discusses advances in traditional methods of AD in relation to museums and architectural artefacts but also explores novel methods which, for example, exploit the sense of touch, smell and sound. This is linked to the concept of presence, as discussed by Fryer and Walczak. In line with the aims of the ADLAB PRO (2016) project to funnel the research into creating a training course for prospective museum describers, the final part of this chapter outlines the course structure and explains how it was derived from the insights gained in the project.

The second part of the volume focuses on new audiences. The contributions in this part of the volume demonstrate how methodological advances in creating AD have led to the development and investigation of different functional varieties of AD, including Easy-to-Read varieties and varieties for cognitively diverse audiences. In Chapter 3 Bernabé and Orero focus on Easy-to-Read AD to extend the use of AD to people with reading difficulties and intellectual disabilities. The authors characterise 'Easy-to-Read' as a functional variety of a national language that has gained momentum in recent years to facilitate the creation of easy-to-understand texts for people with learning difficulties and low reading skills, those with low literacy, and also the elderly, immigrants, refugees or tourists. The authors argue that 'Easy-to-Read' can in principle be exploited in the AD production process, as AD, regardless of whether it is delivered live or as part of a recorded production, is normally scripted. In their chapter, the authors discuss the process of creating easy-to-understand AD and its associated challenges. In addition, hybrid approaches to accessibility services are explored, which include 'Easy-to-Read' as well as other services such as 'Clean Audio', based on improvements of the audio channel on which AD is delivered, and technologies that can be personalised such as fast delivery or synthetic speech. Building on an audience research approach to trialling new methodologies, in Chapter 4 Bardini considers variations in AD style (traditional, cinematic and narrative) for the purposes of understanding and engaging with content as a film consumer. She explores the impact of these diverging styles on efficacy in conveying sentiment and artistic intent, with particular impact afforded to the more interpretive modalities.

In Chapter 5, Starr and Braun then discuss an approach to repurposing AD to assist emotion recognition in autistic children. The authors emphasise the key role played by visual and auditory affective markers—including facial expressions, gestures, body language, verbal prosody and musical scoring—in creating emotional engagement with audiovisual material. Arguing that unless there is a measured and conscious investment in the emotional currency of a film narrative on the part of the viewer, the entertainment value may be compromised, the authors highlight alexithymic individuals, who encounter difficulties in recognising, accessing and interpreting emotions, as a group facing an increased risk of overlooking these salient aspects of film narrative, especially where atypical cognitive frameworks such as autism, or psychological and pathological disorders such as post-traumatic stress syndrome or aphasia, are present. Against this backdrop, Starr and Braun present a study that tested the application of AD for the purpose of delivering emotion-centric information to individuals experiencing emotion recognition difficulties (ERDs). Rather than adopt standard AD techniques designed to meet the needs of blind and partially sighted audiences, an entirely new and *bespoke* style of AD focusing on the description of emotions was created. Working within a functionalist framework, two modalities of this type of AD, emotion labelling and emotion contextualisation, were subsequently trialled with high-functioning autistic children displaying symptoms of ERDs. This chapter focuses on the methods applied to creating and testing this new style of AD, reaching beyond the standard concept of AD, and opening up the potential for AD to become a bespoke service for a wide range of cognitive applications in the future.

The third part is devoted to discussing the impact of emerging technologies on the creation and production of AD. This includes a chapter discussing new approaches to AD in response to the emergence of new media environments such as 3D immersive TV, the latest trends in mainstreaming AD by developing adaptive end-user technologies for its delivery and approaches to automating the production of AD. Chapter 6, by Hughes, Orero and Rai, explores the first systematic effort to create AD for 360-degree TV, based on research currently conducted in the EU-funded H2020 Immersive Accessibility (ImAc) project (2017). The broad objective of this project is to define the requirements for accessibility services within immersive media environments such as 360-degree video, and to explore how these accessibility services can be integrated within immersive media. The chapter presents the initial experiences of blind and partially sighted AD users when interacting with audio described 360-degree content, based on observations and feedback gathered in a focus group discussion. The authors highlight two key findings. The first is the need to consider the differences between the traditional curated linear approach where the viewer consumes the content that the director wishes to show on the screen, and a non-linear approach where the viewer has control over the content and can choose their own path by interacting with the environment. The second is to explore how using audio could enhance the immersive experience and address issues surrounding the creation of a fully accessible interface for 360-degree content.

In Chapter 7, Jankoswka focuses on the use of technology to facilitate mainstreaming AD. Her chapter presents the results of a study carried out within the AudioMovie project, funded by the Polish National Centre for Research and Development, which aims to facilitate mainstreaming accessibility and has developed and tested a mobile app that allows users to play alternative audio tracks (AD and audio subtitles) in cinemas and at home. The app automatically synchronises the selected alternative audio track with the main audio track of the film. This chapter reports on the field study that was carried out to test the app in three cinemas in Poland. The study used a mixed-method design combining quantitative (survey) and qualitative (focus groups) methods. The findings show that the app met with the approval of the respondents, with over 60 per cent of the 58 blind and partially sighted survey respondents stating that the app was easy to use, and most focus group participants expressing an interest in using the app after the completion of the research. The chapter also comments on results obtained from users with other disabilities who participated in the test, including participants with dyslexia, participants with intellectual disabilities and senior citizens. The results obtained from these users suggest that the access services offered in the app are useful to these groups, thus creating synergies with Starr and Braun's findings in relation to AD users with emotion recognition difficulties.

The final chapter in this part of the volume, Chapter 8 by Braun, Starr and Laaksonen, reports on the first systematic initiative to create (semi-)automatic AD for audiovisual material. This initiative is part of the EU-funded H2020 project 'Methods for Managing Audiovisual Data: Combining Automatic Efficiency with Human Accuracy' (MeMAD). The project has its origins in the recent surge of interest in methods for describing audiovisual content, be it for the purposes of automatic image search and retrieval, for advanced visual storytelling, or as a result of an increasing demand in AD following changes in national and European broadcasting legislation to meet the needs of blind and partially sighted audiences. Although the computer vision and natural language processing communities have intensified research into the automatic generation of descriptions, even the automatic description of still images remains challenging in terms of accuracy, completeness and robustness (Husain and Bober, 2016). Descriptions of moving images and visual storytelling pose additional challenges linked to temporality, including co-referencing (Rohrbach *et al.*, 2017) and other features of narrative continuity (Huang *et al.*, 2016). This chapter reports on a study that conducts a systematic comparison of human- and machine-generated descriptions of audiovisual content, with the aim of identifying key characteristics and patterns of manually and automatically produced descriptions, and evaluating each method. The focus of the chapter is on the methodological framework for this comparison, drawing on corpus-based and discourse-based approaches, and on a preliminary evaluation of the two methods (human- and machine-generated). The broader aim of this work is to advance current understanding of multimodal content description and to contribute to enhancing content description services and technologies.

We wish to say a final word about our colleague David Vialard (Texas Tech University), who showed great enthusiasm for this volume and was working on his contribution to it shortly before his tragic and untimely death last year. David had a passion for writing and composition, seeking to turn AD 'on its head' and employ image-to-word techniques to improve creativity in writing within a classroom setting. He considered the translation of image to text inherent in AD as a rich resource for educating students to be responsible and ethical readers, writers and designers of written communication. David appreciated that engaging in the composition and analysis of AD provides an opportunity for students to develop critical modalities of visual literacy, close reading, language analysis and interpretation, regardless of dis/ability. He also believed that composition offers AD a rhetorical perspective that engenders inclusive and thoughtful design and that the intersection of writing studies and AD into a fused pedagogy has the potential to provide insights into each discipline. David's work in this field will be greatly missed, not least by ourselves, since we had selfishly very much looked forward to reading his contribution to this work. It is our sincere hope that David's research mantle will now be taken up by colleagues within the AD community and his valuable contribution used as a foundation for future research in the field of creative writing.

References

ADLAB PRO (2016) *Audio Description: A Laboratory for the Development of a New Professional Profile*. Available at: www.adlabproject.eu (accessed 14 December 2019).

Bardini, F. (2016) 'Audiovisual Translation for the Blind and Partially Sighted: Audio Description, an Indispensable Access Mode', *International Research-to-Practice Conference and Summer School of Audiovisual Translation: Audiovisual Translation in Russia and the World: Dialogue of Cultures in the Changing Global Information Space*, Saint Petersburg, 22–26 August.

Bardini, F. (2017) 'Audio Description Style and the Film Experience of Blind Spectators: Design of a Reception Study', *Rivista Internazionale di Tecnica della Traduzione / International Journal of Translation*, 19, pp. 49–73.

Braun, S. (2008) 'Audio Description Research: State of the Art and Beyond', *Translation Studies in the New Millennium*, 6, pp. 14–30.

Braun, S. (2011) 'Creating Coherence in Audio Description', *Meta*, 56(3), pp. 645–662.

Braun, S. (2016) 'The Importance of Being Relevant? A Cognitive-Pragmatic Framework for Conceptualising Audiovisual Translation', *Target: International Journal of Translation Studies*, 28(2), pp. 302–313.

Braun, S., and Orero, P. (2010) 'Audio Description with Audio Subtitling – an Emergent Modality of Audiovisual Localisation', *Perspectives: Studies in Translatology*, 18(3), pp. 173–188.

Braun, S., and Starr, K. (2019) 'Finding the Right Words: Investigating Machine-Generated Video Description Quality Using a Human-derived Corpus-based Approach', *Journal of Audiovisual Translation*, 2(2), pp. 11–35.

Davila-Montess, J., and Orero, P. (2016) 'Audio Description Washes Brighter? A Study in Brand Names and Advertising', in Matamala and Orero, pp. 123–142.

Described and Captioned Media Program (2012) *Gregory Frazier's Innovation in Audio Description*. Available at: https://dcmp.org/media/7565-gregory-frazier-s-innovation-in-audio-description (accessed 18 December 2019).

EDeAN (2009) *Principles and Practice in Europe for e-Accessibility*. Available at: https://www.toetsenmetenweten.nl/EDeAN_Publication_2009.pdf (accessed 17 December 2019).

Fernández-Torné, A., and Matamala, A. (2015) 'Text-to-Speech vs. Human Voiced Audio Descriptions: A Reception Study in Films Dubbed into Catalan', *Journal of Specialised Translation*, 24, pp. 61–88.

Fresno, N., Castellà, J., and Soler-Vilageliu, O. (2016) ' "What Should I Say?" Tentative Criteria to Prioritize Information in the Audio Description of Film Characters', in Matamala and Orero, pp. 143–167.

Fryer, L. (2016) *An Introduction to Audio Description: A Practical Guide*. Abingdon: Routledge.

Greco, G. M. (2016) 'On Accessibility as a Human Right, with an Application to Media Accessibility', in Matamala and Orero, pp. 11–33.

H2020 Immersive Accessibility (ImAc) Project (2017) Website. Available at: www.imac-project.eu (accessed 14 December 2019).

Hirvonen, M. (2012) 'Contrasting Visual and Verbal Cueing of Space: Strategies and Devices in the Audio Description of Film', *New Voices in Translation Studies*, 8, pp. 21–43.

Hirvonen, M. (2013a) 'Perspektivierungsstrategien und -mittel kontrastiv: Die Verbalisierung der Figurenperspektive in der deutschen und finnischen Audiodeskription', *trans-kom: Zeitschrift für Translationswissenschaft und Fachkommunikation*, 6(1), pp. 8–38.

Hirvonen, M. (2013b) 'Sampling Similarity in Image and Language – Figure and Ground in the Analysis of Filmic Audio Description', *SKY Journal of Linguistics*, 26, pp. 87–115.

Hirvonen, M., and Tiittula, L. (2012) 'Verfahren der Hörbarmachung von Raum: Analyse einer Hörfilmsequenz', in H. Hausendorf, L. Mondada and R. Schmitt (eds.), *Raum als interaktive Ressource*. Tübingen: Narr, pp. 381–427.

Huang, T. H., Ferraro, F., Mostafazadeh, N., Misra, I., Agrawal, A., Devlin, J., Girshick, R., He, X., Kohli, P., Dhruv, B., Zitnick, C., Parikh, D., Vanderwende, L., Galley, M., and Mitchell, M. (2016) 'Visual Storytelling', *Proceedings of Naacl-Hlt*, San Diego, California, 12–17 June, pp. 1233–1239.

Husain, S. S., and Bober, M. (2016) 'Improving Large-scale Image Retrieval through Robust Aggregation of Local Descriptors', *IEEE Transactions on Pattern Analysis and Machine Intelligence*, 39(9), pp. 1783–1796.

Jakobson, R. (1959) 'On Linguistic Aspects of Translation', in R. A. Brower (ed.), *On Translation*, Cambridge, MA: Harvard University Press, pp. 232–239.

Jankowska, A. (2017) 'Accessibility – What Is Stopping Us?', Media Accessibility Platform International Conference, Vigo, Galicia, University of Vigo, 5–6 October.

Jiménez Hurtado, C. (2007) 'Una gramática local del guión audiodescrito: desde la semántica a la pragmática de un nuevo tipo de traducción', in C. Jiménez Hurtado (ed.), *Traducción y accesibilidad: subtitulación para sordos y audiodescripción para ciegos: nuevas modalidades de traducción audiovisual*, Frankfurt: Peter Lang, pp. 55–80.

Kruger, J. L. (2010) 'Audio Narration: Re-narrativising Film', *Perspectives: Studies in Translatology*, 18, pp. 231–249.

Lessiter, J., Freeman, J., Keogh, E., and Davidoff, J. (2001) 'A Cross-media Presence Questionnaire: The ITC-Sense of Presence Inventory', *Presence: Teleoperators & Virtual Environments*, 10(3), pp. 282–297.

Lombard, M., and Ditton, T. B. (1997) 'At the Heart of It All: The Concept of Presence', *Journal of Computer Mediated Communication*, 3(2), pp. 1–39.

Lopez, M., Kerney, G., and Hofstädter, K. (2018) 'Audio Description in the UK: What Works, What Doesn't, and Understanding the Need for Personalising Access', *British Journal of Visual Impairment*, 36(3), pp. 274–291.

Mälzer-Semlinger, N. (2012). 'Narration or Description: What Should Audio Description "Look" Like?', in E. Perego (ed.), *Emerging Topics in Translation: Audio Description*, Trieste: EUT, pp. 29–36.

Mangiron, C., and Zhang, X. 'Game Accessibility for the Blind: Current Overview and the Potential Application of Audio Description as the Way Forward', in Matamala and Orero, pp. 75–95.

Maszerowska, A., Matamala, A. and Orero, P. (eds.) (2014) *Audio Description: New Perspectives Illustrated*. Amsterdam: John Benjamins.

Matamala, A., and Orero, P. (eds.) (2016) *Researching Audio Description: New Approaches*. London: Palgrave Macmillan.

Mazur, I., and Chmiel, A. (2012) 'Audio Description Made to Measure: Reflections on Interpretation in AD Based on the Pear Tree Project Data', in A. Remael, P. Orero, and M. Carroll (eds.), *Audiovisual Translation and Media Accessibility at the Crossroads: Media for All 3*, Amsterdam: Rodopi, pp. 173–188.

Orero, P. (2011) 'Audio Description for Children: Once Upon a Time there Was a Different Audio Description for Characters', in E. Di Giovanni (ed.), *Entre texto y receptor: accesibilidad, doblaje y traducción*, Frankfurt: Peter Lang, pp. 169–184.

Pfanstiehl, M., and Pfanstiehl, C. (1985) 'The Play's the Thing: Audio Description in the Theatre', *British Journal of Visual Impairment*, 3(3), pp. 91–92.

Ramos Caro, M. (2016) 'Testing Audio Narration: The Emotional Impact of Language in Audio Description', *Perspectives: Studies in Translation Theory and Practice*, 24(4), pp. 606–634.

Remael, A., Reviers, N., and Vercauteren, G. (2014) 'Pictures Painted in Words: ADLAB Audio Description Guidelines'. Available at: http://www.adlabproject.eu/Docs/adlab%20book/index.html (accessed 13 December 2019).

Rohrbach, A., Rohrbach, M., Tang, S., Oh, S. J., and Schiele, B. (2017) 'Generating Descriptions with Grounded and Co-referenced People', *Proceedings of the IEEE Conference on Computer Vision and Pattern Recognition*. Available at: https://arxiv.org/abs/1704.01518 (accessed 20 December 2018).

Salway, A. (2007) 'A Corpus-based Analysis of the Language of Audio Description', in J. Diaz Cintas, P. Orero and A. Remael (eds.), *Media for All: Subtitling for the Deaf, Audio Description and Sign Language*, Amsterdam and New York: Rodopi, pp. 151–174.

Story, M. F., Mueller, J. L., and Mace, R. L. (1998) *The Universal Design File: Designing for People of All Ages and Abilities*. Raleigh, NC: Centre for Universal Design. Available at: http://www.ncsu.edu/ncsu/design/cud/pubs_p/pudfiletoc.htm (accessed 13 December 2019).

Szarkowska, A. (2011) 'Text-to-speech Audio Description: Towards Wider Availability of AD', *Journal of Specialised Translation*, 15(1), pp. 142–162.

Szarkowska, A., and Jankowska, A. (2012) 'Text-to-speech Audio Description of Voiced-over Films: A Case Study of Audio Described Volver in Polish', in E. Perego (ed.), *Emerging Topics in Translation: Audio Description*, Trieste: EUT (Edizioni Università di Trieste), pp. 81–98.

Udo, J. P., and Fels, D. I. (2009) 'Suit the Action to the Word, the Word to the Action: An Unconventional Approach to Describing Shakespeare's *Hamlet*', *Journal of Visual Impairment and Blindness*, 103(3), pp. 178–183.

Udo, J. P., and Fels, D. I. (2010) 'Universal Design on Stage: Live Audio Description for Theatrical Performances', *Perspectives: Studies in Translatology*, 18(3), pp. 189–203.

United Nations (2006) *Convention on the Rights of Persons with Disabilities (CRPD)*. Available at: www.un.org/development/desa/disabilities/convention-on-the-rights-of-persons-with-disabilities.html (accessed 14 December 2019).

Vandaele, J. (2012) 'What Meets the Eye: Cognitive Narratology for Audio Description', *Perspectives: Studies in Translatology*, 20(1), pp. 87–102.

Walczak, A., and Fryer, L. (2017) 'Creative Description: The Impact of Audio Description on Presence in Visually Impaired Audiences', *British Journal of Visual Impairment*, 35(1), pp. 6–17.

Walczak, A., and Szarkowska, A. (2012) 'Text-to-speech Audio Description of Educational Materials for Visually Impaired Children', in S. Bruti and E. Di Giovanni (eds.), *Audiovisual Translation across Europe: An Ever-changing Landscape*, Bern: Peter Lang, pp. 209–234.

Wilken, N., and Kruger, J. (2016) 'Putting the Audience in the Picture: Mise-en-Shot and Psychological Immersion in Audio Described Film', *Across Languages and Cultures*, 17(2), pp. 251–270.

Zabrocka, M., and Jankowska, A. (2016) 'How Co-speech Gestures are Rendered in Audio Description: A Case Study', in Matamala and Orero, pp. 123–142.

Filmography

Inglourious Basterds (2009) directed by Quentin Tarantino. [Feature film]. USA: Weinstein Company.

1 Immersion, presence and engagement in audio described material

Louise Fryer and Agnieszka Walczak

1.1 Introduction

Audio description (AD) has been embraced by the rapidly growing field of media accessibility (MA). According to Greco (2018: 206), studies concerned with accessibility have been at the centre of a revolution, gradually 'giving rise to a plethora of fruitful new ideas, methods and models, and becoming an ever more key issue within a process that is reshaping the very fabric of society'. In evidence, Greco cites the United Nations Convention on the Rights of Persons with Disabilities (UNCRPD), which came into force in May 2008. In Matamala and Orero's view (2017) this shifted AD research from being a user-focused service to one considered from the perspective of human rights. This is because the convention requires signatory countries to

> recognize the right of persons with disabilities to take part on an equal basis with others in cultural life, and [...] take all appropriate measures to ensure that persons with disabilities enjoy access to cultural materials in accessible formats.
>
> (UNCRPD, 2008: 22)

Greco (2018: 207) further argues that the 'requirement of access entails that "everyone has an adequate quantity and quality of that object [of a human right], given their particular natural and social circumstances"'.

1.2 Audio description and the search for quality

This shift in focus from quantity to quality echoes the development of research into AD. The earliest research simply reported user response to an audiovisual stimulus, where users viewed the same stimulus with AD and with no AD (e.g. Schmeidler and Kirchner, 1996). According to Matamala and Orero (2017: 8), 'audio description "came of age" once the benefits of adding description had been established, and researchers wanted to tease out the benefits of different styles of AD'. For that to happen, it was necessary to find a measure to assess quality.

However, quality is an elusive concept. In reference to conference interpreting, Shlesinger (1997: 126) asks: 'Quality according to what criteria? Quality for whom? Do our clients know what's good for them?' Considering quality from a marketing perspective, Kurz (2001) cites Kotler and Armstrong (1994), who suggest that customer satisfaction with a purchase depends upon the product's/service's performance relative to a buyer's expectations. If the product's/service's performance falls short of expectations, the customer is dissatisfied. If performance exceeds expectations, the customer is highly satisfied or delighted (Kotler and Armstrong, 1994:553, cited in Kurz, 2001).

Although 'the service provider needs to identify the expectations of target customers concerning service quality' (Kotler and Armstrong, 1994: 646), there have been relatively few studies eliciting what blind and partially sighted people want from AD. This was understandable when the service was new as it is hard to imagine desirable features of a service in the abstract. A decade has passed since Sabine Braun called for more research into 'audience expectations with regard to type and amount of information in the descriptions' (2008: 21). Given that, in the UK at least, AD has been running as a service on television since 2003, and in live theatre since the mid 1990s (Fryer, 2016), it is high time to revisit customer expectations. There have been some attempts to do so (ADLAB PRO, 2017; Lopez *et al.*, 2018; Cavallo and Fryer, 2018). However, Fryer (2019) has also argued that AD users cannot be regarded as customers, as they are not given a choice between different products and suppliers. Their only choice is whether to listen to a product with AD or without. Often, even that limited choice is unavailable.

AD research jumped from testing the binary 'AD yes or no' scenario to testing different styles by manufacturing a 'choice' between an orthodox AD created following the Independent Television Commission (ITC) AD guidelines (ITC, 2000) and an AD style that was more emotive (Fryer and Freeman, 2014; Ramos, 2015), more cinematic (Fryer and Freeman, 2013), more creative (Walczak and Fryer, 2017) or delivered using either a human voice or synthetic speech (Fernández-Torné and Matamala, 2015; Szarkowska, 2011; Walczak and Fryer, 2018; Walczak and Szarkowska, 2012). Rather than asking users to express a simple preference between AD styles, such studies aimed to establish which was of higher quality. Testing whether amateur describers could create high-quality AD, Branje and Fels presented descriptions of a 20-minute comedy programme to 75 people who were blind or had low vision and asked them to rate the AD 'using a number of criteria, including overall quality and entertainment value' (2012: 154).

When asked about the measures used in their study, Fels (2019) replied:

> Our measures were self-developed and we have used them fairly extensively which helps with the internal validity but we have not carried out a full study looking at external validity for them. Quality is an interesting measure as there are technical (e.g., volume, speech clarity, speed, and synchronicity with visuals), and creative elements that must be accounted

for. I would suggest that as AD is ultimately a creative exercise, the concept of 'quality' must be subjectively assessed by users and will relate to expectations, genre, entertainment value, etc.

Fels's observations reflect functional approaches to translation (e.g. Reiss and Vermeer, 2014), where the *skopos* or purpose of the translation should be the lens through which the quality of a translation should be judged. This also matches another definition of quality, taken from the field of data processing, that it be 'fit for purpose' (Greco, 2017). Arguably, the *skopos* of the original content should be considered, not just the *skopos* of the translation. However, the same questions still arise: Who determines the *skopos*? Purpose for whom? Scholars are divided: Ramos (2015: 68) asserts that experiencing emotion is one of the main reasons why we watch movies, go to the theatre or expose ourselves to different audiovisual manifestations'; whereas Vercauteren (2012) proposes that for a feature film 'the intended purpose of the description process is to make the story that is told in that film, accessible to the visually impaired audience'; Fresno (2017) prioritises enjoyment, arguing 'Readers and film viewers engage with books and movies to participate in an experience that will provide some kind of gratification' (2017: 13). If emotional engagement, enjoyment and narrative understanding can be shown to be constituent parts of presence, then it follows that measuring presence is one way of measuring quality.

We argue that the intended purpose of the description process is to make the *production* accessible. This goes beyond the story to include the manner of its telling, not least the way that it is affected by media form. As an example, could Laurence Olivier's film version of Shakespeare's *Hamlet* (1948), shot in black and white with an estimated budget of £500,000, be considered to have the same purpose as the colour version directed by and starring Kenneth Branagh in 1997, with a budget of $18 million? While it is reasonable to assume that the purpose of both was to give the audience a vivid experience of Shakespeare's play, once both versions exist the purpose of the translation might change, allowing audience members to judge which of the two films best achieves the original aim. Although the story remains unchanged, the effect of the two films on the audience is unlikely to be the same. Branagh's film 'is the fullest version of the play ever committed to celluloid, running at over four hours and stuffed with special effects and star cameos' (Smith, 2000: 137) whereas Olivier's was noted for its sparsity. As a reviewer commented at the time:

> He might, too, have filled in his backgrounds more – shown us a laughing, shouting crowd following the players to the Castle and, indoors, a chambermaid passing now and then, a lackey staring fearfully at the goings on. A drama of enormous vitality and excitement is played out in a museum.
>
> (Dixon, 2014)

The Hamlet example suggests that the *skopos* of a translation is not fixed but might shift over time. It might also shift depending on media form. Although the example above features two versions of the same film, in which the media form and the story remain constant, the audience's experience of *Hamlet* on celluloid could be very different from *Hamlet* in a theatre or an opera house. The distinction between different aspects of media form has largely been neglected in AD research in favour of media content. Even content has all too often been regarded as synonymous with plot. This seems reductionist as not all content is driven by plot and such an approach overlooks, for example, the visual aesthetics of the content (for a discussion see Roofthooft *et al.*, 2018).

One way to avoid the decision as to the *skopos* of the content falling on any individual pair of subjective shoulders is to compare the response of the mainstream audience with that of the particular audience for the audio-described version of the same production. A comparative measure obviates the need for the *skopos* to be predefined, thus allowing for unexpected or changing responses. It also aligns with the role AD plays in facilitating social inclusion, which 'requires that people have access to a range of activities regarded as typical of their society' (Farrington and Farrington, 2005: 2).

For these reasons and because of the need for a pre-validated measure to gauge the experience of AD users, Fryer and Freeman (2012) trialled the use of an instrument validated in psychological studies of gaming and virtual reality (VR) designed to measure presence. This was further prompted by the comments of a blind man who stated that he could not assess the quality of the AD of a live performance because he had not noticed the AD that was mediating his experience. Since then, other qualitative research (Cavallo and Fryer, 2018: 33) has shown that this man is not alone in believing that 'the best AD is when you don't really notice it's there'. This 'perceptual illusion of non-mediation' (Lombard and Ditton, 1997: 9) is one definition of presence that underpins its appeal for audiovisual translation (AVT) researchers.

1.3 What is presence?

Lombard and Jones (2015: 30) claim that presence is 'an unusually rich and diverse concept' and is conceived differently by different researchers. The many definitions include 'suspension of disbelief' (Slater and Usoh, 1993), a user's subjective sensation of 'being there' (Barfield *et al.*, 1995), or 'the feeling of being located in a perceptible external world around the self' (Waterworth *et al.*, 2015).

Historically, the first person to mention the concept of presence with regard to 'time and space' was film theorist André Bazin in 1951. In 1959, the sociologist Irving Goffman wrote about co-presence (Lombard and Jones, 2015). Short *et al.* (1976) discussed presence in the context of technology. In 1980, Minsky coined the term 'telepresence', referring to systems that allowed people to operate technology remotely while retaining a sense of proximity summed up as the feeling of 'being there' (1980: 45). In 1997, Lombard and

Ditton theorised about six dimensions of presence: 'presence as social richness' (characterised by the quality of the social interaction), 'presence as realism' (how accurately a virtual environment represents objects, events and people), presence as transportation ('You are there', 'It is here', 'We are together'), 'presence as immersion' (blocking senses to the outside world and making it possible for the user to perceive only the artificial world or having the user mentally absorbed in the world), 'presence as social actor within a medium' (e.g. virtual guides and pets), and 'presence as medium as social actor' (the user responding to the computer itself as a social agent). Although the above vary considerably, they have one central idea in common. They represent one or more aspects that can be formally defined as 'the perceptual illusion of non-mediation' (1997: 9). As Lombard and Ditton (1997: 10) point out:

> Because it is a perceptual illusion, presence is a property of a person. However, it results from an interaction among formal and content characteristics of a medium and characteristics of a media user, and therefore it can and does vary across individuals and across time for the same individual.

It has traditionally been assumed that higher levels of presence occur in VEs characterised by higher levels of immersion. For example a 2-D film would give rise to lower levels of presence than a 3-D film, a radio play would give rise to lower levels of presence than a multi-player computer game (Steuer, 1992). However, numerous subsequent studies suggest that less inter-active media such as television, movies or even books have the potential to trigger surprisingly high levels of presence (see Gysbers *et al.*, 2004; Kim and Biocca, 1997; Wissmath *et al.*, 2009) and there is no direct relationhip between the number of senses addressed by media form and the level of presence experienced.

When it comes to measuring presence, the multiple definitions have led to a number of different instruments, according to Lombard *et al.* (2000), yet 'presence questionnaires are the most widely used measures of presence' (Lombard *et al.*, 2009: 3). In their analysis of the (dis)advantages of different presence instruments, Lombard *et al.* (2009) compare six, ranging from a six-item questionnaire developed by Slater and Usoh (1993), which addresses three aspects of transportation in immersive VEs, to a 32-item Presence Questionnaire (Witmer and Singer, 1998) which is also sensitive to semi-immersive environments. Meanwhile the Measurement Effects, Conditions – Spatial Presence Questionnaire (MEC-SPQ) explicitly distinguishes presence, involvement and attention with three eight-item subscales (Vorderer *et al.*, 2004).

Finally, there is the Independent Television Commission – Sense of Presence Inventory (ITC-SOPI), which comprises four subscales: ecological validity (realism), spatial presence, engagement and negative effects (Lessiter *et al.*, 2001). The ITC-SOPI is discussed below. Of these, Lombard *et al.* (2009: 5) consider that none measures all dimensions of presence and that 'only the MEC-SPQ and ITC-SOPI [...] are cross-media measures of presence that have demonstrated evidence of validity, sensitivity, and reliability'. The next sections discuss some of the dimensions of presence, starting with engagement, which is itself a multi-construct concept that is often used interchangeably with interest, enjoyment and immersion.

1.4 What is engagement?

In their paper introducing the ITC-SOPI, Lessiter *et al.* (2001) suggest that engagement is one of the subscales of presence but that the literature is divided as to whether engagement and its corollary, interest, are determinants or correlates of presence. Fresno settles on curiosity or continuing interest as the distinguishing feature of engagement, arguing that an engaged spectator will 'wish to know what will happen next' (2017: 16). In terms of measuring AD, this way of understanding engagement underlines why presence measures should be favoured over measures of comprehension. Even if audiences are able to answer comprehension questions successfully, the AD may be said to have failed if they 'switch off' either literally or metaphorically because they are not engaged.

Fresno (2017) raises concerns that the term engagement is used interchangeably with enjoyment and immersion. Surprisingly, Fresno's own definition fails to separate two of those three concepts, defining engagement as 'a state in which film spectators are immersed and keep interest in the story' (2017: 14). Similarly, to measure 'presence as engagement', Lombard *et al.* (2009) used two questions, the first of which also conflates engagement and immersion: 'To what extent did you feel mentally immersed in the experience?' and 'How involving was the experience?' Our own understanding of immersion is outlined below. Presence measures were developed with gamers in VEs in mind 'for whom the desire to continue playing is considered a fundamental indicator of engagement' (Schønau-Fog and Bjørner, cited by Fresno, 2017: 14). Turning to the ITC-SOPI, the measure was developed from 63 items to which 604 participants responded. A method of statistical analysis known as Principal Axis Factoring (PAF), which identifies the main factors that account for correlations in a set of variables and therefore sheds light on which ideas contribute to a particular concept, revealed that 13 items in the inventory loaded onto the concept of engagement accounting for 11.1 per cent of the variance between individual responses. These items include a sense of transportation, memorability, enjoyment, intensity, emotion and immersion as well as a desire for the experience to continue.

From this, it is clear that the user's interest in the experience continuing is only one element of engagement. The ITC-SOPI developers conclude that engagement 'provides a measure of a user's involvement and interest in the content of the displayed environment, and their general enjoyment of the media experience' (Lessiter *et al.*, 2001: 293). Later in her argument Fresno rejects enjoyment in favour of comprehension. She suggests that in order for a spectator to become engaged they 'must have experienced some kind of prior psychological involvement with the narrative' (Fresno, 2017: 16). Furthermore, citing Busselle and Bilandzic (2009), she argues that comprehension is a necessary condition to facilitate such involvement, although Busselle and Bilandzic themselves report a weaker correlation between transportation and narrative understanding than between transportation and other factors such as emotional engagement, attentional focus and identification with characters (2009: 338). Fresno clarifies that narrative understanding does not equate to having to understand every aspect of every scene, and research in AD has shown no correlation between comprehension and engagement (e.g. Fryer and Freeman, 2014; Walczak and Fryer, 2017, 2018). These studies replicate earlier findings in computer game research. For example Jennett *et al.* (2008: 643) argue that the game *Myst IV* 'does not have clear goals and it is only through playing the game that the player in time works out what is going on and what needs to be done'; nonetheless players still find it satisfying and immersive.

McShane and Nirenberg (2015) argue that it is sufficient for the listener to understand only enough that they can move on to the actionable part of their goal, which we propose would be enjoyment of the film. Mention of the medium here is a deliberate choice, because the same narrative could be more or less engaging in different media. Presence is known to be affected by media form (Dillon *et al.*, 2000) as well as by media content (Lessiter *et al.*, 2001). As Lessiter *et al.* (2001: 293) express the matter: 'Other questions that comprise this scale [engagement] relate to arousal and emotionality. These are likely to be influenced by the media content, but also intensified by the media form.' Arousal refers to being alert, tense, excited or ready at the high end of the scale and tired, calm, bored or inactive at the other. We return to the role of emotion below.

Research by Lopez *et al.* (2018) into what works for AD users in the UK, found 86 per cent of their 127 blind and partially sighted participants agreed that AD made them feel engaged with the film or television programme. While the participants' understanding of engagement was undefined, it could be presumed to include at least some of the elements discussed above. Whether or not it comprised enjoyment is unclear as Lopez and her colleagues coupled engagement and enjoyment in their list of preferred features of AD from which participants could choose ('increase of enjoyment and engagement') (2018: 287).

As part of their research underpinning the creation of course materials for the training of new audio describers, the ADLAB PRO (2017) project team surveyed one hundred AD users about which aspects of AD they appreciated the most. Multiple answers were possible, making the results hard to interpret. The options distinguished between the narrative contribution of the AD ('the description helps you follow the story') and the degree to which the AD is emotionally engaging ('gives the listener an emotional experience'). This survey conflated engagement and emotion, which proved to be less important for the participants (achieving 47 counts) compared with following the story, which at 71 received the highest number of counts of any option.

It should also be noted that for some presence researchers, engagement is synonymous with attention (Darken *et al.*, 1999). Darken and colleagues found that the addition of sound to visual material increased attention and engagement for sighted participants and that attention correlated well with presence measures.

From this it is clear that while promoting engagement is an important goal for AD, and a hallmark of its quality, scholars have failed to agree on exactly what distinguishes engagement, interest, narrative understanding and immersion. For Slater and Wilbur the distinction lies between the technology and the experience of the individual user, such that 'immersion includes the extent to which the computer displays are extensive, surrounding, inclusive, vivid and matching' whereas 'presence is a state of consciousness, the (psychological) sense of being in the virtual environment' (1997: 603–604). Arguably this presents a problem for the audio describer who has no control over the form of the medium, or the extent to which it is immersive. However, research into hypertext and cognitive schemas by Douglas and Hargadon (2000:1 54) suggests that immersion is not purely determined by media form but also depends on the story:

> The pleasures of immersion stem from our being completely absorbed within the ebb and flow of a familiar narrative schema. The pleasures of engagement tend to come from our ability to recognize a work's overturning or conjoining conflicting schemas from a perspective outside the text, our perspective removed from any single schema. Our enjoyment in engagement lies in our ability to call upon a range of schemas, grappling with an awareness of text, convention, even of secondary criticism and whatever guesses we might venture in the direction of authorial intention.

For Douglas and Hargadon, therefore, immersion equates to absorption whereas engagement allows a small part of our attention (perhaps curiosity, which is discussed in the next section) to monitor the experience for prototypical occurrences and those that defy expectation. Returning to *Hamlet*, then, it is not the story per se that keeps us engaged as we are likely already aware that (spoiler alert) Ophelia will drown herself and that her brother Laertes will be slain. Rather it is the subversions that Branagh makes to Olivier's version and to Shakespeare's original that hook us and draw us in, and provide us with topics of conversation in the bar afterwards.

It is this 'bar mark' that we argue represents the ultimate goal of AD, stemming from some of the earliest AD research, which found that adding AD to science programmes helped legally blind adults feel more comfortable talking about them with sighted people (Schmeidler and Kirchner, 2001).

1.5 Engagement and curiosity

Arnone *et al.* advance a model that links engagement with interest and in particular with curiosity, which they describe as a 'powerful motivator of behaviour, initiating actions directed at exploring one's environment to resolve
uncertainty and make the novel known' (2011: 181). Their model arose from
exploring the use of technology in learning environments where they are also
cautious not to 'overwhelm and distract by providing more information than
can be organized and processed to determine relevance' (2011: 182). Although
AD has mostly been studied in terms of entertainment rather than education,
the issues of AD density, with its potential for cognitive overload, and of
relevance, as a means for determining which visual information to include,
have been of concern to researchers in AD (Braun, 2007, 2011, 2016; Marzà
Ibañez, 2010; Vercauteren, 2012).

1.6 Emotion, engagement and movement

As stated above, more emotive material is deemed to be more immersive. Yet
Bianchi-Berthouze *et al.* (2007) suggest that presence research has overlooked
the importance of body posture and movement as non-verbal means of communicating emotion. Body posture and proxemics function cross-culturally
and are considered important to audio describe (Remael *et al.*, 2015;
Margolies and Smith, forthcoming). Moreover, not only does observed body
posture of characters in a VE influence the emotions experienced by the user,
but also the body posture of the user will influence their affective state in the
course of the experience (Mehrabian and Friar 1969; Peter and Herbon, 2006;
Rambusch 2006).

The research cited above has tended to concentrate on how the player moves
or the manipulation of the controller to play the game, which is of limited relevance to AD. However, it is possible that the interactive and perambulatory
nature of enhanced AD elements such as the touch tour might go some way
to explaining why, amongst all the elements of access provision for an opera,
people with sight loss enjoyed touch tours the most (Eardley-Weaver, 2014).

Having explored the psychological concepts relevant to engagement, this
chapter turns next to those relevant to immersion to further distinguish
the two.

1.7 Immersion

According to the definition postulated by Janet Murray (1997: 98),
immersion is:

> a metaphorical term derived from the physical experience of being
> submerged in water. We seek the same feeling from a psychologically

immersive experience that we do from a plunge in the ocean or swimming pool: the sensation of being surrounded by a completely other reality, as different as water is from air, that takes over all of our attention, our whole perceptual apparatus. We enjoy the movement out of our familiar world, the feeling of alertness that comes from being in this new place, and the delight that comes from learning to move within it.

The use of immersion as a measure of engagement has, like presence, also been developed in the world of online gaming and VEs. For Jennett *et al.* (2008: 642) engagement is but the first of three distinct levels of immersion; the second level they dub 'engrossment', with the third and highest level being 'total immersion'. For Jennett *et al.*, this sense of total immersion equates to presence, 'being cut off from reality to such an extent that the game was all that mattered' (2008: 642). However, in contrast to Lombard and Ditton (1997), for whom presence is a perceptual illusion that might vary depending on individual differences, Jennett *et al.* suggest that 'presence is only a small part of the gaming experience: whereas presence is often viewed as a state of mind, we argue that immersion is an experience in time' (2008: 643). This suggests that an individual may be immersed for the duration of game, play or film, particularly in the latter stages as they get more engrossed, but only be psychologically transported for part of it.

1.8 Systems of measurement

Having established that engagement and immersion are distinct, constituent parts of presence and that presence is a way of measuring quality, this section will discuss ways in which presence measures can be practically administered as well as the challenges they present. As mentioned above, most presence research in AD has used the ITC-SOPI. Participants are asked to rate 44 statements on a 1–5 Likert scale (where 1 = strongly disagree and 5 = strongly agree). One difficulty is that when working with participants with visual impairments, all the items have to be read out by the researcher who then logs the response. This is problematic in a number of respects. First, for both the researcher and the participant, it is tiring and time-consuming; secondly, the lack of anonymity exacerbates the likelihood of the participant saying what they think the researcher wants to hear. This is known as social desirability bias. Furthermore, presence measures are 'self-report', meaning that they are subjective, relying on the participant's own perception of their experience. And finally, the ITC-SOPI has been adapted for use with AD audiences. One item, 'I had eyestrain', was omitted, being deemed inappropriate for use with people who may be more likely to experience eyestrain than the general population, or conversely may not have eyes at all. As this item does not feed into the assessment of engagement, this might not alter the measure's validity for AD purposes. One further issue raised by Kruger (2017, slide 20) is that post hoc questionnaires give only an overview of the whole experience and 'do not allow for the analysis of variation in immersion in the course of the film'. It should be noted that entire films or plays are rarely used as a stimulus. Most studies rely on short clips for the sake of practicality and it is to be wondered whether most are long enough to allow for a sense of presence to develop.

One way around the first two challenges is to use a shortened version of the ITC-SOPI (Fryer amd Freeman, 2014; Walczak and Fryer, 2017, 2018). This has 11 items, only two of which relate to engagement – 'I felt sad that my experience was over'; and, 'I had a sense that I had returned from a journey'. This removes the problem of experimenter and participant fatigue, but does little to improve social desirability bias or the issue of a post hoc questionnaire being non-continuous and dependent on memory. Some researchers have replaced multiple items with a single statement: 'I felt immersed' (Romero-Fresco and Fryer, 2016). Jennett *et al.* (2008) argue that the problem with the single-item questionnaire is that the item tends to be underdefined or undefined and that it requires respondents to have an understanding of what is meant by the item. However, in their own series of experiments, they found that a single-question measure of immersion correlated highly with a multiple-question measure. It also correlated highly with neurophysiological measures. A separate study using eye-tracking (Jennett *et al.*, 2008) showed an increase in eye-movements towards the end of an immersion experiment, which the researchers put down to growing distraction and a decrease in immersion.

Neurophysiological measures have also been employed in AD research (see Fryer *et al.*, 2013; Fryer and Freeman, 2014; Kruger *et al.*, 2016; Ramos, 2015). These have included HR (heart rate), GSR (galvanic skin response) and EEG (electroencephalography). These overcome some of the difficulties raised by self-response measures. Neurophysiological measures are continuous. They cannot be influenced by social desirability bias, as they cannot be faked. They nevertheless introduce problems of their own (see Fryer, 2018 for a discussion). In particular, they are ecologically invalid. In real life, no-one goes to watch a movie with electrodes attached. They are also hard to administer and to interpret. For example Kruger *et al.* (2016) theorise that a decrease in coherence between levels in the beta band (12–30 Hz) of the electrical signal in two parts of the brain – the prefrontal cortex (PFC), which is linked to executive function and attention, and the post parietal cortex (PPC), which is linked to the imagination – indicates a decrease in activity in the amygdala, which controls our imaginative and emotional response. They speculate that this lessens the inhibition of those responses, meaning we are more affected by the stimulus. Yet it could equally be the case that reduced activity in the PFC indicates that the source material is easier to process with the addition of AD or subtitles. Kruger *et al.* argue instead that the additional information from the AVT 'inevitably increases cognitive load' (2016: 173). As much work remains to be done to understand cognitive load, this argument has yet to be substantiated.

The above discussion shows that the weakness of using presence, as a means to measure quality of experience, is its complexity. Yet this can also be seen as an advantage in that it highlights the complexity of an audience's viewing experience. By contrast, measuring immersion and emotional engagement, both of which can be applied to a variety of AD styles and media forms, one avoids the limitations of comprehension and narrative understanding.

1.9 Interactivity, AD and future directions

So far, it has been established that research into AD has appropriated measures from the fields of new technology, namely online gaming and VEs. An immersive VE is defined by Slater and Usoh (1993: 90) as one in which 'sensory input to the user from the external world is, ideally, wholly provided by the computer generated displays'. As the principal products tested in AD research to date have been clips from 2-D films and television, the area where this fit is least complete lies in the sphere of interactivity. For example one of the earliest presence questionnaires (Witmer and Singer, 1998) includes items concerning a sense of control. Witmer and Singer (1998: 227) argue that immersion is reduced to 'the extent that users find interaction with (and control of) a VE awkward'. Although a sense of control is not to be expected with mainstream media, research is beginning into 'possible ways of integrating AD and additional access services [...] in 360 degree contents' (Fidyka and Matamala, 2018: 285). The distinguishing feature of immersive or omnidirectional videos for sighted users is that they offer the viewer a choice of where to look, putting the viewer in control.

A small focus group conducted at the RNIB tested the AD, which was delivered live by a professional audio describer (Roz Chalmers), of a four-minute clip of a David Attenborough documentary about dinosaurs filmed in a 360-degree format[1] (Fidyka and Matamala, 2018). In order to emulate a 360-degree environment, a cursor provided within the video allows the user to shift focus to different views.

> For example, instead of watching David gaze at the dinosaur during the first break in voiceover, the view could be panned left to the mountains in the distance. In the trial, the audio description changed as it referred to the on-screen elements now in view. This resulted in participants mostly feeling disconnected with the storyline and [they] found the description to be repetitive and missing important details.
>
> (Fidyka and Matamala, 2018: 291)

Furthermore, 'although the description was appreciated in terms of making the story clear, some felt it lacked the elements to build the atmosphere needed for an immersive experience' (Fidyka and Matamala, 2018: 291). The researchers concluded that 'a lot more would be needed than just audio description to make the environment more immersive for people with significant sight loss and that getting the right balance without information loss would be difficult' (Fidyka and Matamala, 2018: 291). Given the comments above about attention and sound, it is possible that a more immersive sound-track delivered binaurally would make the media form more immersive for AD users.

1.10 Describing a virtual art gallery: a case study

The concerns of the focus group in relation to a narrative clip may not equally apply to non-narrative source material. For example one problem encountered by the focus group was that 'While the 360 degree movement seemed to enhance the overall immersive experience visually, it was almost impossible to simulate that experience in audio given the brief gaps in voice-over' (Fidyka and Matamala, 2018: 291).

One general shortcoming of AD research is that it has largely ignored what Cámara and Espasa call 'the uncharted territory of dynamic images in non-fictional scientific documents' (2011: 416), for example documentaries. Limited attention has also been addressed to the AD of static images in arts venues and heritage sites. Consequently, the final part of this chapter considers the role of presence measures in relation to the AD of an immersive environment in a non-narrative context, namely a VR recreation of paintings displayed in the Palace of Whitehall, created for the Royal Collection (Surface Impression, n.d.). A contemporary inventory remains from which it was possible to 'place' the virtual paintings in each virtual room in their original positions.

The recreation is accessed from a website. The rooms are navigated on a computer using a mouse, or via an optical head-mounted display where a tilt of the head allows the viewer to 'move' around the room and view more closely whichever picture takes their fancy. For a pilot, the first room was described by VocalEyes. The challenge for the audio describer (the first author) was not only to describe the paintings, but also to recreate the feeling of 'visiting' the room in order to convey a sense of the immersive media form and to repro-duce the sense of presence experienced by sighted virtual visitors.

The description begins with a few lines in the manner of an audio introduc-tion, providing the context both to the Palace and to how it has been recreated, before giving a sense of spatiotemporal setting which is the recommended starting point for all modes of AD (Vercauteren, 2012).

> This is a Virtual Reality recreation of the three Privy Lodging Rooms in the Palace of Whitehall – the main residence of English monarchs from 1530 until it was destroyed by fire in 1698. Here, Charles I housed paintings from his extensive collections.

The use of an external reference frame using compass points (north, south, east and west) was abandoned in favour of an ego-centred reference frame using the viewer's left and right from a single fixed point – the front wall, from which all other points could be determined. Use of the second person pronoun (singular) reinforced this subjective viewpoint. The use of 'you' is regarded as inclusive and can be considered as 'an intervention simply to connect, to show that they are all – writer and readers alike – engaged in the same game and are in a position to draw on shared understandings' (Hyland, 2001: 562).

Features in each wall, such as windows, doors and fireplaces, were also described, not only because they were visible but also more importantly, they could be used to create a sense of movement and as reference points for orientation. Research into the navigation strategies of people with sight loss shows that small non-visual 'milestones' that can be accessed via multimodal features, and attention to surfaces underfoot, help blind people keep on track between major landmarks (Fryer *et al.*, 2013). Consequently, it was felt that incorporating this type of detail would make the AD more ecologically valid and thus give a greater sense of presence.

> Only one piece of furniture is mentioned in the inventory, so in this simulation, the rooms are largely bare. Wooden floorboards are covered by a central carpet, grey with an open weave. The walls are wood-panelled and light comes in through a tall, deep-set window with diamond leaded panes in the front wall. The thickness of the wall creates a window seat. A door in the sidewall close to the windows stands open, leading through to the other rooms in turn. On entering this first room, through a door in one corner near the front wall, immediately to your left on the inside wall a fire flickers in a metal fire basket on a stone hearth. Above the fireplace and cheek by jowl on every wall, even above the doors are paintings, most in ornate gold frames. The First Privy Lodging Room contains twelve: 11 attributed in the inventory to the Venetian artist Titian and one to Correggio. This room is a shrine to Titian whose subjects range from the sacred to the flagrantly erotic. As well as the rooms at the Royal Palace of Alcázar seen in Madrid, Charles I may have been influenced by Sir Anthony van Dyck who also devised a room hung exclusively with paintings by the artist, known as Van Dyck's 'Cabinet de Titian', which Charles would have visited and was perhaps attempting to emulate. As the simulation starts, the room is brought to life, each turn of the head or click of the mouse bringing a different wall of paintings into view.

These opening lines were followed by a list of the painting titles, each augmented by a brief description taken from the seventeenth-century inventory, for example 'Titian: Naked sitting Woman putting on a Smock, with both hands, life-size, half-length, light from the right'.

Clicking on the title above resulted in the AD user hearing the following description, which this time makes use of the first person pronoun (plural):

> Venus sits side on to us filling the frame, her back to a green curtain hanging down the right side that tucks under the curve of her buttock. Her fleshy thigh runs parallel with the lower edge of the painting and its plain

wooden frame. It's not possible to see what she's sitting on and the back-ground is black. Although her body is side on, Venus looks towards us. Her strawberry blonde hair is scraped back from her forehead and secured by a thick plait behind neat ears, only the left being visible. Her arms hold up a white muslin smock, her right arm disappearing into a sleeve. Her left arm bunches the fabric, whether to pull the smock on or having just removed it, isn't clear. Some of the fabric falls across her thigh, drifting across her rounded stomach, close to the swell of her plump left breast and up past her face. She has finely drawn eyebrows, a neat nose, rosebud lips and a faint blush on her cheeks as she eyes us, faintly surprised.

In this way, the VR AD replicated options given in a conventional audio descriptive guide and perhaps simulated the kind of autonomy offered to sighted people whose attention would be captured by a particular painting according to colour, size or any feature that sparked their curiosity, encouraging them to 'zoom' in to see more. It might also be the case that even this degree of control was missing from the 360-degree experiment, perhaps explaining why participants failed to find it immersive.

It remains to be tested whether this limited degree of interactivity is enough to replicate for AD users the experience of sighted viewers. However, it is hoped that this is enough to demonstrate how research into presence can inform the development of AD as more immersive forms of media become mainstream. Furthermore, despite the shortcomings of presence measures, we suggest that they have enabled research in AVT to go beyond user preference to 'tease out the benefits of different styles of AD' as Matamala and Orero (2017) suggest.

1.11 Conclusion

This chapter has endeavoured to untangle the concepts of engagement, immersion and presence and show how they have enabled AD researchers to compare different styles of description, using validated quantitative measures that allow the experiences of mainstream and particular audiences to be compared. Beyond that, an understanding of what makes media immersive and engaging can help inform describers as to the importance of understanding media form and hence which elements to prioritise in their AD. With regards to more immersive media forms, attention should be given to reflecting a sense of movement, adopting an ego-centred reference frame and allowing for user autonomy through interactivity. More consideration should be given to the use of the first/second person in addressing audiences, such that the user feels herself to be within the environment rather than a detached observer of it. Finally, it is hoped that presence measures will be applied to future AD research in order to achieve a greater understanding of the viewer experience.

Note

1   The clip can be accessed here: www.youtube.com/watch?v=rfh-64s5va4.

References

ADLAB PRO (2017) *Audio Description Professional: Profile Definition.* Available at: www.adlabpro.eu/wp-content/uploads/2018/04/IO2-REPORT-Final.pdf (accessed 10 December 2019).

Arnone, M.P., Small, R.V., Chauncey, S.A., and McKenna, H.P. (2011) 'Curiosity, interest and engagement in technology-pervasive learning environments: a new research agenda', *Educational Technology Research and Development*, 59(2), pp. 181–198.,

Barfield, W., Zeltzer, D., Sheridan, T.B., and Slater, M. (1995) 'Presence and performance within virtual environments', in W. Barfield and T.A. Furness (eds.), *Virtual Environments and Advanced Interface Design*. Oxford: Oxford University Press, pp. 473–541.

Bazin, A. (1967) *What Is Cinema?*. Translated by H. Gray. Los Angeles: University of California Press.

Bianchi-Berthouze, N., Kim, W.W., and Patel, D. (2007) 'Does body movement engage you more in digital game play? And why?', in A.C.R. Paiva, R. Prada and R.W. Picard (eds.), *Affective Computing and Intelligent Interaction (ACII)*, Berlin and Heidelberg: Springer, pp. 102–113.

Branje, C.J., and Fels, D.I. (2012) 'Livedescribe: can amateur describers create high-quality audio description?', *Journal of Visual Impairment & Blindness*, 106(3), pp. 154–165.

Braun, S. (2007) 'Audio description from a discourse perspective: a socially relevant framework for research and training', *Linguistica Antverpiensia, New Series – Themes in Translation Studies*, 6, pp. 357–369.

Braun, S. (2008) 'Audio description research: state of the art and beyond', *Translation Studies in the New Millennium*, 6, pp. 14–30.

Braun, S. (2011) 'Creating coherence in audio description', *Meta*, 56(3), pp. 645–662.

Braun, S. (2016) 'The importance of being relevant? A cognitive-pragmatic framework for conceptualising audiovisual translation', *Target: International Journal of Translation Studies*, 28(2), pp. 302–313.

Busselle, R., and Bilandzic, H. (2009) 'Measuring narrative engagement', *Media Psychology*, 12, pp. 321–347.

Cámara, L., and Espasa, E. (2011) 'The audio description of scientific multimedia', *Translator*, 17(2), pp. 415–437.

Cavallo, A., and Fryer, L. (2018) 'Integrated access inquiry 2017–18 report'. Available at: https://extant.org.uk/access/is-it-working (accessed 25 April 2020).

Darken, R.P., Bernatovich, D., Lawson, J.P., and Peterson, B. (1999) 'Quantitative measures of presence in virtual environments: the roles of attention and spatial comprehension', *CyberPsychology & Behavior*, 2(4), pp. 337–347.

Dillon, C., Keogh, E., Freeman, J., and Davidoff, J. (2000) 'Aroused and immersed: the psychophysiology of presence', Proceedings of 3rd International Workshop on Presence, Delft University of Technology, Delft, the Netherlands, 27–28 March.

Dixon, C. (2014) 'Shakespeare: Laurence Olivier as Hamlet: original 1948 Telegraph review'. Available at: www.telegraph.co.uk/culture/theatre/william-shakespeare/10782898/Shakespeare-Laurence-Olivier-as-Hamlet-original-1948-Telegraph-review.html (accessed 5 December 2019).

Douglas, Y., and Hargadon, A. (2000) 'The pleasure principle: immersion, engagement, flow', *Proceedings of the Eleventh ACM on Hypertext and Hypermedia*, San Antonio: ACM, pp. 153–160.

Eardley-Weaver, S. (2014) 'Lifting the Curtain on Opera Translation and Accessibility: Translating Opera for Audiences with Varying Sensory Ability', PhD thesis, Durham University.

Farrington, J., and Farrington, C. (2005) 'Rural accessibility, social inclusion and social justice: towards conceptualisation', *Journal of Transport Geography*, 13(1), pp. 1–12.

Fels, D. (2019) Email to Louise Fryer, 1 October.

Fernández-Torné, A., and Matamala, A. (2015) 'Text-to-speech vs. human voiced audio descriptions: a reception study in films dubbed into Catalan', *Journal of Specialised Translation*, 24, pp. 61–88.

Fidyka, A., and Matamala, A. (2018) 'Audio description in 360° videos', *Translation Spaces*, 7(2), pp. 285–303.

Fresno, N. (2017) 'Approaching engagement in audio description', *Rivista internazionale di tecnica della traduzione / International Journal of Translation*, 19, pp. 13–32.

Fryer, L. (2016) *An Introduction to Audio description: A Practical Guide*. London: Routledge.

Fryer, L. (2018) 'Psycholinguistics and perception in audiovisual translation', in Luis Pérez-González (ed.), *The Routledge Handbook of Audiovisual Translation*, Abingdon: Routledge, pp. 225–240.

Fryer, L. (2019) 'Quality assessment in audio description: lessons learned from interpreting', in E. Huertas-Barros, S. Vandepitte and E. Iglesias-Fernandez (eds.), *Quality assurance and assessment practices in translation and interpreting*, Hershey, PA: IGI Global, pp. 155–177.

Fryer, L., and Freeman, J. (2012) 'Presence in those with and without sight: audio description and its potential for virtual reality applications', *Journal of CyberTherapy and Rehabilitation*, 5(1), pp. 15–23.

Fryer, L., and Freeman, J. (2013) 'Cinematic language and the description of film: keeping AD users in the frame', *Perspectives*, 21(3), pp. 412–426.

Fryer, L., and Freeman, J. (2014) 'Can you feel what I'm saying? The impact of verbal information on emotion elicitation and presence in people with a visual impairment', in A. Felnhofer and O.D. Kothgassner (eds.), *Challenging Presence: Proceedings of the 15th international Conference on Presence*, Vienna: Facultas WUV, pp. 99–107.

Fryer, L., Freeman, J., and Pring, L. (2013) 'What verbal orientation information do blind and partially sighted people need to find their way around? A study of everyday navigation strategies in people with impaired vision', *British Journal of Visual Impairment*, 31(2), pp. 123–138.

Greco, G.M. (2017) 'Understanding media accessibility quality (UMAQ)'. Paper presented at Media Accessibility Platform International Conference (MAPIC), Vigo, 5 October.

Greco, G.M. (2018) 'The nature of accessibility studies', *Journal of Audiovisual Translation*, 1(1), pp. 205–232.

Gysbers, A., Klimmt, C., Hartmann, T., Nosper, A., and Vorderer, P. (2004) 'Exploring the book problem: text design, mental representations of space, and spatial presence in readers', in Proceedings of the 7th International Workshop on Presence, Technical University of Valencia, Valencia, 13–15 October, pp. 13–20.

Hyland, K. (2001) 'Bringing in the reader: addressee features in academic articles', *Written Communication*, 18(4), pp. 549–574.

Independent Television Commission (2000) *ITC Guidance on Standards for Audio Description*. Available at: http://audiodescription.co.uk/uploads/general/itcguide_ sds_audio_desc_word3.pdf (accessed 17 November 2018).

Jennett, C., Cox, A.L., Cairns, P., Dhoparee, S., Epps, A., Tijs, T., and Walton, A. (2008) 'Measuring and defining the experience of immersion in games', *International Journal of Human-Computer Studies*, 66(9), pp. 641–661.

Kim, T., and Biocca, F. (1997) 'Telepresence via television: two dimensions of telepresence may have different connections to memory and persuasion', *Journal of Computer-Mediated Communication*, 3(2). Available at: www.ascusc.org/jcmc/vol3/issue2/kim.html (accessed 12 December 2018).

Kotler, P., and Armstrong, G. (1994) *Principles of Marketing*, 6th edn, Englewood Cliffs, NJ: Prentice-Hall.

Kruger, J. (2017) 'Beta coherence as objective measure of immersion'. Paper presented at Advanced Research Seminar in Audio Description (ARSAD), Barcelona, 16 March. Available at: http://grupsderecerca.uab.cat/arsad/sites/grupsderecerca.uab.cat.arsad/files/kruger_arsad_2017.pdf (23 May 2020).

Kruger, J.L., Sanfiel, M.T.S., Doherty, S., and Ibrahim, R. (2016) 'Towards a cognitive audiovisual translatology', *Reembedding Translation Process Research*, 128, p. 171.

Kurz, I. (2001) 'Conference interpreting: quality in the ears of the user', *Meta: Journal des traducteurs / Meta: Translators' Journal,* 46(2), pp. 394–409.

Lessiter, J., Freeman, J., Keogh, E., and Davidoff, J. (2001) 'A cross-media presence questionnaire: the ITC-Sense of Presence Inventory', *Presence: Teleoperators and Virtual Environments*, 10(3), pp. 282–297.

Lombard, M., and Ditton, T.B. (1997) 'At the heart of it all: the concept of presence', *Journal of Computer Mediated Communication*, 3(2), pp. 1–39.

Lombard, M., Ditton, T.B., Crane, D., Davis, B., Gil-Egui, G., Horvath, K., Rossman, J., and Park, S. (2000) 'Measuring presence: a literature-based approach to the development of a standardized paper-and-pencil instrument', in 3rd International Workshop on Presence, Delft University of Technology, Delft, the Netherlands, 27–28 March.

Lombard, M., Ditton, T.B., and Weinstein, L. (2009) 'Measuring presence: The Temple Presence Inventory', Proceedings of the 12th International Workshop on Presence, University of Southern California Institute for Creative Technologies, Los Angeles, 11–13 November, pp. 1–14. Available at: https://astro.temple.edu/~lombard/ISPR/Proceedings/2009/Lombard_et_al.pdf (accessed 10 December 2019).

Lombard, M., and Jones, M.T. (2015) 'Defining presence', in F. Biocca, W.A. Ijsselsteijn, J. Freeman and M. Lombard (eds.), *Immersed in Media: Telepresence Theory, Measurement & Technology*, New York: Routledge, pp. 13–34.

Lopez, M., Kearney, G., and Hofstädter, K. (2018) 'Audio description in the UK: what works, what doesn't, and understanding the need for personalising access', *British Journal of Visual Impairment*, 36(3), pp. 274–291.

Margolies E., and Smith, K. (forthcoming) 'Translating an embodied gaze: theatre audio description, bodies and burlesque performance', in K. Ganguly and K. Gotman (eds.), *Inflections: Translation, Performance and the Everyday*, Cambridge: Cambridge University Press.

Marzà Ibañez, A. (2010) 'Evaluation criteria and film narrative: a frame to teaching relevance in audio description', *Perspectives: Studies in Translatology*, 18(3), pp. 143–153.

Matamala, A., and and Orero, P. (2017) 'Audio description and social accept-ability', *Rivista internazionale di tecnica della traduzione / International Journal of Translation*, 19, pp. 7–12.

McShane, M., and Nirenburg, S. (2015) 'Decision-making during language understanding by intelligent agents', *Artificial General Intelligence: Lecture Notes in Computer Science*, 9205, pp. 310–319.

Mehrabian, A., and Friar, J. (1969) 'Encoding of attitude by a seated communicator via posture and position cues', *Journal of Consulting and Clinical Psychology*, 33, pp. 330–336.

Minsky, M. (1980) 'Telepresence', *Omni*, June, pp. 45–51.

Murray, J.H. (1997) *Hamlet on the Holodeck: The Future of Narrative in Cyberspace*. Cambridge, MA: MIT Press.

Peter, C., and Herbon, A. (2006) 'Emotion representation and physiology assignments in digital systems', *Interacting with Computers*, 18, pp. 139–170.

Rambusch, J. (2006) 'Situated learning and Galperin's notion of object-oriented activity' *Proceedings of the Annual Meeting of the Cognitive Science Society*, 28, pp. 1998–2003. Available at: https://escholarship.org/uc/item/3vw4n768 (accessed 10 December 2019).

Ramos, M. (2015) 'The emotional experience of films: does audio description make a difference?', *Translator*, 21(1), pp. 68–94.

Reiss, K., and Vermeer, H.J. (2014) *Towards a General Theory of Translational Action: Skopos Theory Explained*. London: Routledge.

Remael, A., Reviers, N., and Vercauteren, G. (2015) 'Pictures painted in words: ADLAB audio description guidelines.' Available at: www.adlabproject.eu/Docs/adlab%20 book/index.html (accessed 25 November 2019).

Romero-Fresco, P., and Fryer, L. (2016) 'The reception of automatic surtitles: viewers' preferences, perception and presence.' Paper presented at Conference Unlimited: International Symposium on Accessible Live Events, University of Antwerp, 29 April.

Roofthooft, H., Remael, A., and Van den Dries, L. (2018) 'Audio description for (postdramatic) theatre: preparing the stage', *JoSTrans: The Journal of Specialised Translation*, 30, pp. 232–248. Available at: www.jostrans.org/issue30/art_ roofthooft_et_al.pdf (accessed 13 December 2019).

Schmeidler, E., and Kirchner, C. (1996) *Adding Audio Description to Television Science Programs: Impact on Legally Blind Viewers (Research Report)*. Washington, DC: National Science Foundation.

Schmeidler, E., and Kirchner, C. (2001) 'Adding audio description: does it make a difference?', *Journal of Visual Impairment & Blindness*, 95 (4), pp. 197–212.

Shlesinger, M. (1997) 'Quality in simultaneous interpreting', *Benjamins Translation Library*, 23, pp. 123–132.

Short, J., Williams, E., and Christie, B. (1976) *The Social Psychology of Telecommunications*. London: Wiley.

Slater, M., and Usoh, M. (1993) 'Presence in immersive virtual environments', in IEEE *Virtual Reality Annual International Symposium*, pp. 90–96.

Slater, M., and Wilbur, S. (1997) 'A framework for immersive virtual environ-ments (FIVE): speculations on the role of presence in virtual environments', *Presence: Teleoperators and Virtual Environments*, 6(6), pp. 603–616.

Smith, E. (2000) 'Either for tragedy, comedy': attitudes to Hamlet in Kenneth Branagh's *In the Bleak Midwinter and Hamlet*, in M.T. Burnett and R. Wray (eds.), *Shakespeare, Film, Fin de Siècle*, London: Palgrave Macmillan, pp. 137–146.

Steuer, J. (1992) 'Defining virtual reality: dimensions determining telepresence', *Journal of Communication*, 42(4), pp. 73–93.

Surface Impression (n.d.) 'The lost collection: Charles I and Whitehall Palace, a digital initiative.' Available at: www.paul-mellon-centre.ac.uk/whats-on/forthcoming/charles-i-and-whitehall-palace (accessed 12 December 2018).

Szarkowska, A. (2011) 'Text-to-speech audio description: towards wider availability of AD', *Journal of Specialised Translation*, 15(1), pp. 142–162.

United Nations (2008) Convention on the Rights of Persons with Disabilities (UNCRPD) Available at: https://www.un.org/development/desa/disabilities/convention-on-the-rights-of-persons-with-disabilities.html#Fulltext

Vercauteren, G. (2012) 'A narratological approach to content selection in audio description: towards a strategy for the description of narratological time', *MonTI*, 4, pp. 207–230.

Vorderer, P., Wirth, W., Gouveia, F.R., Biocca, F., Saari, T., Jäncke, L., ... and Klimmt, C. (2004). MEC Spatial Presence Questionnaire.

Walczak, A., and Fryer, L. (2017) 'Creative description: the impact of audio description style on presence in visually impaired audiences', *British Journal of Visual Impairment*, 35, pp. 6–17.

Walczak, A., and Fryer, L. (2018) 'Vocal delivery of audio description by genre: measuring users' presence', *Perspectives: Studies in Translation Theory and Practice*, 26(1), pp. 69–83.

Walczak, A., and Szarkowska, A. (2012) 'Text-to-speech audio description of educational materials for visually impaired children', in S. Bruti and E. Di Giovanni (eds.), *Audiovisual Translation across Europe: An Ever-changing Landscape*, Bern: Peter Lang, pp. 209–234.

Waterworth, J.A., Waterworth, E.L., Riva, G., and Mantovani, F. (2015) 'Presence: form, content and consciousness', in M. Lombard, F. Biocca, J. Freeman, W. Ijsselsteijn and R.J. Schaevitz (eds.), *Immersed in Media: Telepresence Theory, Measurement & Technology*, New York: Routledge, pp. 35–58.

Wissmath, B., Weibel, D., and Groner, R. (2009) 'Dubbing or subtitling? Effects on spatial presence, transportation, flow, and enjoyment', *Journal of Media Psychology: Theories, Methods, and Applications*, 21(3), pp. 114–125.

Witmer, B.G., and Singer, M.J. (1998) 'Measuring presence in virtual environments: a presence questionnaire', *Presence: Teleoperators and Virtual Environments*, 7(3), pp. 225–240.

Filmography

Hamlet (1948) Directed by L. Olivier. [Feature film]. UK: Rank Film Distributors Ltd.
Hamlet (1997) Directed by K. Branagh. [Feature film]. UK: Sony Pictures Releasing.

2 New approaches to accessibility and audio description in museum environments

Christopher Taylor and Elisa Perego

2.1 Introduction

The theme of this chapter is that of new approaches to accessibility for people with sight loss (PSL), and the particular area of interest is that of museums, architectural works and other kinds of landmark. Audio description (AD) has now established itself as an important element in the semiotic translation spectrum, particularly in relation to film and television access; the audio description of museums, either live or (semi) recorded, is now following in the wake of this pioneering sector, and exploring new areas of access through the exploitation, for example, of the senses of touch, smell and taste. This new approach to AD access comes at a time when new approaches to museum organisation are being put into practice, and when new visions of what a museum should offer are changing the appearance and the function of such institutions. As a result, a new visiting public is being created, and is expanding in those places that have adapted best to the new requirements. The hybrid nature of many modern museums attracts people for reasons that go beyond the mere viewing of exhibits (though this remains the principal raison d'être) to the 'hands-on' approach, which has helped render museums interesting for children, to the merchandising of all manner of products, connected or not to the museum's contents, to the holding of special exhibitions, lectures, courses, even dinners.

This change in the societal role of museums has resulted in massive attendances at major centres, the Tate Modern in London being a particularly good example, where locals and tourists mill around its many spaces in search of exhibits, gadgets, talks, coffee and lunch. Along with the provision of all these amenities, there has also fortunately been a move towards providing more access for the disabled, in the form of ramps for wheelchairs, sign language guides for the deaf and hard of hearing and, though certainly not ubiquitously, audio description and other supports for people with sight loss. The fact that museum AD has had to, and will continue to have to, adapt to these changes is at the base of this discussion of new approaches.

As a result of the above-mentioned innovations, there has been a renewed interest in researching the contemporary museum phenomenon through visitor studies and sociological surveys, while at the same time projects such as ADLAB PRO (2016–2019, financed by the European Union under the Erasmus+ Programme, Key Action 2 – Strategic Partnerships) and initiatives such as the Advanced Research Seminars on Audio Description (ARSAD) have ventured into and supported researching new approaches to providing quality AD in these environments, and by extension into similar areas such as buildings and famous landmarks. The ADLAB PRO project, in its attempt to create the profile of the professional audio describer in all sectors, includes museum AD in its training course structure and has produced a number of prototype ADs for such Italian institutions as the National Archeological Museum in Aquileia and Miramare Castle in Trieste. Architectural works that have been similarly studied include the Aquileia Basilica and St Paul's Cathedral in London. The research and analyses conducted are being funnelled into creating a course structure, within the wider frame of a curriculum for audio describers of all types, for prospective museum describers. It is therefore the purpose of this chapter to explore how AD can be best integrated into the new museum environments and to provide examples based on the ADLAB PRO experience.

2.2 New audiences

Museum visitors have become a very heterogeneous group, but a simple classification ranging from art novice through well-informed patron to art expert indicates the difficulty in catering for all tastes. However, while in the past museums tended to cater more for the better informed end of the spectrum, modern institutions have widened their appeal. This has been in response to visitor behaviour patterns and the results of surveys, interviews and focus groups aimed at gauging audience needs and wishes. Patterson Williams (1985) of the Denver Art Museum, an early innovator, produced an 'Agenda for Reform' back in 1982. The aims of such a reform are described by Samis and Michelson (2017: 52) as consisting of '*installed interpretives*: an evolving array of brochures, games, journals, videos, and analog and digital activities designed to support visitors in developing a deeper relationship with the artworks in the galleries'. Some visitors to museums and art galleries would prefer not to be there (children brought unwillingly by parents, adults having misunderstood what they were coming to see, patrons getting bored after a few hours, etc.) but insightful studies into what visitors want and what each type of visitor wants, have provided many more patrons with interesting and enjoyable visits than was the case when museums gave little thought to the myriad needs of a diverse public. Most museums remain collection-based, but change has come through the way collections are displayed and the way collections are accompanied by or integrated with other services, amenities and innovative practices. For example some museums consist mostly of a single impressive exhibit, such as the massive steam engine at Wigan Pier in northern England, whose attraction also lies in the refurbishment of the adjoining canal with its cafés, bookshops and souvenir stalls. Others place their exhibits in simulated environments, typical of natural history museums; yet others provide comfortable coffee-table-type ambiences such as the Discovery Library at the aforementioned Denver Art Museum.

Different visitors appreciate different facilities but surveys carried out by many institutions have provided a good guide as to what a fair cross-section of the public desires, going from the focused patron who knows what he or she is looking for, the curious visitor looking for something (anything) interesting, to the 'average' patron who spends little time on most exhibits but enjoys the general experience. But what facilities could interest, to varying degrees, all these categories of visitor? Rand (2001) listed a series of visitors' needs in her 'Bill of Rights'. These included comfort (fast, easy access to the building, the toilets, etc.), orientation (clear signing, lifts), welcome (friendly staff), enjoyment (a fun 'hands-on' experience), socialisation (meet and discuss the experience with friends in a café, etc.), respect (no 'dumbing down' and no patronising), communication (help in understanding from captions, audio-guides, staff, etc.), learning (educational aspect for adults and children), control (autonomous decision-making), challenge (tasks that can stimulate interest), and revitalisation (leave the museum refreshed).

2.3 Accessibility

The provision of the amenities, services and considerations encapsulated in Rand's 'Bill of Rights' does not specifically include accessibility for the disabled, but each item on the list can be seen to have relevance in new approaches to museum access. As regards access for people with sight loss, which is our principal interest here, the relevance can be easily observed. For example fast and easy access to the museum and all its facilities is a primary concern, ranging from privileged parking space provision to reduced prices. Cultural access, understood as the provision of a visitor experience of the museum's contents comparable to that of a sighted patron, can be provided by a human guide and/or an audio-guide, the latter preferably containing directional information. Indeed, the question of 'orientation' is fundamental, and this aspect of accessibility is still very much 'work in progress' when it comes to the autonomous use of AD audio-guides. The friendly welcome, the effort made to provide an enjoyable experience and the possibility of socialisation with other visitors and staff are elements that are common to all patrons, as is the 'no dumbing down and no patronising' warning. PSL are particularly sensitive to patronising attitudes even when they are adopted in good faith. They wish to have the same experience as sighted patrons and therefore not to be unduly 'assisted' in their understanding of the museum environment. This antipathy towards condescension has become something of a cliché amongst researchers, practitioners and end-users involved in AD provision, but needs a little clarification.

Certainly PSL want to 'work things out for themselves' and not be 'spoon-fed', and they wish to experience the same feeling as other visitors of being in an important museum or even in a little-known local institution. What Fryer and Freeman (2012) describe as 'presence' is a very useful concept in any attempt to clarify this search for 'the same experience'. Their idea of presence was originally formulated in relation to the enjoyment of a film on the part of PSL; there was more to experiencing a film than simply understanding the story. For example the way a film is shot influences the audience's emotional engagement, and the sense of presence can be replicated for the blind through describing camera shots, and identifying strange sounds. The purpose is to create the perceptual illusion of non-mediation – of 'being there'. Transferring this concept to the museum environment, the PSL need to feel that they are 'there' in the British Museum, or in the local village collection of Roman remains. This requires more than the simple description of exhibits but also a series of other inputs. For instance, the layout of the building needs to be described along with its furnishings and non-exhibit features (a poster-strewn notice board in the entrance hall, a box for donations, uniformed custodians in each room, etc.). These elements definitely do not need copious or lengthy descriptions (sighted users absorb their presence almost instantaneously) but they go towards providing the full picture. As observed by Hutchinson and Eardley (2019), the source text in a museum is a complex entity, which goes far beyond art objects and the decision as to which aspects of their visual information are more relevant, to encompass 'the space and [the] architecture of the museum, [but also] the experience of being in the space and interacting with others within it; in other words, the wider experience of visiting a museum' (2019: 46–47). Selecting a source text in a museum therefore becomes a multi-layered process leading translators to trans- or recreate it, creativity being a key ingredient in the process.

2.4 New forms of access

2.4.1 *'Maximilian e Manet – un incontro multimediale'*

Going back to the observation that 'new visions of what a museum should offer are changing the appearance and the function of such institutions', exhibits are now often presented to the visiting public in ways that transcend the traditional caption affixed below the display cabinet. A recent exhibition at the Miramare Castle in Trieste, linking the history of the Archduke Maximilian of Austria and the painting by Manet of the Archduke's execution in Mexico, contained no actual artefact. Rather, it exploited the multimedial possibilities of sound and vision by having video representations appear in the pages of an open book and on an artist's easel, accompanied by a spoken account backed by the sounds of crowds seeing off the then Emperor of Mexico from Miramare, and the sounds of insurrection on the streets of Mexico City. The video representations were often shown simultaneously on three walls with alternating details from the main image appearing in one or other of the surfaces. Manet's paintings were presented stage by stage so as to show their evolution in the hands of the master. An audio-guide was mandatory for this exhibition, though no audio description version is available.

An audio described version would require a new approach to such exhibitions and have to rely on judiciously chosen details from among the myriad elements on show, in the same way that AD guides recommend for the description of ordinarily displayed objects. However, the overall impression gained by the sighted visitor to the Maximilian exhibition would be a total immersion in imagery. Whereas visitors to a more traditional museum display would spend differing amounts of time on each exhibit, often very little or none at all, in this case the timing of the visit is fixed by the fact that the obligatory audio-guide is activated by entering each room on a fixed itinerary. As the commentary is continuous, apart from a few moments of silence on entry to each room while the video presentation winds slowly and evocatively into gear, there is hardly any space for a description of the images. While the audio-guide gives explanations that a PSL could follow, this whole new experience, as excitingly promoted by the advance publicity, would be totally lost. Thus the AD version of the guide, in attempting to provide a sense of 'presence' and a sense of 'the new', would need to describe not only the historical sequence, but also the effects used to portray it. The length of the itinerary would be the same as for the sighted visitor, as the video sequences are timed to coincide with the audio-guide, so the description would have to move between the historical information, the (judicious) description of the images and an explanation of the special effects. For example in one room, the video presentation evokes the sea around the castle, in another Manet's canvas comes to life as the final version of the execution scene is completed. Such presentations are certain to become ever more sophisticated and it is these that represent the challenges that a new generation of audio describers will have to face.

2.4.2 Ethnographic museums

In the search for a blanket term to include those museums not dedicated wholly or partially to art and sculpture, but to what might be loosely called ethnography, that is, the study of people and cultures, the term 'ethnographic museums' will be used. Such institutions, which are in constant expansion, are charged with:

> il compito di raccogliere, conservare e valorizzare le testimonianze demo-etno-antropologiche del territorio che rappresenta[no].

> the task of collecting, conserving and valuing the demo-ethno-anthropological findings in the area they represent.

> (Fo.cu.s., 2018)

In many places 'there is a "museum boom" going on right now' (Mason *et al.*, 2018: 2) and the ethnographic variety is a part of this phenomenon. As a case study, the proposal for an accessible tour of the Museum of Manufacturing Art (Museo dell'Arte Fabbrile e delle Coltellerie) in Maniago (D'Andrea, 2018) is a useful indicator of the challenges audio describers will continue to experience, also in this field. The museum in question tells the story of the production of knives and similar instruments in the small town of Maniago in the Friuli region of northern Italy. Providing an audio-described tour of this environment requires a very different approach to that used in more artistically based museums.

Here the description needs to move from the physical form of the actual exhibits to the more invisible concepts of social and economic history that lie behind the objects. This aspect is assisted by the modern approach to presentation adopted by the museum itself. Despite the seemingly banal, everyday objects on display (knives), the visitor is offered a multisensorial historical tour of this now redimensioned industry which was so important to the development of the town of Maniago. As well as setting the exhibits in real-life situations through the use of models and simulations, the tour consists of 'hands-on' tactile experiences, video showings, spoken commentaries, re-evocations of the sounds of the workshop and even the opportunity to appreciate the smells of the industry. The whole exhibition is surrounded by gigantic photographs of the heyday of the industry. An audio description, especially an autonomous audio-guide with AD, thus needs to contextualize the exhibits physically and historically, direct the PSL visitors around the loosely chronological arrangement of exhibits, and assist them in negotiating the multisensorial components of touch, sound and smell, providing the necessary spoken input. The purpose is to give the PSL the impression that they are fully immersed in each situation, reliving and not just observing the essentially mundane artefacts (D'Andrea, 2018: 81). As a result, the AD will have to take a new form, where the description of the visual details is limited to the very core, to be complemented by a multisensory experience and by the verbal description of a close link between form and (practical as well as cultural) function of each object. Objects have a value because they explain a culture and tell a story rather than because of their aesthetics and details. This can be explained to the visitor in the AD, as in the excerpt below, where the visitor is warned of the complexity and the unmanageable size of the donkey mallet (D'Andrea, 2018: 105):

> puoi prenderti del tempo per […] analizzare più nel dettaglio i vari componenti del maglio a testa d'asino. È difficile riuscire a individuarli tutti, e capirne la funzione, perché sono molti e piuttosto tecnici, ma sicuramente puoi renderti conto che si tratta di un macchinario grande e pesante, impossibile da manovrare a mano e composto di molti materiali.

you can take your time to [...] analyse the various components of the donkey mallet in more detail. It is difficult to identify them all, and understand their function, because they are many and rather technical, but surely you can realize that this is a large and heavy machine, impossible to manoeuvre by hand and composite of many materials.

Similarly, the following AD excerpt (D'Andrea, 2018: 103) shows how an anvil is not 'painted in words' for the benefit of PSL, but its shape is offered through the experience of touch and by verbally lingering on physical details which have a precise function (e.g. bumps and holes on the surface of the anvil resulting from hammer blows; or the wooden plinth where the anvil is set down which enables blacksmiths to stand comfortably while working):

> Prova a salire sulla pedana e ad allungare le mani davanti a te: potrai sentire l'acciaio freddo e liscio dell'incudine, che insieme al martello costituisce la base e quindi uno degli strumenti fondamentali per il lavoro del fabbro. Scorrendo le mani sulla superficie superiore dell'incudine, sentirai delle irregolarità e dei buchi: sono i segni lasciati dalle forti martellate con cui il fabbro dà forma all'acciaio a seconda della funzione che lo strumento che sta forgiando avrà nella vita di ogni giorno. Prova ora a portare le mani verso le estremità dell'incudine: sentirai sicuramente che si concludono in due coni. Questi hanno la funzione di estendere la superficie su cui battere e hanno forme diverse: uno è tondeggiante e l'altro squadrato, per permettere di modellare l'acciaio della forma desiderata per creare curve o spigoli nell'attrezzo che viene forgiato. Scendi con le mani verso terra: potrai notare il basamento in legno su cui poggia l'incudine, che permette di rialzarla in modo che il fabbro la possa usare stando in piedi.

> Try to get on the platform and stretch your hands in front of you: you can feel the cold and smooth steel of the anvil, which together with the hammer forms the basis and therefore one of the fundamental tools for the work of the blacksmith. Sliding the hands on the upper surface of the anvil, you will feel irregularities and holes: these are the marks left by the strong hammering with which the blacksmith gives shape to the steel according to the function that the tool that he is forging will have in everyday life. Try now to bring your hands to the ends of the anvil: you will surely feel that they end in two cones. These have the function of extending the surface on which to beat and have different shapes: one is round and the other square, to allow you to shape the steel to the desired shape to create curves or edges in the tool that is forged. Go down with your hands to the ground: you will notice the wooden base on which the anvil rests, which allows it to be raised up so that the blacksmith can use it while standing.

The AD would then be followed by the insertion of the noise of the hammer on steel, a noise that is supposed to fade until it disappears before the narration starts again, with an emphasis on the importance of listening to the hammer noise and linking this to a tough working reality, and with direct involvement of the visitor who can try the hammer for him/herself (D'Andrea, 2018: 103):

> Ascolta il rumore dei colpi del martello sull'incudine: senti la frequenza con cui si ripetono e prova a immaginare la fatica di un operaio che per ore e ore deve fare lo stesso movimento ad intensità elevate. Puoi provare a farlo tu stesso con l'aiuto della tua guida.

> Listen to the sound of the hammer blows on the anvil: feel the frequency with which they repeat and try to imagine the labour of a worker who for hours and hours must make the same movement at high intensity. You can try to do it yourself with the help of your guide.

This is in line with the recent idea of the improved effectiveness of 'enriched audio description' (Eardley *et al.*, 2017; Neves, 2016) and in general of multisensory approaches to audio describing art and environments (Dobbin *et al.*, 2016; Eardley *et al.*, 2016; Neves, 2012) – which are considered to be not only more engaging but also more inclusive, accessible and pleasing for all, and favouring long-term memory of the museum experience.

As in art gallery AD, it will not be possible to cover every exhibit, except perhaps in the case of very small institutions, and the usual judicious choices must be made. However, unlike art galleries where exhibits are arranged either according to theme, or artistic period, or nationality, or even randomly, ethnographic museums usually arrange their objects in a chronological or some other logical order to tell a story. The describer has thus to consider not only which exhibits to describe but how to connect one to another without losing track of the narrative. Considerable research is required into historical sources, museum catalogues and so on (see Altin, 2007, 2012).

2.4.3 The Fan Museum

Taking another, very different, example of an ethnographic institution, at the Fan Museum in Greenwich, London, the describer cannot restrict his or her work to describing a selection of the beautiful fans on display, as he or she might describe a selection of paintings in an art gallery. This would be uninformative and essentially pointless to an interested visitor. The museum exhibits are arranged so as to provide a history of the production and use of fans throughout the world, but the museum is situated in a small house where movement is restricted, and the exhibits are arranged in the small space available. A lady welcomes visitors and provides printed information. Otherwise, the set-up is rather traditional since there is no room for special effects and multisensoriality. The describer would need to acquaint him or herself with the logistics of such a visit. Normally there are few visitors and thus even a private viewing could be arranged. The task would be relatively straightforward: follow the short itinerary, give the historical narrative and choose the best specimens to describe. In these conditions, even an autonomous audio-guide with AD could be used with relative ease. However, on the day this author visited the Fan Museum, a party was booked in and movement was difficult, if not hazardous. In these conditions a human guide is necessary, either a professional who is knowledgeable about the museum contents, or a lay person who can guide a PSL in crowded spaces and then rely on an audio-guide to explain the details. These latter considerations are also relevant to PSL visits to large but popular venues such as the British Museum.

2.4.4 Outdoor areas

2.4.4.1 Miramare Castle

A further challenge facing museum audio describers is that of coping with outdoor scenarios. A number of museums in northeast Italy, for example, have an outdoor section, including the aforementioned National Archeological Museum in Aquileia and the Castle of Miramare in Trieste. An AD has been prepared for this latter institution (Biscuola, 2018) with a tour of the interior followed by a tour of the surrounding park which contains a number of places of interest such as the Stables, the Holm-oak Avenue, Castle Square, the Round Terrace, the Amazon and another 20 or so selected elements. This outdoor section requires a different AD approach than that used for the museum housed in the Castle. The AD described here was designed for use as an audio-guide and thus as an autonomous tool for people with sight loss. It begins with the following introduction (Biscuola, 2018: 88):

> Welcome to Miramare park. This descriptive guide has been designed to talk you through your visit to the most accessible part of the park, and it will last about 45 minutes. For safety reasons, only some of the outstanding features of the park will be described. Every time, indications will be given on how to find your way through the park from one stop to the next: an approximate count of the necessary steps will be provided, as well as the time required. The instructions will be given at the beginning of each track, to give you time to comfortably reach your destination. The park being an open space, please take extra care while you walk around, as the path might be wet or slippery.

The introduction stresses the accessibility factor, pointing out that only safely accessible elements will be described and also providing warnings relating to possible weather conditions. It gives the required information in terms of orientation (find your way through the park), distance (the necessary steps) and time (overall 45 minutes and time required at each stop). As can be imagined, the creation of this outdoor guide required meticulous preparation, of a kind that transcends that required for the more common indoor experience. The attention to time and direction are common to both, but the dimensions involved and the planning of a viable itinerary require a more innovative approach.

The tour begins as follows with the Stables:

> Our visit starts here, from the stables. It is an average-size building, cream-coloured and with green, sloping roofs. Located on two floors, several windows are painted in brown, with shutters and jalousies, a feature that is typical of windows in Trieste.
>
> (Biscuola, 2018)

The description is of a building seen from the outside and limits itself to this aspect, though adding just a couple of lines on its history. The contentious use of technical terms (jalousies) is supplemented by the information that these are 'typical of windows in Trieste'. As regards the interior the following suggestion is added (Biscuola, 2018): 'You can now enter the stables if you wish to visit the current exhibition.' Here a different AD will be provided for the temporary exhibitions which are held regularly in the stables. The AD continues (Biscuola, 2018):

> Otherwise, we shall continue the visit. Proceed on the road following the pavement to your left. Please be careful of the cars, as they can travel on this road from both directions. You can step on the pavement if you prefer to do so, but please be careful as there are trees on it. Keep walking until you reach the entrance to the park, marked out by a large arch. Once you've stepped beyond the arch, you will have reached a pedestrian zone, so you will be able to walk more freely. At this point, select the next track.

The instructions rightly stress the safety aspect up to the point where the pedestrian zone is reached. The audio-guide itself gives the instruction to 'select the next track'. The next track describes the Holm-oak Avenue, again a very different element to the artefacts found in the museum (Biscuola, 2018):

> The road is flanked by a stone parapet to your left, with a series of street lamps on top [...] The road overlooks the Adriatic Sea, whose waves you can probably hear and smell. On your right is the actual park, uphill, resembling a real wood. Reforestation efforts resulted in a rich laurel and viburnum undergrowth and in the presence of holm-oaks on both sides of the avenue, hence the name 'Holm-oak Avenue'. The tree branches meet above the avenue and form a sort of arch, that on sunny days creates a nice light-shadow play on the ground. When you are ready, keep walking

along the avenue for about three minutes, following the pavement to your left, until you reach the Castle Square.

Being in the open air, the description can encompass other senses (hearing and smell). The origin of the name of the avenue is explained. While a description of the various trees is not provided (unnecessary detail?), the description of the effect of the overhanging branches is arguably more evocative. In order to reach the next stop the PSL is told to 'keep walking along the avenue for about three minutes'. This may represent one of the limits to this kind of autonomous guide, in that three minutes is a long time in which to lose a sense of orientation, even on a straight road. However, in the absence of human assistance, the incorporation of sonar 'beacons' could solve the problem. In this way the audio-guide appliance is automatically activated when the next stop is reached.

As it is, the AD in question continues with directional information such as the following, between the statue of the Amazon and the Round Terrace (Biscuola, 2018).

The wall we have described so far is about as tall as a person and about one metre wide. After you reach the end of it, you will find another entrance on your right. Take it and enter the colonnade. Keep walking for a few metres on the pebbled avenue, following the short wall on your left. When you reach a round terrace, select the next track.

The dimensions are illustrated through comparison (as tall as a person) and measurements (about a metre wide), covering both approaches to size, and provide more easily followable distance markers (a few metres). This brief glimpse at a well-prepared AD of an outdoor environment still needs to be assessed through user feedback, but gives an idea of the new approaches that will be needed for this kind of audio description.

2.4.4.2 *The National Angkor Museum (Cambodia)*

The above account of the audio description designed for the museum and the park at Miramare in Trieste foresaw the production of two distinct entities. Indeed the one can be experienced and enjoyed separately from the other. There is little direct connection between the exhibits in the castle itself and the places of interest in the grounds. A further challenge to audio describers is represented, on the other hand, by the Angkor Wat complex of temples in Siem Reap, Cambodia. The still very poor country of Cambodia boasts a now famous massive complex of ancient temples visited annually by millions of tourists and a state of the art museum in the city of Siem Reap. Whether the museum is visited before the temples or vice versa, the two are intrinsic-ally connected. The precise itinerary offered to visitors is generally decided by the tourist organisations which provide the guides and the transport, without which and without whom the visits would be arduous. As yet there would seem to be no official form of access to either the museum or the temples for people with sight loss.

The provision of such access would ideally cover the whole experience, starting, say, with the National Angkor Museum. This impressive institution is equipped with the latest technological innovations, including audio-visual content, innovative lighting effects, the possibility to touch statues and other artefacts relating to the ancient Khmer culture, and the simulation of elements of the actual temple complex to be visited later.

The second stage of the experience would then be to move outdoors and several kilometres to the many temple sites. The temples are empty of any furniture or objects other than statues, but contain magnificent examples of sculpted surfaces and bas-reliefs stretching many hundreds of metres, all of which are potentially open to tactile exploration. The temples themselves provide breathtaking views, especially at sunset and at sunrise when hordes of tourists rise at five o'clock in the morning to capture the unique chromatic experience. In order to profit from the complete Angkor Wat experience, people with sight loss would firstly need a human guide or an audio-guide to the museum incorporating AD, or a combination of the two, and for the temple visit, very definitely a human guide with the possible accompaniment of an audio-guide for individual artefacts. The challenge for the creator of an audio description lies first in the selection of elements to describe, not only from the point of view of relative importance, but from how the itinerary is organised. There are a great many temples worth visiting, often quite distant one from the other, and even the most determined sighted tourist rarely goes to all, and certainly does not devote the same attention to all those visited. Consequently the potential AD, already at the museum stage, must concentrate on those elements that will be visited on the chosen itinerary. The examples described above, one in an area where museum AD has already made inroads (Miramare) and the other in a context ripe for its introduction (Angkor), show first where innovation in AD technique is emerging, and secondly where more concentrated efforts are now needed to produce solutions in more complicated environments and where little is yet available.

2.4.5 *The museum at the university: a case study*

Examples of multisensoriality have already been discussed in relation to the Miramare, Maniago and Angkor museums, but at this point, we can go into more detail on particular aspects of this growing phenomenon. Many institutions have already introduced the practice of tactile tours, where PSL visitors can touch or feel exhibits accompanied by some form of audio description. This can be a standard description, leaving the PSL to augment understanding by touching the object (Grassini, 2015), or it can take the form of a more holistic model where the speaker (the describer or a voice talent trained in this practice) accompanies the PSL physically by positioning the hands, the palms and the fingertips in such a way as to achieve a more fulfilling experience. A pioneer in this type of tactile approach, the Tactile Museum of Ancient and Modern Painting Anteros in Bologna, with qualified staff dealing exclusively with PSL visitors, has documented evidence of the efficacy of this method (see Secchi 2004, 2010, 2014). At the Anteros Museum, founded in 1999 within the F. Cavazza Blind Institute and directed by Loretta Secchi, a team of specialised artists of the School of Applied Sculpture of Bologna is in charge of hand-sculpting plaster or resin perspective bas-relief models of some representative pictorial artworks by famous painters.[1] These can be explored through touch and a careful live description offered by an expert guide. The 'traditional' contact with the artwork can be followed in some cases by creative activities where visitors can try to reproduce what they have 'seen' in clay. And this approach, with inevitable variations depending on the type of museum and the way exhibits are displayed, represents another aspect of the new approaches to accessibility required for museums.

The experience of touching a painting that has been translated into a relief is very intense and it can be best exploited if the visitor is already acquainted both with art-related notions and with tactile literacy. In any case, it might be demanding to access more than one painting on the same day. This is one of the reasons that made the authors decide to acquire a three-dimensional reproduction of the painting of the Greek myth 'Atalanta and Hippomenes' (Reni, 1625a,b) (Figure 2.1) to be exhibited and touched at the Department of Legal, Language, Interpreting and Translation Studies at the University of Trieste.[2]

The bas-relief has been safely hung and located in a visible, accessible and well-lit place in the department entrance hall, and a recorded AD (in a standard and in a simplified version for children: Canestrari, 2017; Venier, 2017) has been produced and made available to visitors in several languages through a QR code linking to the YouTube channel *Audio for All* (Figure 2.2).

Tactile tours should be accompanied by an experienced human guide to work best (Figure 2.3). A face-to-face encounter lends itself to the immersive experience: it is more interactive, it offers the chance for the visitor to ask questions, and it allows describers to tailor their description around an individual's particular interests (Eardley *et al.*, 2017). During a live touch tour, the guide can also direct the visitor's hands to the right spots on the replica, as shown in the picture. In fact, the tactile exploration procedure is no random process. However, audio-guides can be a functional substitute in given circumstances. When having to rely on prerecorded ADs, it might be useful to put into practice some expedients, especially as far as the reference to the tactile activity is concerned.

As shown in the following excerpt, in the introductory section of the AD, it is crucial to give clear instructions on the role, extent and scope of the

Figure 2.1 Photographic reproduction (above) and plaster reproduction (below) of 'Atalanta and Hippomenes' by Guido Reni (1625).

Figure 2.2 QR codes of AD of 'Atalanta and Hippomenes' in several languages.

reference to tactility, and to leave enough freedom for the visitor-listener to decide whether to touch the relief or just to enjoy its verbal description. Not all visitors feel comfortable with touching objects and they might prefer to avoid this experience. A further crucial issue pertains to the degree of independence offered to the visitor. It is not wise to force the listener to stick to the pace of the narration or to touch while listening: visitors have different backgrounds and needs, and these have to be taken into account.

> You can either listen to the audio guide without touching the relief, or explore it with your hands independently or following the instructions given by the audio. If you want to touch the relief while listening, make sure you are standing comfortably. You can check the distance from the relief by stretching your arms in front of you to see if your hands can reach the surface without problems.
>
> (Audio For All, 2018a)

Offering the option to stop the narration and take the time necessary to explore the painting when this is more convenient is another important factor. This might help especially those visitors that are not yet acquainted with the reading of haptic supports. Understanding artworks through touch

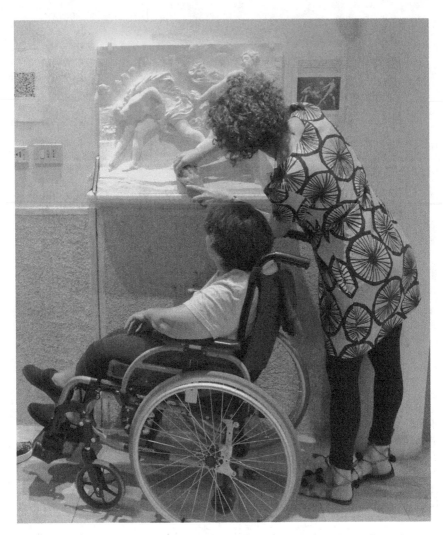

Figure 2.3 Guided tactile experience at the University of Trieste.

is a process which takes more time than visual perception and is not immediate but 'successive, slow, analytical, and active' (De Coster and Loots,
2004: 331). Furthermore, art appreciation through touch can depend on several factors, including for instance the visitors' familiarity and experience
with art; their previous experiences whilst still having sight; their cultural,
historical and individual differences. These are the reasons why instructions
on how to use hands during exploration have been included in the AD
introduction:

Some pauses were introduced in the audio guide [and] these pauses will enable you to pause the audio and have more time to make particular movements during the tactile exploration or to focus on some details of the work and appreciate them more. However, you can choose to touch the relief at any moment and explore it with two hands using your palms, your fingers and fingertips to better feel the physical features of the smooth surface, its three-dimensionality and the layout of its components. Take your time: seeing with your hands is an exciting yet challenging experience!

(Audio For All, 2018a)

Reference to touch has been made also in the descriptive section of the AD, where more detailed (yet not overwhelming) instructions are offered. These include reference to both macro and micro tactile processes. Visitors should be aware that the process should begin by exploring the outer edges (to convey a rough idea of the dimensions of the object) and to later move to the centre, for a deeper exploration into tactile aspects that might otherwise be overlooked. For instance:

The tension in the muscles and tendons of his body caused by the effort of running is clear to the touch. If the reader lingers over his left leg stretched forward, the surge of the body can be imagined, as well as the shift of weight caused by the surge itself.

(Audio For All, 2018b)

Acquiring a bas-relief in our department has been a challenge, but has proven to be a formidable means in offering a sensory and inclusive experience to students, university staff and local PSL (who might not have the chance to visit a tactile museum), but also to any inquiring 'outsider', thus offering the chance to enhance awareness especially in sighted viewers regarding crucial themes such as sensory disabilities.

Besides functioning as an awareness-enhancer, the bas-relief has proven to work as a powerful didactic tool for students who want to experiment with a tactile experience and for those who want to practise guiding while audio describing. We can now use the relief when we teach in class, and show a concrete example of tactile painting (vs. theory), in order to offer a more comprehensive and authentic learning experience to our students.

Last but not least, bringing the museum into the university has enabled us to draw attention to important sensitive themes through an attractive and eye-catching decorative feature.

2.4.6 Easy-to-Read language to enhance museum accessibility

Given the diversity of the target audience for museum ADs, as well as the widespread idea of creating texts that are accessible for all rather than for a restricted subgroup of users, the idea of taking into account various degrees of simplification strategies is gaining momentum. The recently launched EU project EASIT (Easy Access for Social Inclusion Training, financed by the European Union under the Erasmus+ Programme, Key Action 2 – Strategic Partnerships, http://pagines.uab.cat/easit/en) focuses on the integration of easy-to-understand language with audiovisual translation, and though in its infancy (2018–2021), it suggests the importance of considering the need to implement Easy-to-Read language and plain language also in enriched AD contexts (see also Chapter 3 in this volume).

Museum ADs, and more general ADs of art objects, environments, architecture, etc., can be very complex, especially when they are very detailed. An interesting example is the AD of St Paul's Cathedral by VocalEyes. Located within the central City of London, it is an Anglican cathedral, one of the most famous and most recognisable sights of London. Designed and built (1675–1710) under the supervision of Sir Christopher Wren in a baroque style with medieval influences, it also incorporates neoclassical and Gothic elements.

The description of the Great West Doors, for instance, is vivid, lexically and semantically rich, and exploits art jargon and technical terms that could put off any visitor not acquainted with this type of lexicon and style. The AD is complete and imaginative, resembling a poem. Whether it is easy to follow for most visitors should be tested. The flow of information that it delivers in a few lines is enormous:

> About 10 metres beyond the font are the Great West Doors. Made of deep brown oak, they're 9 metres high and about 4 metres wide, in a deep, arched alcove. Artwork is often exhibited in front. The doors are decorated by carved rows, alternating squares and rectangles, interspersed with semi-spheres, the size of an eating apple, small enough to cup in your hand. This grand entrance is reserved for when visitors such as HM The Queen attend the cathedral, while most visitors enter through the smaller doors on either side.
>
> (VocalEyes, 2012)

One way to make information accessible to a large number of users, including people with intellectual and learning disabilities, would be to adopt Easy-to-Read language, which would facilitate greater access to learning opportunities and encourage broader cultural engagement. This implies a reduction in the volume and complexity of information and language materials, in order to produce an immediate, clear, empathetic and concise communication.

The rules to be followed are not many and they are apparently simple – one sentence per line, simple words, explanation of their meaning, etc. (Inclusion Europe, 2016; Mencap, 2000). However, the creation of these texts is not immediate. Simplification processes need to be learnt and practised and Easy-to-Read texts must undergo review (or validation) by a person with intellectual disability before being released, thus implying quite a long chain of work. Because there are different levels of intellectual capacity, the results might

not be universally accessible, but they should reach a larger number of bene-
ficiaries than the use of only standard texts. In the example above, the text
would be reconceived as follows:

> The Great West Doors are beyond the font.
> They are made of brown oak.
> Oak is a type of hard durable wood.
> They are very big.
> They are 9 metres high
> and 4 metres wide.
> They form an arch at the top.
> Often, artists display their work
> in front of these doors.
> Rows of squares and rectangles
> decorate the doors.
> Half spheres decorate the doors too.
> The squares, rectangles and half spheres
> are cut with care into the wood.
> Only important visitors use these doors.
> For example,
> Her Majesty The Queen can use these doors.
> Ordinary visitors use smaller doors.

2.5 Concluding remarks

Thanks to new technologies and new sensibilities in the realm of social inclusion and accessibility, new forms of access in the museum and art environments are being tested and exploited. Such a variety of forms of accessibility
is beneficial to the heterogeneous target group of users, which has been
expanding to encompass new audiences, including people with sensory disabilities as well as people with a limited time (or wish) to visit a given exhibition, people who are not art experts but want to give it a try, children, elderly
visitors, visitors with a range of disabilities, etc.

The work done in this area is substantial, and it involves a high degree of
interaction between different fields of study that might appear to be far from
that of accessible translation. They include psychology and specialist pedagogy, linguistics, reading studies, disability studies, as well as graphic design,
architecture and engineering.

Special training is therefore an ever growing need in this area, where
experts dealing with accessible art need to acquire specialist skills and compe-
tencies, and absorb concepts derived from many different disciplines. Recently
concluded projects such as ACT, as well as ongoing projects such as ADLAB
PRO and EASIT, have focused or are focusing on identifying the necessary
elements to be passed on to newly trained accessible translation experts, and

entail the development of specific training materials that can be exploited in these new contexts.

Acknowledgements

Both authors contributed equally to the scientific content of the manuscript. C. Taylor dealt specifically with 2.4.1, 2.4.3, 2.4.4; E. Perego dealt specifically with 2.4.2, 2.4.5, 2.4.6.This project has been made available thanks to the support of the ADLAB PRO project Audio Description: A Laboratory for the Development of a New Professional Profile, www.adlabproject.eu (2016–2019, Project number: 2016-1-IT02-KA203-024311) coordinated by Elisa Perego, and by the EASIT project Easy Access for Social Inclusion Training, http://pagines.uab.cat/easit/en (2018–2021, Project number: 2018-1-ES01-KA203-05275) coordinated by Anna Matamala, both financed by the EU under Erasmus+ Programme, Key Action 2 – Strategic Partnerships.

Notes

1   Bas-reliefs are both produced for internal use or sculpted on request and delivered to other museums or institutions.
2   This project has been made available thanks to the support of FRA 2015, University of Trieste Research Fund, 'Accessibility through Translation: Museum AD' (2015–2017) and the ADLAB PRO project (Audio Description: A Laboratory for the Development of a New Professional Profile, www.adlabproject.eu) financed by the EU under Erasmus+ Programme, Key Action 2 – Strategic Partnerships (2016–2019) (Project number:2016-1-IT02-KA203-024311), both coordinated by Elisa Perego.

References

Altin, R. (2007) 'Il museo della coltelleria di Maniago', *Antropologia Museale*, 17, 30–33.
Altin, R. (2012) *Coricama: lo specchio della comunità – Catalogo MAFC – Museo dell'Arte Fabbrile e delle Coltellerie di Maniago*. Lito Immagine.
Audio For All (2018a) *Atalanta and Hippomenes (ENG) – Introduction*. 28 July. Available at: www.youtube.com/watch?v=eWci4hXDcX0 (accessed 4 December 2019).
Audio For All (2018b) *Atalanta and Hippomenes (ENG) – Description of the Work*. 28 July. Available at: https://www.youtube.com/watch?v=DP8ASB8u2SM (accessed 4 December 2019).
Biscuola, F. (2018) 'Il castello di Miramare e il suo parco: un progetto di audio descrizione.' Unpublished thesis. University of Trieste.
Cansestrari, M. (2017) ' "Atalanta e Ippomene" di Guido Reni: Audiodescrizione per un pubblico dell'infanzia. Analisi, semplificazione e traduzione verso l'inglese.' Unpublished thesis. University of Trieste.
D'Andrea, G. (2018) 'Oltre l'audiodescrizione: proposta di percorso museale accessibile per il Museo dell'Arte Fabbrile e delle Coltellerie di Maniago.' Unpublished thesis. University of Trieste.

De Coster, K., and Loots, G. (2004) 'Somewhere in between touch and vision: in search of a meaningful art education for blind Individuals', *International Journal of Art & Design Education*, 23(3), pp. 326–334.

Dobbin, C., Eardley, A. F., and Neves, J. (2016) 'Ektashif: art through senses: families shaping museum programmes in Qatar', *Multaqa: Professional Journal of the Gulf Museum Educators Network*, 2, pp. 11–19.

Eardley, A. F., Fryer, L., Hutchinson, R., Cock, M., Ride, P., and Neves, J. (2017) 'Enriched audio description: working towards an inclusive museum experience', in S. Halder and L. C. Assaf (eds.), *Inclusion, Disability and Culture: An Ethnographic Perspective Traversing Abilities and Challenges*. Cham: Springer, pp. 195–209.

Eardley, A. F., Mineiro, C., Neves, J., and Ride, P. (2016) 'Redefining access: embracing multimodality, memorability and shared experiences in museums', *Curator: The Museum Journal*, 59(3), pp. 263–286.

Fo.cu.s. (Fondazione Culture Santarcangelo) (2018) 'MET – Museo Etnografico.' Available at: www.focusantarcangelo.it/poli-istituti/met-museo-etnografico (accessed 28 November 2019).

Fryer, L., and Freeman, J. (2012) 'Presence in those with and without sight: audio description and its potential for virtual reality applications', *Journal of CyberTherapy and Rehabilitation*, 5(1), pp. 15–23.

Grassini, A. (2015) *Per un'estetica della tattilità*. Rome: Armando.

Hutchinson, R. S., and Eardley, A. F. (2019) 'Museum audio description: the problem of textual fidelity', *Perspectives*, 27(1), pp. 42–57.

Inclusion Europe (2016) 'European standards for making information easy to read and understand.' Available at: https://easy-to-read.eu (accessed 25 November 2019).

Mason, R., Robinson, A., and Coffield, C. (2018) *Museum and Gallery Studies: The Basics*. London: Routledge.

Mencap (2000) *Am I Making Myself Clear? Mencap's Guidelines for Accessible Writing*. London: Mencap.

Neves, J. (2012) 'Multi-sensory approaches to (audio) describing the visual arts', *MonTI*, 4, pp. 277–293.

Neves, J. (2016) 'Enriched descriptive guides: a case for collaborative meaning-making in museums', *Cultus*, 9(2), pp. 137–153.

Rand, J. (2001) 'Why we need a Visitor's Bill of Rights', *Curator: The Museum Journal*, 44(1), pp. 7–14.

Reni, G. (1625a) 'Atalanta and Hippomenes' [Oil on canvas]. Available at: https://commons.wikimedia.org/wiki/File:Guido_Reni_-_Atalanta_e_Ippomene_ (Museo_di_Capodimonte).jpg (accessed 25 November 2019).

Reni, G. (1625b) 'Atalanta and Hippomenes' [Gesso]. Instituto Dei Ciechi Francesco Cavazza Onlus. Available at: https://commons.wikimedia.org/wiki/File:Atalanta_ e_Ippomene_-_Guido_Reni_(Bassorilievo_tattile_del_%22Museo_Anteros%22). jpg (accessed 25 November 2019).

Samis, P., and Michaelson, M. (2017) *Creating the Visitor-centred Museum*. London: Routledge.

Secchi, L. (2004) *L'educazione estetica per l'integrazione*. Rome: Carocci Editore.

Secchi, L. (2010) *Le metodologie dell'esplorazione tattile: per una conoscenza delle forme della rappresentazione ed estensione di senso dell'aptica. Contributo in occasione della manifestazione Libri che prendono forma*. Rome: MiBAC-FNIPC.

Secchi, L. (2014) 'Between sense and intellect: blindness and the strength of inner vision', in D. de Kerckhove and C. M. de Almeida (eds.), *The Point of Being*, Newcastle-upon-Tyne: Cambridge Scholars, pp.197–212.

Venier, G. (2017) *"Atalanta e Ippomene" di Guido Reni: analisi, audiodescrizione e traduzione verso l'inglese*. Unpublished thesis. University of Trieste.

VocalEyes (2012) *London beyond Sight: On St Paul's Cathedral*. Available at: https://vocaleyes.co.uk/audio-clip/london-beyond-sight/#player=837&track=31 (accessed 4 December 2019).

Williams, P. (1985) 'Educational excellence in art museums: an agenda for reform', *Journal of Aesthetic Education*, 19(2), pp. 105–123.

3 Easier audio description
Exploring the potential of Easy-to-Read principles in simplifying AD

Rocío Bernabé and Pilar Orero

3.1 Introduction

The audio describer has a similar function to that of the language translator, who has to render the work written in a source language into a target language. The audio describer translates visual language into written text, which is later read aloud. Research on audio description (AD) has focused on both the source and target texts (Braun, 2011). The source text alone is a multi-semiotic and complex matter as it could be anything from a film, a play, an opera or a picture displayed in a museum. An audio description of a Picasso painting, for example, explains not only the picture but also where it hangs, the frame, its size and so forth. The equivalence of the target AD text to its source text is an interesting issue which has received much attention in research (Orero, 2012).

Film is the genre with most AD research (Fryer and Freeman, 2012a, 2014; Fryer *et al.*, 2013; Perego, 2014). Some authors have focused on specific film components such as light (Maszerowska, 2012), secondary details (Orero and Vilaró, 2012), film credits (Matamala and Orero, 2011), leitmotifs (Vilaró and Orero, 2013) and sound (Szarkowska and Orero, 2014; Orero *et al.*, 2016). Paying attention to the source text, Fels *et al.* (2006) looked at text genre, in particular at comedy, and Orero (2016) at TV series. Udo and Fels (2009) narrowed down their research to audio describing theatrical productions, focusing in particular on Shakespeare.

Research on AD has also been undertaken to study the adequacy of the target text and its reception by the audience, i.e. persons with sight loss. The theoretical vacuum regarding concepts such as equivalence or adequacy in AD has been compensated for by the acknowledgement of bottom-up reception studies to understand issues such as audience engagement (Afonso *et al.*, 2010; Chmiel and Mazur, 2012, 2016; Fels *et al.*, 2006; Fryer and Freeman, 2012b, 2014; Wilken and Kruger, 2016). Some authors have narrowed down the audience to children (Schmeidler and Kirchner, 2001; Palomo López, 2008; Orero, 2012, Krejtz *et al.*, 2012) or autistic children (Starr and Braun, Chapter 5 in this volume). Starr and Braun experimented with bespoke (emotive) AD target texts, moving away from visually oriented scripts to consider applications for end-users with cognitive needs. Other authors proposed changes to the target audio-described text to aid comprehension and engagement (Fryer, 2018). These include the audio description delivery speed (Cabeza-Cácares, 2013), the change from third to first person narrative (Udo and Fels, 2009) and the move from traditionally 'flat' to highly creative audio descriptions (Walczak and Fryer, 2017).

There is clear interest from researchers with regards to exploring how AD scripts are produced as a way of understanding what is considered—though never defined—to be quality AD (Fryer, 2018), and furthermore, how this material can best trigger an entertainment experience in the sight-impaired viewer which equates to that experienced by the general audience (ISO/IEC, 2015). Though much research has been carried out on this hybrid, written-oral text type, little research has been performed in relation to efficiency of AD listening and understanding or comprehensibility (Fryer, 2018), nor on enhancing AD (Sade *et al.*, 2012). To fill this gap, the present chapter focuses on two fundamental features of AD: listening and understanding. The hypothesis is that an audio description that is easier to listen to and understand will elicit a better audience comprehension performance and AD which is easy to listen to and easy to understand would contribute to mainstreaming AD.

3.2 Audio description audiences and functions

Considering the advantages of mainstreaming AD for all audiences, away from the specific needs of persons with disability, and drawing on the Universal Design approach (Story *et al.*, 1998) of working towards a diverse society is a timely task (Orero and Tor-Carroggio, 2018). More specifically, the observation that audio descriptions are useful for audiences other than blind and low-sighted persons opens the opportunity to optimise them both in financial terms (Sade *et al.*, 2012) and for those who benefit from easier-to-understand texts. Moving from the specificity of a blind and partially sighted audience to society in general implies a tweak in the traditional service towards AD for all. It makes it possible to take into consideration new audiences, such as the elderly, who are neither blind nor deaf, but have both hearing and sight loss, or people with learning difficulties and low-level reading skills, children, non-native speakers (including second-language learners) and readers with reduced literacy arising from, for example dyslexia, aphasia or deafness (Shardlow, 2014; Fajardo *et al.*, 2014; Arfe *et al.*, 2017; Inclusion Europe, 2009; European Commission, 2017; Siddharthan, 2014). The rise of this new AD-for-all service will go beyond the classic AD accessibility function. The proposed tweak to the known, existing service is to enhance understandability in order to aid all users. The new AD-for-all service should factor in sound and semantic content in order to aid comprehension.

AD is considered to be an accessibility service, working towards the fulfilment of the UN Convention for the Rights of Persons with Disabilities (CRPD) (Bachmeier, 2014). The traditional function of AD is to offer an alternative communication channel to an audiovisual text, when one of the main channels—the visual channel—is challenged. However, AD has also been found to work towards aiding learning and comprehension (Schmeidler and Kirchner, 2001; Krejtz *et al.*, 2012). Learning both content and languages, and increasing end-user attention (Starr, 2018), have been proved to be areas where the functions of AD have some collateral benefits.

Ultimately however, end-user profiles are too numerous to allow for personalised audio descriptions. The same can be said regarding any cognitive activity: no two users are exactly the same and what one finds easy, engaging or interesting, another may find pointless. Even the same person at different stages or in various situations will have a different response to the same cognitive stimuli. As with AD (for blind or low-sighted persons), text simplification users (second-language learners or low-literacy readers) may react differently; what is simple for one user may be more complex for another. However, Shardlow's (2014: 59) comment that 'a text which is made slightly simpler for one user will generally be easier for most other users' can be applied to audio description, leading to the hypothesis that an easier-to-process audio described text will benefit all.

3.3 The two departing points for easier audio description

Given the dual nature of the audio description text type—as a text to be read aloud or as an oral text—both writing and listening stages can be made easier to understand. The two points of departure are a simplification of the text and the sound, described in the next two sections respectively.

3.3.1 Text simplification and Easy-to-Read

There is no general agreement on the definition and naming of the two most common text simplification approaches: Plain Language and Easy-to-Read. According to Shardlow (2014: 59) 'Text Simplification (TS) is the process of modifying natural language to reduce its complexity and improve both readability and understandability. It may involve modifications to the syntax, the lexicon or both.' There are many text simplification models, and all focus on easing information processing (Siddharthan, 2014) and enhancing the cognitive accessibility of texts (Drndarevic *et al.*, 2012). A decreased effort in understanding reduces the cognitive load and the audience's freed resources can be dedicated to enjoyment (Berliner, 2017). Within TS, there are two important elements to define, namely, readability and understandability. The former deals with Easy-to-Read text and is related to complexity of grammar, length of sentences and familiarity with the vocabulary. The latter according to Shardlow (2014: 59) is

the amount of information a user may gain from a piece of text. This can be affected by factors such as the user's familiarity with the source vocabulary, their understanding of key concepts or the time and care taken to read the text. It may be the case that a text has high readability, but low understandability.

Text simplification relies on both since text can be more readable after lexical and syntactic modifications but still not be understandable, and vice versa. Within the context of this article, it should also be stressed that while readability can be assessed automatically or by humans, understandability requires the involvement of the target audiences (Shardlow, 2014).

As such, readability is extrinsic to the reader and influences the individual resources dedicated to the decoding task (Brueggeman, 2000) whereas understandability is intrinsic and depends on the reader's familiarity with the source vocabulary, their understanding of key concepts or the time and care that were taken to read the text. In this article, readability is considered a concept that relates to linguistic parameters which make a text more or less complex, but also to legibility (Burtt, 1949; European Commission, 2009; Siddharthan, 2014; Fajardo *et al.*, 2014). As already defined by Tinker (1963), legibility parameters influence the first interaction between the reader and paratextual elements. These are design-related, language-independent and range from typographical variables such as font-size or font-type to layout ratios such as contrast or text-to-white space (Inclusion Europe, 2009; Yuste Frías, 2012; Nietzio *et al.*, 2014).

Easy-to-Read (E2R) as a user-centric writing workflow includes a validation stage performed by the target audience and has fixed creation guidelines as well as recommendations. Looking at the first issued guidelines by an official standardisation agency—the Spanish Association for Standardisation and Certification (AENOR)—an E2R text has two production avenues: (i) creation or adaptation, which in turn should go through (ii) a validation stage, which is performed not by the writer or adaptor, but by the end user (CEAPAT, 2017). A good example of E2R is the text 'Lead in water' in Figure 3.1 and its adaptation to Plain English and Easy-to-Read.

Easy-to-Read is related not only to text but also paratextual features, as can be seen in the previous example, where illustrations are added to aid comprehension. Easy-to-Read is one of the most studied simplification methods exclusively for printed text (García, 2012) and currently is receiving more attention in digital content (Nietzio *et al.*, 2014). Finally, Easy-to-Read displays spoken and written characteristics and some have conceptualised it as a distinct language variety (Bredel and Maaß, 2016).

Easy-to-Read can be studied and defined from points of view ranging from linguistics to psychology and graphic design. E2R relates to all linguistic, textual and paratextual elements, and can be studied from any of these areas. The report *Guidelines for Easy-to-Read Materials* issued by the International Federation of Library Associations and Institutions (IFLA) points out the discrepancy regarding its definition:

Lead in Water

Original	Plain English	Easy to Read
Infants and children who drink water containing lead in excess of the action level could experience delays in their physical or mental development. Children could show slight deficits in attention span and learning abilities. Adults who drink this water over many years could develop kidney problems or high blood pressure.	Lead in drinking water can make you sick. Here are some possible health effects of high lead levels in your drinking water: **Children:** ○ Delayed growth ○ Learning disabilities ○ Short attention span **Adults:** ○ Kidney problems ○ High blood pressure	**Lead** is a metal. We can find lead in nature under the ground. Lead can be toxic to humans and animals. That means that lots of lead in drinking water can make you sick. Lead makes children and adults sick in different ways. Children: • grow slower • learn harder • have trouble concentrating Adults: • have problems with kidneys • have high blood pressure

The Original and the Plain English text © www.plainlanguage.gov
Easy to Read text © EASIT
Pictures © www.healthdirect.gov.au, toxictapbrisbane.wordpress.com, guidingexceptionalparents.com, geology.com

Figure 3.1 Example of text simplification.

There are two slightly different definitions of the term "easy-to-read". One means a linguistic adaptation of a text that makes it easier to read than the average text but which does not make it easier to comprehend; the other definition means an adaptation that makes both reading and comprehension easier.

(IFLA, 2010: 3)

Bernabé and Orero (2019) consider E2R as an accessible service which shares linguistic and extra-linguistic aspects with the standard language, while differing from it when it comes to improving readability and comprehension for all, but especially for people with reading, learning or comprehension difficulties.

3.3.2 Easy-to-listen audio descriptions

The reception of audio description is always as a voice service, a soundtrack to be listened to by an audience. As with any soundtrack, it has to be produced, mixed and distributed. AD can be distributed over many platforms, mainly by broadcast or broadband, and in fact by any technology delivering sound. The proliferation of devices allows for AD to be received via any streaming service: that is, a broadcast TV as a separate audio track, on TV as a mixed audio track, via video-on-demand content such as Netflix, from the radio, etc. In relation to AD there are three issues regarding sound: the sound itself, its recording and mixing, and its delivery. Looking at AD sound literature, only two authors (Van der Heidjen, 2007; Rodríguez, 2017) have raised the issue of sound quality, examining in particular sound mixing, and the intelligibility resulting from careless sound treatment. Some AD guidelines touch upon the issue of AD sound delivery, but on a very superficial level. Most guidelines invariably recommend quality—while avoiding its definition. An exception is the UK regulator OFCOM (2000: 10), stating:

> When descriptive commentary is inserted into a programme, the background level of programme audio needs to be reduced so that the description can be clearly heard. [...] The narrative voice is fixed at a constant level at the start of the recording but the background level can be adjusted. [...] If possible, music should be faded in and out at the beginning or end of a phrase (as is done by some disc jockeys when talking over music).

This recommendation has, to date, never been objected to or even contrasted with existing sound mix standards dealing with loudness, such as EBU R128 o W3 G56 (W3 G56, n.d.). There are plenty of studies regarding the sound mix when dealing with adverts on TV. A common practice is the automatic increase of the TV sound volume when adverts are shown. To protect consumers from abusively loud sound, standards are applied (EBU R 128, 2014). The loudness adjustment in TV adverts could be compared to that of audio description. There is also audio engineering technology to improve dialogue intelligibility, such as speech enhancement (Dixit and Mulge, 2014) or noise reduction (Chen *et al.*, 2006). In all cases, the objective is to highlight the dialogue with the aim of improving accessibility.

There are many ways to produce the AD soundtrack. The first is in a live context when the AD is produced simultaneously with the described event, and the audio describer is part of the audience. A good example would be a live fashion show. The second is the sound recording by the audio describer with the audio description editor. The third is the automatic text-to-sound reproduction by an application. Finally, a sound recording studio may record, and then manually mix the different soundtracks: background music, ambient noise, and sound effects. The many additional sounds, which are present for various narrative or aesthetic purposes, may interfere with dialogue intelligibility, and can be modified to improve its reception. Noise reduction and speech enhancement are the most common and current techniques for processing soundtracks in such a way, and could be applied to audio description to improve the original version of the sound by mixing it with the AD track.

Another issue present when delivering audio description is the delivery or reading speed. Some studies point towards the impact of reading speed on AD reception, and advise on controlling the delivery rate (Fels and Udo, 2010; Udo *et al.*, 2010; Fryer, 2016). Snyder (2014) suggested a reading speed of 160 words per minute, which has been adopted by the media industry (Netflix, n.d.), as compared to the average oral reading rate of 183 wpm (Brysbaert, 2019). This reading rate is independent of language and genre. Some studies have determined the reading rate by analysing existing content. This is the case for Ballester (2007) in the Spanish language, where she found the delivery speed variant of 150 to 180 wpm. For English, and looking specifically at children, McGonigle (2007) determined 175 wpm, and Cabeza-Cáceres (2013) found an average of 17 characters per second (CPS) as the delivery rate in Catalan. Jankowska *et al.* (2017) analysed reading rates for Polish in three films from different genres. The average AD reading rate was calculated at 13.95 CPS for a drama *Ida* (2013), 15.7 CPS for a comedy *Day of the Wacko* (2002), and 15.75 CPS for an action movie *Yuma* (2012). Only one study has carried out experimental research on reception. Cabeza-Cáceres (2013) tested for comprehension and enjoyment of AD delivered at three different speeds: slow 14, medium 17 and fast 20 characters per second, finding that while reading rate does not influence enjoyment, using a slower speed has a positive influence on comprehension.

Despite these advised delivery rates, we find humans do not have a standard ability to process speech (Fields, 2010a, 2010b). The difference in processing may be due to personal disposition or to the incoming sound. As already pointed out, the reception of a sound is influenced by the volume of the sound, prosodic features of the voice, and the level of semantic complexity in the text. Technology now allows personalisation beyond the classic settings such as volume, brightness or contrast on most screens—from TV sets to tablets or smartphones. Choosing the size of subtitles, their position and background is now a potential reality (Mas and Orero, 2017) for audio reproduction in almost all media players.

As with any service that can be personalised, it may seem that no specific research is required. Once its usability has been established, each person will choose the settings preferred either by personal requirements or the situation. A different sound volume is needed when listening to an AD from a smartphone at home or at an open event such as cinema (Walczak, 2017b). The same can be said for audio reproduction, i.e. the end user is able to set the preferred speed, but when reproducing audio description, a high-speed option opens the door to including more text in the available space. This is an interesting proposition: AD text length will depend on the reproduction speed, allowing for more description to be included. Existing media players, such as VLC or Windows, allow for a fast reproduction personalisation. This function applied to AD would allow for a longer and perhaps more explicit narrative, which may lead to an easier-to-understand text depending on the type of semantic content added (Bernabé, 2020).

Finally, research in automation and its reception is also a dynamic area in audio description advancement. In an effort to mainstream accessibility services and to match UN and local regulatory requirements, some work towards automation is being conducted (Starr and Braun, Chapter 5 in this volume). Industry players already offer some solutions as is the case with Microsoft[1] and the Japanese public broadcaster NHK.[2] Within the Audio Description Project, the American Council of the Blind is developing the Algorithmic

Automated Description (AAD).[3] The AAD is exploring automatic visual tagging technology.

> to automate specific aspects of description such as camera motion, scene changes, face identification, and the reading of printed text. Such events could be identified by computer models that automatically add annotations to the video. This would allow such things as the automated announcement of scene changes, or the use of text-to-speech for the reading of on-screen text.

Furthermore there has been testing for acceptance of the delivery of AD by synthetic speech through text-to-speech technology, which was carried out by Szarkowska (2011), Szarkowska and Jankowska (2012), and Fernández-Torné and Matamala (2015). Their research was performed on persons with low vision or blindness as end users, across audiovisual genres and different voices.

The results from all research on the audio channel of the audio description point towards the need to guarantee sound quality. The end user may have an excellent audio description created by a professional team and tested by end users, and yet a bad recording or sound mix will render the AD poor in quality, ultimately becoming a liability to accessibility. This has been shown by Rodríguez (2017) and also in recent work by Walczak and Fryer (2017) through examining the impact of AD delivery. The search for good-quality sound to create an easy-listening AD should be a priority, and prioritised when benchmarking for overall AD quality.

3.4 Easy-to-understand audio descriptions

Easy-to-understand accessibility services are not established yet as either access services or an academic course. However, the growing demand for cognitively accessible services—triggered by the need to comply with national and international regulations as well as the increased number of scientific publications—has attracted the attention of experts such as linguists, sociolinguists, translators, persons-with-disability associations, social workers and even typeface designers. In this chapter, it is considered in relation to the audiovisual modality, audio description.

After examining the two ways in which to generate an easier-to-understand text (Section 3.3.1) and easier-to-listen audio description, (Section 3.3.2) this section describes steps towards the creation of easier audio descriptions. The approach is based on the combination of four sets of guidelines: (a) existing AD guidelines, (b) Easy-to-Read guidelines, (c) W3C (2018) guidelines WCAG 2.1, and (d) sound mix guidelines. For each step, analysis of the source text, scripting and reviewing, with the aim to facilitate understanding, will be prioritised.

3.4.1 Steps in the creation of an easier-to-understand audio description

The three steps are analysis of the source text, scripting and reviewing.

3.4.1.1 First step

The first step in creating easier-to-understand audio description is to check on existing research and guidelines. AD and E2R guidelines recommend a thorough analysis of the source text as the first step (e.g. Remael *et al.*, 2014 for AD; Inclusion Europe, 2009 for E2R). There are two aims: first, to classify the text according to the type, genre, intention and other characteristics, and second, to identify content which is inaccessible or challenging for the viewer, either visually or cognitively.

With regard to AD, the purpose of describing identified cues is to help viewers to more easily understand specific content, establish meaningful connections between elements, and comprehend the global argument. The importance of a robust coherence when generating an audio description was established by Braun (2007) as a cornerstone of AD creation. According to van Dijk and Kintsch (1983), identifying coherence breaks is an important preliminary step in cognitive text simplification. Coherence gaps may be caused by the order in which the information is presented or by the absence of cues, which force viewers to make their own inferences (Braun, 2007). In easy audio descriptions, coherence needs to be maintained at two levels: for the content itself, and for the operability of the service. Service-related AD materials will be aimed at helping the user understand the functionality of the service and at operating it autonomously during the interaction. Inclusion Europe (2009) has already identified necessary cues for service-related content such as the introduction of the service itself and how to control it, and to present the background voice and its purpose, in for example an audio introduction. A lack of such cues could lead by implication to a lack of coherence.

The identification of content-related AD cues to facilitate coherence is less straightforward. Both IFLA (2010) and Inclusion Europe (2009) superficially address how to identify potential coherence gaps, breaks or difficulties. Both approach it methodologically by providing recommendations and advice involving users in the process. However, both offer limited support with implementation. At this point, it can be argued that all recommendations and guidelines related to creation can also be used to identify coherence gaps. In line with this, all paratextual, linguistic (e.g. lexical, syntactic) and global recommendations can become metrics for coherence. For instance, recommendations such as informing the audience beforehand about the topic or explaining relevant words or concepts and complex words or relationships would help to identify necessary content-related cues. Also of assistance is the recommendation to avoid difficult words. In this case, the Spanish UNE 153101 EX (AENOR, 2018) provides one specific technique, that is, to identify words that cannot be substituted by a suitable synonym. In such a case, a content-related cue explaining the meaning would be necessary.

The fact that we assume in this article that visual accessibility is always subordinated to cognitive accessibility in easy audio descriptions, yields two new types of content-related cues. These are, on the one hand, cues providing information that has already been presented multimodally but needs to be repeated vocally through the AD channel (repetition cues); and on the other, AD cues that can be excluded to avoid cognitive overload, if there are no losses of coherence. Vilaró and Orero (2013) further analysed these cues, also known as 'leitmotifs', and their function as 'anchoring' according to three AD elements: character, object and situation. Through the analysis of leitmotifs in different films and the anchoring effect, Vilaró and Orero (*ibid.*) studied the double coding effect and its function.

Another set of guidelines to be consulted are those issued by the World Wide Web Consortium (W3C, 2018) accessibility guidelines WCAG 2.1. These guidelines offer the possibility of achieving either an AA level of compliance or AAA, the highest level. The recommendations for AA status audio descriptions (pre-recorded) which are housed in Section 1.2.5 of WCAG 2.1, exclusively refer to content that is conveyed visually. In the 1.2.7 Extended Audio Description (pre-recorded) category, which incorporates periodic freezing of the synchronised media presentation so that supplementary audio description can be added (regarded as level AAA), Easy AD for W3C is simply required to be 'easy to understand'.

The criteria for successful understanding as defined in WCAG 2.1 are presented in several sections and are as follows (W3C, 2016):

3.1.1 Language of page
3.1.2 Language of parts
3.1.3 Unusual words
3.1.4 Abbreviations
3.1.5 Reading level
3.1.6 Pronunciation delivers further identification metrics

The first two criteria refer to the need for specifying the main language of a text and those parts that are written in a different language. By doing this, assistive technologies can recognise the language and render the text with the right pronunciation. The third criterion advises using known words instead of figurative language or technical terms. The fourth recommends both avoiding abbreviations because they might be unknown to users and providing access to their written-out form. The fifth criterion concerns the need for providing users either with supplementary information or easier-to-understand versions of content which require proficiency reading levels. As for the last criterion, it demands the provision of support when understanding the meaning of a word depends on a specific pronunciation.

As for service-related content, WCAG 2.1 (W3C, 2018) section 'Understanding Success Criterion 1.3.6: Identify Purpose' (AAA) points out the need for user-understandable interoperability. Though these guidelines are succinct, and drafted primarily with websites in mind, they offer good examples and information regarding the content creation of audio description. For instance, they advise explaining the purpose of the service so that users can benefit from personalisation options without having to know terms that might or might not be familiar to them.

3.4.1.2 Second step

The second step in AD creation is scripting and the aim is to deliver an easy-to-understand script. Text simplification requires the reduction of the linguistic complexity of a text, adding linguistic information and text elaboration by varying degrees (Arfe *et al.*, 2017). This definition is based on the assumption that removing linguistic complexity at lexical or grammatical levels alone does not necessarily aid (inferential) comprehension, as shown in young less-able readers (Di Mascio *et al.*, 2011) and in second-language learners (Urano, 2000). Current E2R guidelines and recommendations provide text elaboration, text addition and text simplification strategies.

Text elaboration is a process that aims to clarify and explain information and to make connections explicit in a text (Aluísio and Gasperin, 2010). E2R guidelines recognise the benefits of two main techniques, repetitions and explicitness. For instance, the guidelines issued by Inclusion Europe state: 'It is OK to repeat important information', 'Explain the subject', 'Explain difficult words' and 'Use examples to explain things'. Further, the guidelines suggest: 'Where possible, explain the words at the time you are using them' and 'When you change the place of filming, explain where the new place is so people do not get confused' (Inclusion Europe, 2009: 11, 9, 10, 15, 34). As for linguistic additions, in terms of additions of new information, the above E2R guidelines and recommendations also apply: 'Make sure you explain the subject clearly and also explain any difficult words to do with that subject', and 'Always make sure you give people all the information they need' (IFLA, 2010: 9). The risk of potential overload related to text elaboration and text additions is mentioned as well: 'Do not give people more information than they need to understand your point. Only give them the important information' (IFLA, 2010: 17). For the implementation of both elaborations and additions, they refer to linguistic simplification and advise against the use of relative clauses: 'write short sentences' (IFLA, 2010: 22). 'Always keep your sentences short' and 'Use the right language' (Inclusion Europe, 2009: 11, 9).

Van Dyck and Kintsch (1983: 27) stated that 'complex semantic contents can only be expressed or understood clearly with the help of syntax, and syntax can make language communication more efficient'. E2R guidelines also refer to text simplification as lexical and syntactic reduction of the complexity of a text, while trying to preserve meaning and information (Aluísio and Gasperin, 2010). Both IFLA (2010) and Inclusion Europe (2009) include many recommendations. 'Use easy to understand words that people will know well', 'Stick as much as possible to reality', 'Use the same word to describe the same thing throughout your document', 'Do not use words from other languages' (Inclusion Europe, 2009: 10); 'avoid abstract words', 'Do not use difficult ideas such as metaphors' (IFLA, 2010). Syntactic recommendations include using short and positive propositions, avoiding passive language, as well as writing information in a logical and chronological order: 'Always put your information in an order that is easy to understand and follow' and 'Group the information about the same topic together.' However, although these references might suggest the validity of the E2R guidelines, they are experience-based (IFLA, 2010) and still need to be empirically validated as their efficiency can only be proven by the target audience.

3.4.1.3 *Third step*

The third step is reviewing, which is often accomplished in standard AD by working together with a blind or visually impaired collaborator (Benecke, 2014; ADLAB, 2014). Easy-to-Read guidelines refer to this task as checking or validation (Inclusion Europe, 2009) and endorse the involvement of the final user. The aim is to validate whether the provided AD cues help the audience to understand the content more easily and to make observations regarding its reception. Thus, validation relates to language and perceivability of the voiced texts through the auditory channel and, additionally, to the viewer's experience.

Regarding perceivability, the reception of audio description depends on the perception and comprehension skills of the viewer. Inclusion Europe (2009) specifies ways to facilitate listening comprehension in general. Clear and high-quality sound, good volume and avoidance of interferences or background noise are necessary in order to support acoustic segmentation and lexical access. The voice should be clear, without accent or dialect, and focused on good pronunciation and clear articulation. There are specific E2R recommendations related to delivery. Inclusion Europe (2009) recommends the insertion of pauses at appropriate points, and to read the text in a way that allows emotions to be perceived. It also states: 'Do not be in a hurry. Do not speak too fast.' A steady motion is preferred. Although there is no direct reference to audio descriptions, these audio recommendations and those regarding consistency in the delivery cannot be ignored at this point.

The brief review presented in this chapter suggests that the creation of Easy AD by combining AD and E2R guidelines and recommendations could help to deliver a pathway for its implementation. Along the way, similarities in approach with other forms of Easy-to-Read have been identified as well as implementation metrics and traits. Dissimilarities were also found, deriving from the predominant role given to cognitive accessibility, to avoid both cognitive overload and loss of coherence. The final aspect of methodological transfer, language adaptation, is discussed in the next section.

3.4.2 *Language adaptation for Easy AD*

Writing easy audio descriptions involves multi-semiotic translations and text simplifications that support the enjoyment of multimodal content. As intersemiotic translations, they act as the spoken word, supplying image elements that are conveyed visually—facial expressions, scene changes and sound elements that can only be understood within a visual context. For instance, the sound of a door slamming does not give any indication of the action, whether or not a person is arriving or leaving, or even about the type of door. As text simplifications, Easy AD would be modifications applied to natural language (Shardlow, 2014) to increase understandability. Shardlow (2014) also states that the term 'simple' is mostly used in these contexts when in contrast with a complex language. While traditional AD uses rich language, easy audio descriptions would employ less complex or simplified language.

Language in audio descriptions is discussed across all guidelines and recommendations. The overall aim is to avoid tiring the listener due to saturation of information or causing anxiety due to a lack of information. A comparative study conducted by Rai *et al.* (2010) showed a high overlap in language recommendations between research projects. In AD, consistency, accuracy and objectivity prevail whilst also making use of the richness of the language. It is advised to use clear and unambiguous words, as well as impartial and factual language that expresses with precision and details actions and visuals on the screen or display. The use of vivid language is recommended in order to engage the listener. Variety, especially with verbs, is important in order to create images, with adverbs and adjectives tagged as useful, provided they are not subjective. Technical terms should be explained or avoided. Finally, the use of the present tense should be obvious, and sentences simple and short (ADLAB, 2014; American Council of the Blind, 2010).

In Easy AD language, the extent to which these recommendations can be implemented would be subordinate to the primary goals of text simplification and the E2R features. Lexical simplification according to UNE 153101 EX (AENOR, 2018) and the guidelines of Inclusion Europe (2009) seem to rely on finding substitution candidates based on word frequency, word length and sense disambiguation. They recommend using simple, short and common words that do not contain difficult syllables which, for instance, sound the same, as well as avoiding abstract and foreign words. Moreover, they advise against the use of metaphors, irony, proverbs and idioms. They also pinpoint the pitfalls of ambiguity and warn about the use of words that do not clearly designate a concept, such as the words 'thing' or 'something' as well as homonyms and homophones, which should be used only if the context makes clear which concept is signified. The proposed simplifications are illustrated in the following example:

1. *He approached the bank. His mother was waiting.*
    In this utterance it is not clear what type of bank the author is referring to.
2. *He approached the bank. His mother was waiting inside.*
    In this version the second sentence helps to understand the type of 'bank' but the utterance can still be misunderstood.
3. *He approached the bank building. His mother was waiting for him inside.*
    This version is less ambiguous.

Regarding syntactic simplification, current E2R guidelines focus on syntactic reordering, sentence splitting, deletions and insertions. They advise only using pronouns if the reference is clear, avoiding passive and progressive constructions, prioritising short sentences without coordinate or subordinate clauses, and using positive sentences over negative ones where possible, or at least avoiding two negative sentences in a row (Inclusion Europe, 2009; AENOR, 2018). Morphological simplifications are also generally considered and addressed in detail according to the particular language: for instance, the Spanish guidelines in UNE 153101 EX advise against using the progressive form as well as verbal periphrases (AENOR, 2018), whereas the German guidelines warn about the use of genitive case, subjunctive mood and past simple tenses (Suter *et al.*, 2016).

Adoption of Easy AD would create an individualistic, hybrid narrative style through the deliberately applied modifications and restrictions, be they lexical and syntactic simplifications, word repetition and choices, text elaborations and additions (explanations, examples, analogies, other) or linear syntactic structures. The yielded descriptions might then be considered as linguistically and stylistically adapted. As with standard AD, their effectiveness will depend on their degree of cohesion with the other elements of the source text—images, dialogues, sounds, other—and the viewers' reception, which will be evaluated at the validation stage.

3.5 Conclusion

Contrary to some guidelines proposing rich audio description, in this chapter we propose a shorter, more concise and compact narrative with an enhanced audio. Given the complex nature of audio description production and delivery, improvements can be introduced at all stages to increase its reception (listening) and understanding (comprehension): from a high-quality, clean-sound mix (which should be an objective value measured in decibels) to a script, taking into account Easy-to-Read guidelines. There are also many technological possibilities for the personalisation of AD delivery to make it align with audience needs. This paper has only outlined three areas of audio description components where technology exists and can be successfully implemented to generate a quality, personalised, easy-listening, enhanced audio description. While this chapter has proposed a theoretical approach, the overall objective is to generate a high-quality service that fulfils end-user requirements and expectations.

To summarise, the current framework of Easy-to-Read guidelines across several languages shows that hybrid easy audio descriptions could already be implemented. This article is the conceptual point of departure for a study that will be carried out to analyse the validity of the issues reported. Validation of Easy AD through experience-based results and parallel scientific research will allow us to move forward, paving the way for further hybrid, and multiservice settings such as the combination of easy audio descriptions and subtitling, or Easy-to-Read or easy-to-understand subtitles. As for the latter, authors have already created E2U subtitles within the framework of the EU Horizon 2020 project ImAc,[4] which have been validated by end users in Spain and are currently being tested.

Acknowledgements

This chapter has been partially funded by the EU project IMAC grant number 761974, EASIT 2018-1-ES01-KA203-050275, RAD PGC2018-096566-B-I00, and the Catalan Research Council grant number SGR113.

Notes

1 www.microsoft.com/en-us/seeing-ai.
2 www.nhk.or.jp/strl/open2017/tenji/13_e.html.
3 http://acb.org/adp/articles/vdrdc.html.
4 www.imac-project.eu.

References

ADLAB (2014) 'Audio description: lifelong access for the blind'. Available at: www. adlabproject.eu/home (accessed 28 April 2020).
AENOR (2018) Norma 153101 EX Lectura fácil: pautas y recomendaciones para la elaboración de documentos. Madrid: AENOR.
Afonso, A., Blum, A., Katz, B. F., Tarroux P., Borst G., and Denis, M. (2010) 'Structural properties of spatial representations in blind people: scanning images constructed from haptic exploration or from locomotion in a 3-D audio virtual environment', *Memory and Cognition*, 38(5), pp. 591–604.
Aluísio, S., and Gasperin, C. (2010) 'Fostering digital inclusion and accessibility: the PorSimples project for simplificaction of Portugues texts', *Proceedings of the NAACL HLT 2010 Young Investigators Workshop on Computational Approaches to Languages of the Americas*, Los Angeles, 6 June, pp. 46–53.
American Council of the Blind (2010) 'The Audio Description Project.' Available at: www.acb.org/audio-description-project (accessed 28 April 2020).
Arfe, B., Mason, L., and Fajardo, I. (2017) 'Simplifying informational text structure for struggling readers', *Reading and Writing*, 31, pp. 2191–2210.

Bachmeier, C. (2014) 'Barrier-free access to audiovisual content: a fundamental human right', in S. Nikoltchev (ed.), Enabling Access to the Media for All, Strasbourg: European Audiovisual Observatory, pp. 7–22.

Ballester, A. (2007) 'La audiodescripción: apuntes sobre el estado de la cuestión y las perspectivas de investigación', *TradTerm*, 13, pp. 151–169.

Benecke, B. (2014) *Audiodeskription als partielle Translation: Modell und Methode*. Münster: LIT.

Berliner, T. (2017) *Hollywood Aesthetic: Pleasure in American Cinema*. Oxford: Oxford University Press.

Bernabé, R. (2020) 'New taxonomy of easy-to-understand access services', in M. Richart-Marset and F. Calamita (eds.), *Traducción y accesibilidad en los medios de comunicación: de la teoría a la práctica*, MonTI, 12, pp. 345–380.

Bernabé, R., and Orero, P. (2019) 'Easy to Read as multimode accessibility service', *Hermeneus*, 21, pp. 53–74.

Braun, S. (2007) 'Audio description from a discourse perspective: a socially relevant framework for research and training', *Linguistica Antverpiensia, New Series – Themes in Translation Studies*, 6, pp. 357–369.

Braun, S. (2011) 'Creating coherence in audio description', *Meta*, 56(3), pp. 645–662.

Bredel, U., and Maaß, C. (2016) *Leichte Sprache: theoretische Grundlagen. Orientierung für die Praxis*. Berlin: Dudenverlag.

Brueggeman, L. (2000) 'Fourth graders' literal and inferential reading comprehension: effects of readability and answer format', unpublished PhD thesis, University of Washington.

Brysbaert, M. (2019) 'How many words do we read per minute? A review and meta-analysis of reading rate', PsyArXiv Preprints. Available at: https://doi.org/10.31234/osf.io/xynwg (accessed 28 April 2020).

Burtt, H. (1949) 'Typography and readability', *Elementary English*, 26(4), pp. 212–221.

Cabeza-Cáceres, C. (2013) 'Audiodescripció i recepció: efecte de la velocitat de narració, l'entonació i l'explicitació en la comprensió fílmica' [Audio description and reception: the effect of speed of narration, intonation and explicitation in film comprehension], unpublished PhD thesis, Universitat Autònoma de Barcelona. Available at: www.academia.edu/23388431/Audiodescripció_i_recepció_efecte_de_la_velocitat_de_narració_lentonació_i_lexplicitació_en_la_comprensió_fílmica (accessed 1 May 2020).

CEAPAT (2017) Decálogo de apoyo a la Lectura Fácil. Available at: www.ceapat.es/InterPresent2/groups/imserso/documents/binario/decalogo_apoyo_lfacil.pdf (accessed 9 July 2017).

Chen, J., Benesty, J., Yiteng, H., and Doclo, S. (2006) 'New insights into the noise reduction Wiener filter', *IEEE Transactions on Audio, Speech, and Language Processing*, 14(4), pp. 1218–1234.

Chmiel A., and Mazur, I. (2012) 'AD reception research: some methodological considerations', in E. Perego (ed.), *Emerging Topics in Translation: Audio Description*. Trieste: Edizioni Università di Trieste, pp. 57–80.

Chmiel, A., and Mazur, I. (2016) 'Researching preferences of audio description users – limitations and solutions', *Across Languages and Cultures*, 17(2), pp. 271–288.

Di Mascio, T., Gennari, R., and Vittorini, P. (2011) 'The design of the TERENCE adaptive learning system', in T. Bastiaens and M. Ebner (eds.), *Proceedings of ED-MEDIA 2011–World Conference on Educational Multimedia, Hypermedia and*

Telecommunications, Lisbon, 27 June – 1 July, pp. 1609–1617. Available at: www. learntechlib.org/primary/p/38077 (accessed 25 July 2017).

Dixit, S., and Mulge, Y. (2014) 'Review on speech enhancement techniques', *International Journal of Computer Science and Mobile Computing*, 3(8), pp. 285–290.

Drndarevic, B., Štajner, S., and Saggion, H. (2012) 'Reporting simply: a lexical simplification strategy for enhancing text accessibility', in *Easy-to-Read on the Web Online Symposium 3 December 2012: Proceedings 2012*, Cambridge, MA. Available at: https://ub-madoc.bib.uni-mannheim.de/41359 (accessed 8 November 2019).

EBU R 128 (2014) 'Loudness normalisation and permitted maximum level of audio signals.' Available at: https://tech.ebu.ch/docs/r/r128-2014.pdf (accessed 8 November 2019).

European Commission (2009) 'Guideline on the readability of the labelling and package leaflet of medicinal products for human use.' Available at: https://ec.europa.eu/ health/sites/health/files/files/eudralex/vol-2/c/2009_01_12_readability_guideline_ final_en.pdf (accessed 6 September 2018).

European Commission (2017) 'Progress report on the implementation of the European Disability Strategy (2010–2020).' Available at: www.eud.eu/news/public-hearing-crpds-committee-concluding-observations-eu-two-years-after (accessed 4 August 2018).

Fajardo, I., Ávila, V., Ferrer, A., Tavares, G., Gómez, M., and Hernández, A. (2014) 'Easy-to-read texts for students with intellectual disability: linguistic factors affecting comprehension', *Journal of Applied Research in Intellectual Disabilities*, 27(3), pp. 212–225.

Fels D., Udo, J. P., Diamond J. E., and Diamond J. I. (2006) 'A comparison of alternative narrative approaches to video description for animated comedy', *Journal of Visual Impairment and Blindness*, 100(5), pp. 295–305.

Fels, D., and Udo, J. P. (2010) 'Re-fashioning fashion: an exploratory study of a live audio described fashion show', *Universal Access in the Information Society*, 9(1), pp. 63–75.

Fernández, A., and Matamala, A. (2015) 'Text-to-speech vs human voiced audio description: a reception study in films dubbed into Catalan', Jostrans: Journal of Specialised Translation, 24, pp. 61–88. Available at: www.jostrans.org/issue24/art_ fernandez.pdf (accessed 28 April 2020).

Fields, D. (2010a) 'Why can some blind people process speech far faster than sighted persons?', *Scientific American*, 13 December. Available at: www.scientificamerican. com/article/why-can-some-blind-people-process (accessed 23 July 2017).

Fields, D. (2010b) 'Extraordinary ability of blind people to hear ultrafast speech', *Brain Waves*, 14 December. Available at: https://rdouglasfields.wordpress.com/2010/12/ 14/extraordinary-ability-of-blind-people-to-hear-ultrafast-speech (accessed 23 July 2017).

Fryer, L. (2016) *An Introduction to Audio Description: A Practical Guide*. London: Routledge.

Fryer, L. (2018) 'Quality assessment in audio description', in E. Huertas-Barros, S. Vandepitte and E. Iglesias-Fernández (eds.), *Quality Assurance and Assessment Practices in Translation and Interpreting*, Hershey, PA: IGI Global, pp.155–177.

Fryer, L., and Freeman, J. (2012a) 'Cinematic language and the description of film: keeping AD users in the frame', *Perspectives: Studies in Translatology*, 21(3), pp. 412–426.

Fryer, L., and Freeman, J. (2012b) 'Presence in those with and without sight: implications for virtual reality and audio description', *Journal of Cybertherapy and Rehabilitation*, 5(1), pp. 15–23.

Fryer L., Pring, L., and Freeman, J. (2013) 'Audio drama and the imagination: the influence of sound effects on presence in people with and without sight', *Journal of Media Psychology*, 25, pp. 65–71.

Fryer L., and Freeman J. (2014) 'Can you feel what I'm saying? The impact of verbal information on emotion elicitation and presence in people with a visual impairment', in A. Felnhofer and O. D. Kothgassner (eds.), *Challenging Presence: Proceedings of the 15th International Conference on Presence*, Vienna, 17–19 March, pp. 99–107.

García, O. (2012) *Lectura fácil: métodos de redacción y evaluación*. Available at: www.plenainclusion.org/sites/default/files/lectura-facil-metodos.pdf (accessed 21 August 2018).

Inclusion Europe (2009) *Information for All: European Standards for Making Information Easy to Read and Understand*. Available at: www.inclusion-europe.eu/easy-to-read (accessed 30 April 2020).

IFLA (International Federation of Library Associations and Institutions) (2010) *Guidelines for Easy-to-Read materials*. Available at: www.ifla.org/files/assets/hq/publications/professional-report/120.pdf (accessed 23 July 2017).

ISO/IEC (2015) '20071-21 Information technology – user interface component accessibility – Part 21: guidance on audio descriptions.' Available at: www.iso.org/standard/63061.html (accessed 21 July 2017).

Jankowska, A., Ziółko, B., Igras-Cybulska, M., and Psiuk, A. (2017) 'Reading rate in filmic audio description', *International Journal of Translation*, 19, pp. 75–97.

Krejtz, I., Szarkowska, A., Krejtz, K., Walczak, A., and Duchowski, A. (2012) 'Audio description as an aural guide of children's visual attention: evidence from an eye-tracking study', *Proceedings of the ACM Symposium on Eye Tracking Research and Applications Conference*, New York, ACM, 28–30 March, pp. 99–106.

Mas, L. and Orero, P. (2017) 'New subtitling possibilities: testing subtitle usability in HbbTV', *Translation Spaces*, 7(2), pp. 263–284.

Maszerowska, A. (2012) 'Casting the light on cinema: how luminance and contrast patterns create meaning', *MonTi*, 4, pp. 65–85.

Matamala, A., and Orero, P. (2011) 'Opening credit sequences: audio describing films within films', *International Journal of Translation*, 23(2), pp. 35–58.

McGonigle, F. (2007) 'The audio description of children's films.' Unpublished MA dissertation, University of Surrey.

Nietzio, A., Naber, D., and Bühler, C. (2014), 'Towards techniques for Easy-to-Read Web content', *Procedia Computer Science*, 27, pp. 343–349.

NETFLIX (n.d.) 'Netflix audio description style guide V1.0.' Available at: https://backlothelp.netflix.com/hc/en-us/articles/215510667-Audio-Description-Style-Guide-v1-0 (accessed 5 August 2017).

OFCOM (2000) 'ITC guidance on standards for audio description UK: Independent Television Commission.' Available at: www.ofcom.org.uk/static/archive/itc/itc_publications/codes_guidance/audio_description/index.asp.html (accessed 23 July 2017).

Orero, P. (2011) 'Audio description for children: once upon a time there was a different audio description for characters', in E. di Giovanni (ed.), *Entre texto y receptor:*

Accesibilidad, doblaje y traducción [Between Text and Audience: Accessibility, Dubbing and Translation]. Frankfurt: Peter Lang, pp. 169–184.

Orero, P. (2012) 'Film reading for writing audio descriptions: a word is worth a thousand images?', in E. Perego (ed.), *Emerging Topics in Translation: Audio Description*, Trieste: Edizioni Università di Trieste, pp. 13–28.

Orero, P. (2016) 'Audio describing the TV series *The West Wing*', *TRAlinea: Online Translation Journal*, 18.

Orero, P., and Tor-Carroggio, I. (2018) 'User requirements when designing learning e-content: interaction for all', in E. Kapros and M. Koutsombogera (eds.), *Designing for the User Experience in Learning Systems*, Cham: Springer, pp. 105–121.

Orero, P., and Vilaró, A. (2012) 'Eye tracking analysis of minor details in films for audio description', *MonTi*, 4, pp. 295–319.

Orero, P., Maszerowska, A., and Cassacuberta, D. (2016) 'Audio describing silence: lost for words', in A. Jankowska and A. Szarkowska (eds.), *New Points of View in Audiovisual Translation*, Oxford: Peter Lang, pp. 219–236.

Palomo López, A. (2008) 'Audio description as language development and language learning for blind and low vision children', in R. Hyde Parker and K. Guadarrama García (eds.), *Thinking Translation: Perspectives from Within and Without*. Boca Ratón, FL: Brown Walker Press, pp. 113–133.

Perego, E. (2014) 'Film language and tools', in A. Maszerowska, A. Matamala and P. Orero (eds), *Audio Description: New Perspectives Illustrated*, Amsterdam: John Benjamins, pp. 81–101.

Rai, S., Greening, J., and Petré, L. (2010) '*A Comparative Study of Audio Description Guidelines Prevalent in Different Countries*', London: Media and Culture Department, Royal National Institute of Blind People. Available at: http://audiodescription. co.uk/uploads/general/RNIB._AD_standards.pdf (accessed 21 May 2019).

Remael, A., Reviers, N., and Vercauteren, G. (2014) 'Pictures painted in words: ADLAB audio description guidelines.' Available at: http://www.adlabproject.eu/Docs/ adlab%20book/index.html (accessed 21 May 2019).

Rodríguez, A. (2017) *Audiodescripción y propuesta de estandarización de volumen de audio: hacia una producción sistematizada*. Unpublished PhD thesis, Universitat Autònoma de Barcelona. Available at: https://www.tdx.cat/bitstream/handle/ 10803/459247/alro1de1.pdf?sequence=1&isAllowed=y (accessed 20 May 2019).

Sade, J., Naz, K., and Plaza, M. (2012) 'Enhancing audio description: a value added approach', *ICCHP '12 Proceedings of the 13th International Conference on Computers Helping People with Special Needs*, Linz, 11–13 July.

Schmeidler, E., and Kirchner, C. (2001) 'Adding audio description: does it make a difference?', *Journal of Visual Impairment and Blindness*, 95(4), pp. 198–212.

Shardlow, M. (2014) 'A survey of automated text simplification', *International Journal of Advanced Computer Science and Applications*.

Siddharthan, A. (2014) 'A survey on text simplification', *International Journal of Applied Linguistics*, 165(2), pp. 259–298.

Snyder, J. (2014) *The Visual Made Verbal: A Comprehensive Training Manual and Guide to the History and Applications of Audio Description*. Arlington: American Council of the Blind.

Starr, K. L. (2018) 'Audio description and cognitive diversity: a bespoke approach to facilitating access to the emotional content in multimodal narrative texts for autistic audiences.' PhD thesis, University of Surrey.

Story, M. F., Mueller, J. L., and Mace, R. L. (1998) *The Universal Design File: Designing for People of All Ages and Abilities*. Raleigh: North Carolina State University Center for Universal Design. Available at: https://eric.ed.gov/?id=ED460554 (accessed 4 November 2019).

Suter, J., Ebling, S., and Volk, M. (2016) 'Rule-based automatic text simplification for German', in *The 13th Conference on Natural Language Processing* (KONVENS 2016), Bochum, Germany.

Szarkowska, A. (2011) 'Text-to-speech audio description: towards wider availability of AD', *Jostrans: Journal of Specialised Translation*, 15, pp. 142–162. Available at: www.jostrans.org/issue15/art_szarkowska.pdf (accessed 28 April 2020).

Szarkowska, A., and Jankowska, A. (2012) 'Text-to-speech audio description of voiced-over films: a case study of audio described *Volver* in Polish', in E. Perego (ed.), *Emerging Topics in Translation: Audio Description*. Trieste: Edizioni Università di Trieste, pp. 81–98.

Szarkowska, A., and Orero, P. (2014) 'The importance of sound in audio description', in A. Maszerowska, A. Matamala and P. Orero (eds.), *Audio Description: New Perspectives Illustrated*, Amsterdam: John Benjamins, pp. 121–139.

The American Council of the Blind. (2010) 'The Audio Description Project.' Available at: https://www.acb.org/audio-description-project (accessed 28 April 2020).

Tinker, M. A. (1963) *Legibility of Print*. Ames: Iowa State University Press.

Udo J. P., and Fels, D. I. (2009) 'Suit the action to the word, the word to the action: an unconventional approach to describing Shakespeare's Hamlet', *Journal of Visual Impairment and Blindness*, 103(3), pp. 178–183.

Udo, J. P., Acevedo B., and Fels D. I. (2010) 'Horatio audio-describes Shakespeare's Hamlet', *British Journal of Visual Impairment*, 28(2), pp. 139–156.

Urano, K. (2000) 'Lexical simplification and elaboration: an experiment in sentence comprehension and incidental vocabulary acquisition.' Unpublished Master's thesis, University of Hawaii. Available at: www.urano-ken.com/research/thesis.pdf (accessed 9 November 2019).

Van der Heijden, M. (2007) 'Making film and television accessible to the blind and visually impaired.' Master's thesis, Utrecht School of the Arts. Available at: https://static.aminer.org/pdf/PDF/000/288/838/spoken_subtitles_making_subtitled_tv_programmes_accessible.pdf (accessed 28 April 2020).

Van Dijk, T. A., and Kintsch, W. (1983) *Strategies of Discourse Comprehension*. New York: Academic Press.

Vilaró, A., and Orero, P. (2013) 'The audio description of leitmotifs', *International Journal of Humanities and Social Science*, 3(5), pp. 56–64.

W3 G56 (n.d.) 'Mixing audio files so that non-speech sounds are at least 20 decibels lower than the speech audio content.' Available at: https://www.w3.org/TR/WCAG20-TECHS/G56.html (accessed 23 July 2017).

W3C (2016) 'Readable: understanding guideline 3.1.' Available at: www.w3.org/TR/UNDERSTANDING-WCAG20/meaning-other-lang-id.html (accessed 8 November 2019).

W3C (2018) 'Web accessibility content guidelines.' Available at: www.w3.org/TR/WCAG21 (accessed 20 May 2019).

Walczak, A. (2017a) 'Creative description: audio describing artistic films for individuals with visual impairments', *Journal of Visual Impairment and Blindness*, 111(4), pp. 387–391.

Walczak, A. (2017b) 'Audio description on smartphones: making cinema accessible for visually impaired audiences', *Universal Access in the Information Society*, 17(4), pp. 833–840.

Walczak, A., and Fryer, L. (2017) 'Vocal delivery of audio description by genre: measuring users' presence', *Perspectives: Studies in Translatology*, 26(1), pp. 69–83.

Wilken, N., and Kruger, J. L. (2016) 'Putting the audience in the picture: *mise-en-shot* and psychological immersion in audio described film', *Across Languages and Cultures*, 17(2), pp. 251–270.

Yuste Frías, J. (2012) 'Paratextual elements in translation: paratranslating titles in children's literature', in A. Gil-Bajardí, P. Orero and S. Rovira-Esteva (eds.), *Translation Peripheries*. Bern and New York: Peter Lang, pp. 117–134.

Filmography

Day of the Wacko (2002) Directed by M. Koterski. [Feature film]. Poland: Vision Film Production.

Ida (2013) Directed by P. Pawlikowski. [Feature film]. Poland: Solopan.

Yuma (2012) Directed by P. Mularuk. [Feature film]. Poland: Yeti Films.

4 Film language, film experience and film interpretation in a reception study comparing conventional and interpretative audio description styles

Floriane Bardini

4.1 Introduction

Audio description (AD) is a form of intersemiotic translation whose purpose is to translate visual elements into the verbal system for those who do not have access to the visual channel. The shift in semiotic systems implies a shift of mode (non-verbal to verbal) and channel (visual to auditory). According to Zabalbeascoa (2008), all modes and channels are equally important for generating an audiovisual message. Yet their presence and balance vary in the original and in the audio described version of the audiovisual text. The auditory channel normally contains a combination of non-verbal elements in the form of music and sound effects, and a verbal component in the form of dialogue, song lyrics and/or narration. In the visual channel, on the contrary, there is a clear prevalence of the non-verbal mode: images are the essence of the audio-visual text. Hence, film language relies on infinite ways to create meaning and express a message through verbal and non-verbal cues and the interplay of visual and auditory information.

Important insights into how meaning is created in film come from Peirce's "second trichotomy of the sign" (Wollen, 2013: 102). According to this theory, meaning emerges at iconic, indexical and symbolic levels (*ibid.*). Icons resemble the object they represent: an image of a pipe represents a pipe. Indices bear an existential relationship with the object they represent and are essential in cinema. They can be visual (e.g. footprints on a path mean that somebody walked this way) or auditory (e.g. Darth Vader's theme in *Star Wars* (1977) means that the villain is there or that his arrival is imminent). Finally, symbols are arbitrary signs, like words, or a red ribbon as a symbol of solidarity with people living with AIDS. Schmid (2014: 22) argues that viewers interpret films by 'combining the multi-layered verbal, visual and musical impulses to form a semantic, sensual and emotional impression in which a maximum of symbols, icons and indexes of the multimedia-based cinematographic "text" is foregrounded'. In cinema, the use of symbols and indices relies on well-known conventions, such as the shot/reverse shot technique (Kuhn and Westwell, 2012), but can also be reinvented by each film director. Carroll (2008: 121) believes that 'insofar as cinema is an artform, motion picture makers need not regard any rule as inviolable' and, according to Plantinga (2010: 94), 'the filmmaker can affect the spectator through all of the various parameters of film style, from shot composition, to movement, to editing, to colour, to sound and music', which illustrates the infinite array of creative possibilities open to filmmakers—and the challenge for viewers to interpret the meaning of film. These insights from cognitive film theory reflect the importance of creative decisions behind film language, which go well beyond the level of iconic representation and imply that complex cognitive processes are involved in the interpretation of film.

Although interpretation is at the core of the film-watching activity, most AD guidelines advocate objective descriptions: audio describers should not interpret any element of the film but provide the necessary information for blind and partially sighted viewers to make their own interpretation (Dosch and Benecke, 2004; AENOR, 2005; Morisset and Gonant, 2008). Furthermore, the use of cinematic terminology (e.g. 'close-up', 'pan-down') is also not encouraged because, according to guidelines, these terms might not be meaningful for all AD users, depending on their visual memory and previous exposure to cinema (Ofcom, 2000; Dosch and Benecke, 2004; Morisset and Gonant, 2008). These requirements both clash with film theory as, in practice, it is often impossible for audio describers to depict a cinematic effect without using any technical terms or interpreting the effect of the technique employed, because of time constraints and because, in contrast to the 'impressionistic' quality of the visual mode, verbal language is emitted and processed sequentially, which could lead to a cognitive overload if a film effect were to be depicted denotatively (Braun, 2008: 20). This contradiction between AD guidelines and film theory has been pointed out by several researchers (Braun, 2007; Orero, 2012; Perego, 2014) and different user studies have been conducted to tackle these inconsistencies. For example in the UK, Fryer and Freeman tested a cinematic description with blind and partially sighted viewers, breaking AD conventions by including multiple cinematic terms to describe camera work and editing techniques: most participants expressed greater satisfaction with the cinematic AD version than with conventional audio description (Fryer and Freeman, 2013: 7). Szarkowska (2013) tested *auteur* description with a group of blind and partially sighted viewers in Poland, i.e. an AD style 'which incorporates the director's creative vision in the AD script through the use of a screenplay (or other available materials, such as interviews and reviews) and thus gives the audio describer the artistic licence to depart from the dictate of objectivism' (Szarkowska, 2013: 383). Most participants enjoyed the *auteur* description of *Volver* (2006) and approved of this alternative AD style, which 'gave the film a more entertaining character and enabled them to gain a better understanding of the motivations of the characters and to follow the plot' (Szarkowska, 2013: 386). In Spain, Ramos Caro tested a neutral AD versus subjective AD that included emotional details in the description of different film clips. Her results suggest that the subjective version 'elicits a stronger emotional response in the audience in most cases, especially for scenes of fear and sadness' (Ramos Caro, 2016: 21). Finally, in Poland again, Walczak (2017a) tested a 'creative audio description', an AD style that includes interpretation of film language, colloquial language and an explicit rendering of the scenes. She conducted her study with Polish participants using the film *The Mighty Angel* (2014) and most of her audience also expressed their preference for the non-conventional audio description.

The reception study presented in this chapter was conducted in Catalonia and adds to the body of user studies on alternative audio description styles. We tested a conventional, denotative AD against two interpretative audio descriptions: a cinematic AD and a narrative AD. In the following sections, we will present our methodological framework and experimental design as well as our results on film interpretation and AD evaluation.

4.2 Methodology

In the Catalan context, AD user studies were conducted by Cabeza-Cáceres (2013), on the effects of speech rate, intonation and explicitation on film comprehension, and by Fernández-Torné and Matamala (2015) on natural versus synthetic voices. Following their steps, we drew on principles from social research and adopted a mixed-methods approach with questionnaires and interviews. In this section, we present this methodological framework: first, the creation of the three AD styles to be tested, and then the experimental setting.

4.2.1 AD styles

We adopted a functional approach to define three different AD styles which pursue the same goal using different strategies. Following Nord's affirmation that 'the intended communicative function of the target text is the crucial criterion for the translator's decisions in the translation process' (1997: 48), we identified a common communicative function to be achieved by all three AD versions, which corresponds to the general aim fixed by the Spanish audio description standard UNE 153020 (AENOR, 2005) that applies in Catalonia. This document states that spectators with visual impairment should 'perceive the message as a harmonious work which is as similar as possible to that which is perceived by the sighted' (AENOR, 2005: 4, trans. Utray *et al.*, 2009: 249). This can be achieved by different means and our AD styles all approach film language and include input from film studies in different ways. One is a conventional AD style that describes what is shown on screen at a denotative level and thus barely includes film language. The other two styles are more interpretative: the cinematic AD style includes film language as a result of interpreting the meaning of film techniques and using cinematic terminology to describe them, and the narrative AD style is devoted to interpreting the film's message to formulate a coherent narration. The following detailed definitions of the three AD styles are given in Bardini (2020):

- Conventional AD style (AD1) is a denotative AD style which describes what is shown at an iconic level, according to the WYSIWYS (What You See Is What You Say) paradigm (Snyder, 2007), thus avoiding any kind of interpretation or mention of film techniques. The main aim of this AD style is to give a matter-of-fact depiction of what appears onscreen, so that BPS (blind and partially sighted) audiences can reconstruct the meaning of the images for themselves.

- Cinematic AD style (AD2) is an interpretative AD style which offers a balance between iconic description, use of cinematic terminology and interpretation of film language. Cinematic terminology comes into play most particularly to describe elements that are specific to film, such as camera movements and editing techniques (Casetti and di Chio, 1991). Besides, when the describer considers it helpful to interpret the meaning of a film technique, it can be done instead of, or in addition to, using cinematic terminology. The main aim of the cinematic AD style is to transmit both the iconic content of the pictures and the feeling and meaning of film techniques, in an attempt to boost the audience's immersion in the film's style and contents.

- Narrative AD style (AD3) concentrates on interpreting film language and integrating the visual information into a coherent and flowing narration, which incorporates film dialogue and can be read as a single piece of text. It is an interpretative AD style which does not always depict the images in full detail or in the exact moment they are shown but instead offers a narrative recreation of the feelings raised and of the meaning channelled through film language. Here too, the aim is to offer an immersive experience that is as similar as possible to that of sighted viewers.

To illustrate these definitions, we will take an example from our three audio descriptions of *Nuit Blanche* (2009), the short film we chose for the reception study. *Nuit Blanche* is a black and white short film which mixes modern 3D visual effects with film noir atmosphere, to tell the story of a fleeting moment between two strangers who exchange a look from across the street (Manoukian, 2010). As the man and the woman look into each other's eyes, the film switches to slow-motion. They start walking towards one another but instead of going out through the door, the woman breaks through the window of the restaurant she has been sitting in. She emerges surrounded by a halo of glittering glass and walks towards the man. As for the man, he is hit by a car as he crosses the street, but it is the car which is destroyed by the shock, while he merely bends to the side and continues walking towards the woman. Finally, they meet in the middle of the street surrounded by glass shards and lyrical music rises in crescendo as they are about to kiss, in what seems to be an allegory of the force of the attraction they feel for each other. This is the film's climax and the *dénouement* is a return to reality: slow-motion stops, the lyrical music is replaced by the sounds of the street, and the zoomed-in image of the two faces dissolves into that of the woman, sitting at the restaurant, smiling, looking at the man. The last shot before the end credits is one of the man, standing on the other side of the street, looking at the woman. Although the three AD styles apply distinct strategies to approach the audio description of film language, we kept differences in the AD scripts to a minimum, to ensure that the different experiences of participants were due to these specific differences between AD styles. To create our three ADs, we worked from a first draft, written by professional describer Carme Guillamon, and applied selective modifications in keeping with each AD style, at key moments chosen following an in-depth film analysis. Other than the script, all AD aspects such as text density, pauses, coherence with the soundtrack, voice, intonation and sound level were kept as similar as possible in the three versions. The three audio descriptions of the *dénouement* of *Nuit Blanche*, as well as their translation into English and the original draft in Catalan and English, are presented in Table 4.1.

The conventional AD offers an iconic reading of the scene which does not interpret the return to reality but gives clues for the blind and partially sighted audience to interpret it themselves: it mentions the return to normal speed, which occurs at the same time as a change in the soundtrack—a clue that is accessible to blind and partially sighted viewers and acquires meaning along with the information on the end of slow-motion. The description also includes details about objects that were lost during the short film that are back in place (the man's hat and briefcase) and about characters' position. In the cinematic version, there is the intention to transmit the cinematic effect used for the return to reality by saying that '[the frame] passes beyond them [their lips]' and we considered that its indexical meaning should also be interpreted, so we added that the frame 'returns to reality'. Finally, in the narrative version, the indexical signification of film language is also interpreted, and the situation is rendered in a flowing narration where 'everything goes back to reality'. Apart from translating the feeling of the transition, the economy in words made with this interpretation allowed us to mention the wind, which is a reminder of the feeling of the exposition phase of the short film. Besides, both interpretative versions ('cinematic' and 'narrative') focus on the characters 'looking at each other' to reinforce the idea of a shared moment between them, while in the denotative ('conventional') version, the lingering of the camera on each character does not allow for such a description as it would amount to interpreting the situation.

The denotative AD gives access to the elements seen on screen and to the keys necessary to understand the film, but both interpretative approaches consider that a mere iconic depiction is not enough to access the complexity of the filmic message, so that a different approach is taken to bring forth the film experience to the blind and partially sighted audience. While the cinematic AD tries to take the spectators into the moving image for them to feel

Table 4.1 Nuit Blanche: *dénouement* in three AD styles and original AD draft

Original AD draft	*Quan són a un pam l'un de l'altre, es miren els llavis i tanquen els ulls, **a punt per rebre el petó**. L'enquadrament se centra en els llavis, quasi a tocar. Els **depassa, i apareix, darrere, la dona asseguda** al Cafè de Flore, somrient, **mirant cap a l'home**, que resta dret a l'altra vorera, **amb barret i un maletí a la mà esquerra, mirant-se-la**.* When they are a few inches from each other, they look at their lips and close their eyes **as they are about to kiss**. The **frame focuses** on their lips, which nearly touch. It **passes beyond** them and, **behind it, the woman appears**, sitting at the Café de Flore, smiling, **looking at the man**, who stands on the other side of the street with **hat and a briefcase in his left hand, looking at her**.
Conventional AD	*Quan són a un pam l'un de l'altre, tanquen els ulls i acosten els llavis. **A velocitat normal**. La dona seu al Cafè de Flore, i somriu **mirant cap a l'home**, que resta dret a l'altra vorera, **amb barret i maletí, mirant-se-la**.* When they are a few inches from each other, they close their eyes and bring their lips closer. **At normal speed**. The woman sits at the Café de Flore and smiles, **looking at the man**, who stands on the other side of the street with **his hat and briefcase, looking at her**.
Cinematic AD	*Quan són a un pam l'un de l'altre, es miren els llavis i tanquen els ulls, **a punt per rebre el petó**. L'enquadrament se centra en els llavis, quasi a tocar. Els **depassa, i torna a la realitat, a velocitat normal**: la dona seu al Cafè de Flore i somriu mirant cap a l'home, que resta dret a l'altra vorera. **Es miren als ulls**.* When they are a few inches from each other, they close their eyes and bring their lips closer **as they are about to kiss**. The **frame focuses** on their lips, which nearly touch. It **passes beyond** them and **returns to reality**, at **normal speed**. The woman sits at the Café de Flore and smiles, looking at the man, who stands on the other side of the street. **They look into each other's eyes**.
Narrative AD	*Davant per davant, es miren els llavis i tanquen els ulls, **a punt per rebre el petó**. De cop, **tot torna a la realitat**: el vent **bufa**, i la dona seu al Cafè de Flore, somrient. L'home, **amb barret i maletí**, resta dret a l'altra vorera. **Es miren als ulls**.* In front of one another, they look at each other's lips and close their eyes **as they are about to kiss**. Suddenly, **everything goes back to reality**. The **wind blows** and the woman sits at the Café de Flore, smiling. The man, **with his hat and briefcase**, stands on the other side of the street. **They look into each other's eyes**.

its effects, the narrative version slightly drifts away from the images to better reproduce their effect through a verbal narration. In both cases, the indexical meaning of film language is interpreted to ease comprehension and provide better access to the feeling of the film, but the interpretation of the symbolic meaning of the scene (Was it a thought? A fantasy? Do the characters know each other?) is left to the blind and partially sighted audience. In the following section, we will detail the experimental procedure according to which we tested these three AD styles.

4.2.2 Experimental groups and procedure

To begin with, we conducted a pre-study with sighted participants (SP). A hundred participants answered an online questionnaire after watching *Nuit Blanche* (2009). This pre-study had a double objective: first, it would allow us to gather quantitative reference data on the film experience of sighted audiences with the short film selected for our reception study; second, it would serve as a pilot test of our questionnaire before using it with blind and partially sighted participants (BPSP). SP with varied backgrounds were recruited via personal contacts and social networks, mainly in Catalonia (47 per cent), but also in the rest of the EU and in South America—ensuring that they were all exposed to the cinematographic culture of the Western world. They were invited to watch the video clip without AD and to complete the questionnaire anonymously online. A link to a website where the experiment was explained was distributed in Catalan and Spanish (https://goo.gl/h9udXA), and a link was also distributed to the SoGoSurvey platform where the questionnaire was published (https://www.sogosurvey.com/preview1.aspx?k=YsRRVSPsS&). On the questionnaire page, instructions were given to watch the short film once (a link to the film on the Vimeo video platform was available): and answer the questionnaire immediately afterwards.

The questionnaire entailed the following sections: socio-demographic questions, questions on the emotional reception of the short film, on the interpretation of the short film, and on the evaluation of the film experience. The section on emotional reception and short film interpretation entailed mostly multiple-choice questions and some open-ended questions, while film experience was to be evaluated on a 6-point Likert scale across four items.

Following the online pre-study with sighted viewers, BPSP were recruited to participate in a live study. For them, we added a section on AD evaluation with the same Likert scale model (see 3.6). We also decided to modify the section on emotional reception by including mostly rating-scale questions instead of multiple-choice, because the large number of choices for each question in this section seemed less adequate for a group interview setting than it was for an online survey. The remaining questions were left identical so that the data collected on film experience and film interpretation could be compared for sighted and blind and partially sighted participants.

BPSP were recruited through two user organizations: ONCE (the National Organization of the Spanish Blind) and ACIC (the Catalan Association for the Integration of the Blind)—which we both heartily thank for their interest and support. Forty-five blind and partially sighted persons participated in the study, so that each AD version was heard by fifteen participants. In spite of

Table 4.2 BPSP experimental groups

AD version	Gender		Age group				Education					Blindness			
	F.	*M.*	*18–29*	*30–44*	*45–59*	*60+*	*CE*	*VT*	*AL*	*HE*	*n/a*	*B*	*C*	*A*	*n/a*
AD1	9	6	0	3	6	6	4	1	2	3	5	1	2	12	0
AD2	8	7	1	4	5	5	2	3	3	2	5	3	3	7	2
AD3	1	14	0	6	6	3	10	2	1	2	0	4	2	7	2

F. = female; M. = male; 60+ = age 60 and above; CE = compulsory education; VT = vocational training; AL = A-Level; HE = higher education; B = blind from birth; C = blindness acquired in childhood; A = blindness acquired in adulthood; n/a = data not available.

the support of user associations, access to the sample population proved to be too difficult to work with random selection, so we opted for 'relative comparison between non-equivalent groups' (Trochim and Donnelly, 2006): in practice, the groups were created by the two user organizations themselves depending on participants' availability to attend an experimental session, and groups naturally presented a heterogeneity of gender, age and blindness type, which made them comparable between each other. The composition of the three experimental groups is represented in Table 4.2.

Experimental sessions consisted of both individual and group interviews: a total of fourteen group interviews of two to four people were conducted, plus three individual interviews. Each session began with the presentation of the project and the signing of consent forms following the procedure approved by the Ethics Committee of the University of Vic – Central University of Catalonia. Socio-demographic questions were asked of each participant and subsequently, participants were presented with the AD version assigned to their group, played on an ASUS X540LJ laptop (85 per cent volume; laptop speakers). We played the sound only, so that all participants would equally concentrate on the audio description, even those with some degree of residual sight. Immediately after the AD was presented, we proceeded with the remaining sections of the questionnaire. Rating-scale and multiple-choice questions were answered with a specially made one-rod abacus with six beads (Figure 4.1), so that only the researcher could see the answers, thus avoiding a contagion effect among participants (Le Bon, 1960). After each section of the questionnaire and after open-ended questions, an open group discussion took place. The data gathered during the sessions was recorded in an MS Excel spreadsheet, which was used to centralise the data and subsequently facilitate their analysis with statistical methods and values (percentage; mean and standard deviation; one-way ANOVA and Tukey post hoc test), as well as with qualitative methods (tagging and identification of patterns). Our results are presented in the following section.

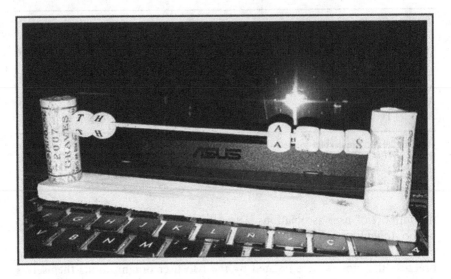

Figure 4.1 Abacus to answer rating-scale questions.

4.3 Results

As the BPSP experimental groups were relatively modest in number (45 participants in total), percentages and mean values for the expressed answers allow for relevant comparisons only when bigger differences are observed, so we will comment on such differences only if they affect at least one third of the group or if the difference in 'means' is at least one point (of six). When a difference appears between BPSP groups, which have comparable sizes, a one-way ANOVA allows us to determine if this difference is statistically significant or not (Fink, 1995). For space reasons, in this chapter, we will mainly report on questions related to the interpretation of the short film and the evaluation of the audio description—emotional reception and the evaluation of the film experience are dealt with extensively in Bardini (2020).

4.3.1 Story reconstruction

4.3.1.1 Narrative space and time

Nuit Blanche (2009) is a timeless allegory of the strength and intensity of a look exchanged between two strangers. The narrative space and time are not clearly expressed and are not crucial to the story, but certain elements of the film orientate the viewer. There is no specific mention of a city or an epoch, the information is not essential and yet it is present, scattered across the film, which makes it challenging for audio describers to transfer the information. The clothes and

Table 4.3 Participants' opinion on where the story takes place

Group	Paris	Paris or other	Other	Not associated with any existing city
AD1	0%	0%	22.2%	77.8%
AD2	0%	0%	8.3%	91.7%
AD3	14.3%	0%	14.3%	71.4%
SP	34%	15%	27%	24%

Table 4.4 Participants' opinion on when the story takes place

Group	20th c. beginning (until 1930)	Mid 20th c. (1930–1960)	20th c. end (after 1960)	Contemporary	Not associated with any particular epoch
AD1	0%	22.2%	11.1%	0%	66.7%
AD2	16.7%	25%	16.7%	8.3%	33.3%
AD3	14.3%	35.7%	7.1%	14.3%	28.6%
SP	10%	66%	6%	0%	18%

accessories, the car model, the smoking chimneys, and the film noir atmosphere give a sense of the mid twentieth century that evokes a relatively recent past—and could arouse emotions such as nostalgia. As for the place, the name of the restaurant in French and the zinc roofs in the foreground during the introduction evoke Paris, while other elements such as the dome could belong to another European city, and a corporate building with glass windows looks North American. As a matter of fact, the city and the cityscape were created for the film from images of Paris and Toronto (*Making of Nuit Blanche*, 2009).

Participants had to answer the following questions about the spatio-temporal setting of the film; results are presented in Tables 4.3 and 4.4:

- Even if it is not clearly mentioned, some elements can suggest the place where the story happens:
  (1) I have not given importance to the place.
  (2) I think it happens in: _____.
- Even if it is not clearly mentioned, some elements can suggest the epoch when the story happens:
  (1) I have not given importance to the epoch.
  (2) I think it happens in: _____.

As far as place is concerned, we can see in Table 4.3 that the result is homogenous between all versions of AD, showing that BPSP did not identify or imagine any particular city as the place of the action, while most SP thought of Paris, some of another city (Florence and London came up several times) and only a minority did not associate the film with any existing city. A one-way ANOVA between the BPSP groups to compare the effect of AD style on the identification of no existing city as the possible place of the action confirms there was no significant effect of AD style at the $p < .05$ level [$F(2, 32) = 0.81$, $p = .453$].

As for the narrative time, results reported in Table 4.4 show that participants who do not associate the narrative time to a real time in history represent less than 20 per cent of the SP group and only about one third of the BPSP groups with AD2 and AD3, while two thirds of BPSP who listened to AD1 did not associate the film with any specific epoch. Although there seems to be a relevant difference between the conventional style (AD1) and the interpretative styles (AD2 and AD3) here, running a one-way ANOVA between the three BPSP groups for 'not associated with any particular epoch' does not show any statistically significant effect of AD style on not identifying any specific epoch at the $p < .05$ level [$F(2, 32) = 1.86$, $p = .172$]. On the other hand, there is a trend among SP to situate the action in the mid twentieth century, which is the epoch we discerned when analysing the film. It was also the most voted option among BPSP with the narrative version, while in the other BPSP groups it was second to 'not associated with any particular epoch'. Again, a one-way ANOVA between BPSP groups reveals no significant effect at the $p < .05$ level [$F(2, 32) = 0.28$, $p = .757$].

Overall, these results show that in our sample population, both conventional and interpretative AD styles struggle to transmit information on the narrative space and time that are not clearly expressed but rather spread out along the short film. Our results point at narrative AD being the most favourable option in this respect, but further research should be conducted on this specific issue to determine if and how interpretation can improve the audio description of such elements.

4.3.1.2 Narrative theme

Two key aspects of the narrative theme that should be transmitted by a quality audio description were tested in the questionnaire: the attraction between the two characters, and the fiction within fiction—be it a thought, a dream or a fantasy. Participants were asked if they had felt the attraction between the characters, and their answers are presented in Table 4.5. In relation to the fiction within fiction, SP were asked if they had noticed that the film was moving away from reality when the woman breaks through the window and BPSP if they had noticed, and *when*, that the action was moving away from reality, so we could differentiate between BPSP who had noticed the shift before the end of the film and those who had realised it at the *dénouement*, which is the latest point in the short film where clear clues are given to indicate that there is a shift from reality to fiction and back. Finally, some BPSP had

Table 4.5 Perception of the attraction between characters

Group	Yes	No
AD1	81.8%	18.2%
AD2	83.3%	16.7%
AD3	100%	0%
SP	90%	10%

Table 4.6 Perception of the shift from reality

Group	Before the dénouement	At the dénouement	Not at all
AD1	45.5%	54.5%	13.3%
AD2	25%	75%	35.7%
AD3	38.5%	61.5%	13.3%
SP	79.2%	n/a	n/a

not noticed the shift at all, which is reported as a third category. Results are presented in Table 4.6.

As shown in Table 4.5, most participants noticed the attraction between characters, BPSP in all groups as well as sighted viewers. A one-way ANOVA between BPSP groups reveals no statistically significant effect of AD style on this aspect at the p < .05 level [F(2, 28) = 0.77; p = .474].

As far as the shift from reality is concerned, a majority of BPSP with all versions reports to have noticed that the short film had moved away from reality only at the end—when the return to reality is made clear—while a vast majority of sighted participants noticed the shift *before* the end of the film. Nevertheless, it is only a minority of BPSP with all versions who did not realise *at all* that the short film had moved away from reality, so that we consider that all three AD styles succeeded at giving access to this key narrative aspect—although only AD2 and AD3 mentioned the return to reality explicitly. However, it is a relatively large minority (over one third) of participants with AD2 who did not understand *at all* that part of the action takes place out of reality. Although a one-way ANOVA does not reveal any statistically significant effect of AD style on this aspect [F(2, 41) = 1.47, p = .242 at the p < .05 level], the profile of participants affected by this comprehension difficulty showed up in our qualitative analysis because of a misunderstanding of the car crash scene, which is explained in 3.5.

4.3.2 Film language reception

To analyse how film language is perceived by BPSP with the different AD styles, we tested the reception of slow-motion. This film technique is used in

Table 4.7 Sensations aroused by slow-motion

Group	An aesthetic sensation	That time had stopped	That something important would happen	That the action was moving beyond reality	Something else	None
AD1	36.4%	27.3%	36.4%	27.3%	18%	45.4%
AD2	25%	41.7%	16.7%	25%	28%	41.7%
AD3	70%	100%	0%	60%	20%	0%
SP	44%	53%	37%	27%	10%	1%

Nuit Blanche as a distinctive trait of the 'fiction within fiction' phase. Slow-motion was described in different ways in each AD version. In AD1 (conventional AD), we used the expression 'in slow-motion': conventional audio description usually refrains from using cinematic terms, but slow-motion is such a common technique that in practice it is often mentioned, so we decided to use the term, as the alternative would have been an omission, which was not advisable for such a prominent feature. In the cinematic AD style (AD2), we said that 'the image slows down', to describe both the technique and its effect. Finally, in the narrative AD style (AD3), we took a holistic approach embracing the slow-motion technique, its effect and the general feeling transmitted by the combination of moving image and music (which also changes at this moment and gets slower) by saying that 'everything slows down'. Participants were asked what sensation the slow-motion gave them; answers are presented in Table 4.7. Participants could select several answers so that the totals may be over 100 per cent.

Answers are varied, of course, just as are individual film interpretations. However, it is pertinent to concentrate on one specific point: participants who did not feel anything special in relation to slow-motion. Sighted participants had something to report in 99 per cent of cases, while things look more complicated for blind and partially sighted participants. All BPSP with the narrative version reported some effect of the slow-motion, while only around 60 per cent did with the cinematic and the conventional versions. These differences are confirmed when running a one-way ANOVA between the three BPSP groups, which shows a statistically significant effect of AD style on bringing about some sensation related to the use of slow-motion in the short film at $p < .05$ [$F(2, 30) = 3.52$, $p = .042$]. A Tukey post hoc test reveals a difference between AD1 and AD3, and between AD2 and AD3, but not between AD1 and AD2. In other words, in our sample, narrative audio description (AD3) is significantly better than the other AD versions at transmitting the sensations aroused by slow-motion. It is interesting to note that the narrative AD style is the one that distances itself most from the images and it is precisely the one that manages to give an experience most similar to that of sighted viewers, by saying that 'everything slows down', thus giving access to the feeling of slow-motion. Interpretation of the slow-motion technique is varied and personal, but our results indicate that access to the very possibility of interpreting its meaning is best gained through an interpretation and rewording of its indexical signification which allows blind and partially sighted viewers to dedicate all their cognitive resources to interpreting its symbolic meaning. The same thought lies behind the decision to verbalise the return to reality at the end of the short film in interpretative AD versions by saying that we are 'back to reality' (see Table 4.1 in 2.1).

4.3.3 Emotional reception

As we said earlier, the emotional reception of the film is dealt with in detail in a separate publication but, here, we will comment on one question, related to participants' mood after the short film. Answers are shown in Table 4.8. Here too, participants could select several answers, so that the totals may be over 100 per cent.

Reactions to the short film are diverse: again, the wide range of answers is a matter of subjectivity in relation to individual spectators and was to be expected, but the most important observation is that a majority of spectators were affected emotionally by the short film. The director himself insists on the importance of the emotional dimension of the short film (Manoukian, 2010) and the lyrical orchestral music is a 'musical treat' (Jullier, 2012: 258) that clearly aims at arousing an emotional response in the audience. In this sense, it is interesting to check whether the three groups of BPSP as well as SP have been emotionally affected by the short film. In the SP group, only 15 per cent report not to have felt in any particular mood after watching the short film, and not one BPSP encountering the cinematic or narrative version was left unaffected. By contrast, over one third of participants with the denotative version was unmoved. A one-way ANOVA between BPSP groups shows a statistically significant effect of AD style at the $p < .05$ level $[F(2, 36) = 7.38$, $p = .002]$ and a Tukey post hoc test confirms a statistically significant difference between AD1 and AD2, and AD1 and AD3, but not between AD2 and AD3. In other words, the interpretative AD versions, cinematic AD (AD2)

Table 4.8 Mood after watching the short film

Group	Joyful	Happy	Senti-mental	Admi-rative	Sad	Disap-pointed	Pensive	Nostalgic or melan-cholic	None
AD1	18.2%	9.1%	45.5%	36.4%	18.2%	18.2%	36.4%	9.1%	36.4%
AD2	46.2%	38.5%	53.8%	46.2%	22.2%	11.1%	100%	44.4%	0%
AD3	86.7%	86.7%	60.0%	46.7%	40.0%	26.7%	20.0%	33.3%	0%
SP	10%	11%	36%	13%	5%	6%	31%	34%	15%

Table 4.9 Immersion according to AD version

Group	Immersion	No immersion	No views expressed
AD1	5	5	5
AD2	7	1	7
AD3	8	0	7

and narrative AD (AD3), appear to have a positive effect on BPSP's emotional reception of the short film, while conventional AD (AD1) seems to offer a less intense emotional experience.

4.3.4 *Immersion*

Wilken and Kruger (2016: 258) define immersion as 'an umbrella term for the sensation of viewers of being transported into the story world, and of being swept up in this world to such an extent that it takes priority over their experience of their immediate surroundings' (see also Fryer and Walczak, Chapter 1 in this volume). We have not directly tested or asked questions about immersion in our study, therefore we do not have data for all participants. However, the analysis of the data collected during the interviews shows that a substantial number of participants reported being particularly involved or immersed in the short film or, on the contrary, the opposite feeling. For example participant 15 (female, AD1) said that she got carried away by the short film and felt sorry that everything was unreal. By contrast, participant 39 (male, AD1) said the film had not aroused any feeling, that something was missing.[1] The number of BPSP who expressed immersion or the contrary, and the AD version they heard, is represented in Table 4.9.

Around half of the participants with an interpretative AD version (AD2 and AD3) reported immersion, and only one (with AD2) reported the opposite. Conversely, with AD1 (conventional AD), it is only one third of participants who explicitly report immersion, while another third reports the opposite. This information points at the potential of interpretative audio descriptions to offer a more immersive experience than conventional audio description, but a follow-up study with questions and/or measurements designed exclusively to investigate this point would be necessary to reach clear conclusions on immersion with cinematic and narrative versus conventional audio description styles.

4.3.5 *Comprehension issue*

As we have shown, the three AD versions tested gave our sample population keys to the comprehension of the story, so that a majority of BPSP understood

Table 4.10 Profile of BPSP who misunderstood the car crash scene

BPSP number	AD version	Gender	Age group	Blind from...	"Access to comprehension" score (1 to 6)	Immersion
5	2	M	60+	adulthood	4	n/a
7	2	M	30–44	adulthood	n/a	n/a
8	1	F	45–59	adulthood	n/a	n/a
9	1	F	60+	adulthood	n/a	n/a
21	2	F	60+	birth	5	n/a
22	2	M	60+	childhood	1	NO
28	2	M	45–59	adulthood	4	YES
32	3	M	60+	adulthood	6	YES
33	3	M	45–59	adulthood	6	YES

that most of the action was taking place out of reality, even if some understood it only at the end of the short film, at the moment when the action returns to reality. Nevertheless, some participants were confused and there was a recurrent misunderstanding when the car crashes into the man: several BPSP thought it was a real accident and gave it a narrative importance. This affected their understanding of the film as they tried to reconstruct the whole story around it. For example participant 5 (male, AD2) said that they [the characters] meet in surprising circumstances, that *everything happens because of the accident*—and that it was very nice.[2] In Table 4.10, the profile of affected participants is represented.

The issue affected 9 BPSP, both men and women, especially in age groups over 45 years old. Most of them had become blind in adulthood—as is the case of a majority of participants in the study. Most participants affected evaluated the item 'did the audio description give you access to the elements necessary to understand the short film' (see 3.6) with a positive score (4 to 6), which indicates that they were not aware that they did not understand the situation. As explained above, we do not have data on immersion for all participants affected, but three of the participants who reported immersion misunderstood the car crash scene. This suggests that AD allowing spectators to feel transported into the film is no guarantee of film comprehension. Finally, only two participants with AD1 and two with AD3 were affected, as opposed to five participants with AD2. Although results show no statistically significant effect of AD style on the transmission of narrative contents (see Section 4.3.1.2), it is of concern that most participants who encountered this misunderstanding received AD2. The difficulty may be due to a cognitive overload, as the inclusion of cinematic terms makes the cinematic AD necessarily denser than the other versions. Moreover, these terms need to be understood and/or interpreted, which is an additional difficulty for the audience.

4.3.6 AD evaluation

Participants' evaluation of the audio description allows us to understand their responses as a function of the style of AD they received. The audio description was evaluated on a six-point Likert scale with four items. The ratings from 1 to 6 corresponded with: 'not at all', 'little', 'rather no', 'rather yes', 'quite a lot' and 'very much'. The items to be reported on concerned access to different elements through audio description: participants were asked to rate the access to the elements they considered necessary to understand the short film, to the stylistic and aesthetic elements of the film, to emotional aspects, and to an enjoyable experience. Participants' answers are presented in Table 4.11.

Participants' AD evaluations reveal that BPSP perceived that they had access to 'story comprehension' and to 'an enjoyable experience' with all three versions. In spite of the comprehension difficulties experienced by some participants with AD2 (see 3.5), the mean score on that item is very high—but the standard deviation too, which shows that some participants have given a very low rating. Therefore, it seems that cinematic AD can be very helpful for some users but exclude others, such that further research needs to be conducted on this AD style before potentially recommending its use in Catalonia. Anyway, in this study, a one-way ANOVA does not show any statistically significant difference between the three AD styles at the $p < .05$ level, neither for comprehension [$F(2, 34) = 1.99$, $p = .152$] nor for enjoyment [$F(2, 34) = 0.05$, $p = .955$]. On the contrary, we observe considerable differences between versions for the two other items: access to 'film style and aesthetics' and 'emotional aspects' obtained noticeably lower scores with the conventional AD (AD1) than with the cinematic AD (AD2) and the narrative AD (AD3). A one-way ANOVA shows an effect of AD style for 'stylistic and aesthetic elements' only at the $p < .10$ level [($F(2, 34) = 2.50$; $p = .097$)], but a statistically significant effect of AD style for 'emotional aspects' is observed at the $p < .05$ level [($F(2, 34) = 3.57$; $p = 0.039$)]. Tukey post hoc tests confirm a difference between AD1 and AD2 for stylistic and aesthetic elements, as well as for AD1 and AD2, and AD1 and AD3 for emotional aspects. In light of these results, we can say that conventional, cinematic and narrative AD style all offer satisfactory access to the film, but it seems that both interpretative AD

Table 4.11 AD evaluation on a scale of 1 to 6 [M (SD)]

Group	Film comprehension	Film style and aesthetics	Emotional aspects	Enjoyable experience
AD1	4.3 (1.0)	3.4 (0.9)	3.4 (1.3)	4.9 (0.8)
AD2	4.9 (1.4)	4.8 (1.2)	4.8 (1.5)	4.8 (1.9)
AD3	5.3 (0.8)	4.3 (1.1)	4.7 (1.1)	5.0 (1.1)

styles, cinematic and narrative, may have a more effective approach to elements expressed through film language, transmitting emotion and film style, thus offering an experience more similar to that of sighted viewers. In the end, the AD evaluation by blind and partially sighted participants reinforces the results outlined earlier in this chapter.

4.4 Conclusions

We conducted a reception study on AD styles which had the particularity of testing two interpretative AD styles that approach film language audio description from different angles. We compared the film experience of three groups of blind and partially sighted participants, who saw the film with sound only, to explore differences in film reception with the conventional (denotative) AD, a cinematic and a narrative AD. We also compared participants' answers to those of sighted viewers who had seen the same film with sound and image but without AD and answered the same questionnaire, which was designed to explore participants' film experience.

Our data show that the conventional as well as both interpretative AD styles convey the information necessary to understand the story and enjoy the short film. This confirms that even in the case of a film with prominent use of film language such as *Nuit Blanche*, a conventional, denotative AD can give blind and partially sighted spectators access to the film.

However, conventional AD seems less adequate than interpretative ADs for transmitting elements that are not indispensable to the story comprehension but participate in shaping the film experience. In our example, slow-motion and visual effects of floating, glittering glass were combined with lyrical orchestral music to produce an intense aesthetic and emotional effect that was reported to a higher rate by BPSP with the cinematic and narrative ADs than with the conventional AD. This is in line with the results of researchers mentioned earlier in this chapter (e.g. Szarkowska, 2013; Walczak, 2017a), who found that viewers preferred alternative descriptions that deviate from guidelines and help them to 'feel' the film beyond essential narrative elements. To strengthen these conclusions, further investigation on emotional aspects should include emotional self-evaluation before watching the film and could incorporate physiological measures such as heart rate metrics (Iturregui-Gallardo, 2019; Ramos Caro, 2016).

Interpretation, as long as it is practised ethically and does not involve any patronising retelling, opens a new range of possibilities to enhance the film experience of the blind and partially sighted audience and bring it closer to that of sighted viewers. For example none of our three ADs of *Nuit Blanche* mentioned the narrative place, because it was never clearly stated in the short film and we did not want to create a gap between versions for the experiment. Yet, a describer adopting an interpretative approach could say something like 'a cityscape that evokes Paris or Florence' to transmit the same non-specific sense of place experienced by sighted viewers from the city features onscreen, which gets lost with a denotative description. Another example is the shift from reality, which a majority of BPSP noticed only at the *dénouement* and which, in an interpretative AD, could be made explicit at the moment when it happens. Further research should be conducted in this direction to determine how far interpretation can go to be considered helpful and not intrusive for a majority of blind and partially sighted AD users.

During the interviews, more participants with the cinematic and narrative audio descriptions reported immersion than those with the conventional audio description. This observation concurs with Walczak's results on presence levels with a creative AD style: in her case all participants with the alternative AD showed higher levels of presence (2017b: 43) that indicate more immersion in the audio described film. Immersion is one of the key aspects of film experience and further research is needed in this complex area (see theoretical framework by Fresno, 2017) to refine academic proposals on immersive AD styles.

On the basis of our results, cinematic and narrative AD appear to be interesting alternatives that offer the blind and partially sighted audience a better film experience, more closely matched to that of sighted viewers than that offered by conventional audio description. In our study, cinematic AD was linked to a comprehension issue, which was not statistically significant but recurrent. Possible explanations could be that cinematic audio descriptions are more complex to process or lie in the cinematic cultural background of AD users in Catalonia. Nevertheless, this description style remains an alternative worth exploring: Fryer and Freeman (2013) achieved positive results on user satisfaction and did not detect any comprehension problem in their reception study on cinematic AD conducted in the UK.

We would like to end this chapter with an emphasis on narrative audio description, which obtained the best results in our sample, although it contravenes AD guidelines by interpreting images and not constantly respecting the iconic content and synchronicity with the visuals. Adapting the AD script to a verbal delivery mode, rather than writing within the constraints imposed by the original visual mode, allowed us to produce an audio description which offered a quality film experience, closer to that of the sighted audience than with the conventional approach to AD creation.

Notes

1 Original comments in Catalan:
   • Participant 15: 'M'he deixat portar pel curt, m'ha *sapigut* greu que tot fos irreal.'
   • Participant 39: 'No m'ha despertat sentiments, no m'ha arribat, faltava alguna cosa.'
2 Participant 5's original comment in Catalan: 'Es troben en circumstàncies menys esperades, tot surt arran de l'accident. Ha estat molt bé.'

References

AENOR (2005) 'UNE 153020: Audiodescripción para personas con discapacidad visual', in *Requisitos para la audiodescripción y elaboración de audioguías*. Madrid: AENOR.

Bardini, F. (2020) 'Film language, film emotions and the experience of blind and partially sighted viewers: a reception study', *JoSTrans: Journal of Specialized Translation*, 33.

Braun, S. (2007) 'Audio description from a discourse perspective: a socially relevant framework for research and training', *Linguistica Antverpiensia, New Series*, 6, pp. 357–369. Available at: http://epubs.surrey.ac.uk/303024/1/fulltext.pdf (accessed 26 July 2019).

Braun, S. (2008) 'Audio description research: state of the art and beyond', *Translation Studies in the New Millennium*, 6, pp. 14–30.

Cabeza-Cáceres, C. (2013) 'Audiodescripció i recepció. Efecte de la velocitat de narració, l'entonació i l'explicitació en la comprensió fílmica.' PhD thesis, Universitat Autònoma de Barcelona.

Carroll, N. (2008) *The Philosophy of Motion Pictures*. Malden, MA: Blackwell.

Casetti, F., and di Chio, F. (1991) *Cómo analizar un film*. Translated by C. Losilla. Barcelona: Paidós.

Dosch, E., and Benecke, B. (2004) *Wenn aus Bilder Wörter werden*. Munich: Bayerischer Rundfunk.

Fernández-Torné, A., and Matamala, A. (2015) 'Text-to-speech vs. human voiced audio descriptions: a reception study in films dubbed into Catalan', *JoSTrans: The Journal of Specialized Translation*, 24. Available at: www.jostrans.org/issue24/art_fernandez.php (accessed 26 July 2019).

Fink, A. (1995) *The Survey Handbook*. Thousand Oaks, CA: SAGE.

Fresno, N. (2017) 'Approaching engagement in audio description', *Rivista Internazionale di Tecnica della Traduzione*, 19, pp. 13–32. Available at: www.openstarts.units.it/bitstream/10077/17349/1/Ritt19_Fresno.pdf (accessed 26 July 2019).

Fryer, L., and Freeman, J. (2013) 'Cinematic language and the description of film: keeping AD users in the frame', *Perspectives: Studies in Translation Theory and Practice*, 21(3), pp. 412–426.

Iturregui-Gallardo, G. (2019) 'Audio subtitling: voicing strategies and their effect on emotional activation.' PhD thesis, Universitat Autònoma de Barcelona.

Jullier, L. (2012) *Analyser un film: de l'émotion à l'interprétation*. Paris: Flammarion.

Kuhn, A., and Westwell, G. (2012) *A Dictionary of Film Studies*. Oxford: Oxford University Press.

Le Bon, G. (1960) *The Crowd*. 1st edn 1885. New York: Viking.

Manoukian, A. (2010) 'Slow-Motion Car Crash Speeds Filmmaker's Career.' Interviewed by H. Hart for *Wired*, 4 September. Available at: www.wired.com/2010/04/nuit-blanche (accessed 26 July 2019).

Morisset, L., and Gonant, F. (2008) *La charte de l'audiodescription*. Available at: www.enaparte.org/charte (accessed 26 July 2019).

Nord, C. (1997) 'Defining translation functions: the translation brief as a guideline for the trainee translator', *Ilha do Desterro: A Journal of English Language, Literatures in English and Cultural Studies*, 33, pp. 39–54.

Ofcom (2000) *ITC Guidance on Standards for Audio Description*. London: Ofcom.

Orero, P. (2012) 'Film reading for writing audio descriptions: a word is worth a thousand images?', in E. Perego (ed.), *Emerging Topics in Translation: Audio Description*, Trieste: Edizione Università di Trieste, pp. 13–28.

Perego, E. (2014) 'Film language and tools', in A. Maszerowska, A. Matamala and P. Orero (eds.), *Audio Description: New Perspectives Illustrated*, Amsterdam: John Benjamins, pp. 81–101. ·

Plantinga, C. (2010) 'Emotion and affect', in C. Plantinga and P. Livingstone (eds.), *The Routledge Companion to Philosophy and Film*, London: Routledge, pp. 86–96.

Ramos Caro, M. (2016) 'Testing audio narration: the emotional impact of language in audio description', *Perspectives: Studies in Translation Theory and Practice*, 24(4), pp. 606–634.

Schmid, W. (2014) 'The selection and concretization of elements in verbal and filmic narration', in J. Alber and P.K. Hansen (eds.), *Beyond Classical Narration: Unnatural and Transmedial Challenges*, Berlin: De Gruyter, pp. 15–24.

Snyder, J. (2007) 'Audio description: the visual made verbal', *International Journal of the Arts in Society*, 2, pp. 99–104. Available at: https://audiodescribe.com/about/articles/ad_international_journal_07.pdf (accessed 26 July 2019).

Szarkowska, A. (2013) 'Auteur description: from the director's creative vision to audio description', *Journal of Visual Impairment & Blindness*, 107, pp. 383–387.

Trochim, W., and Donnelly, J. P. (2006) *The Research Methods Knowledge Base*. Cincinnati: Atomic Dog.

Utray, F., Perera, A. M., and Orero, P. (2009) 'The present and future of audio description and subtitling for the deaf and the hard of hearing in Spain', *Meta*, 54(2), pp. 248–263.

Walczak, A. (2017a) 'Creative description: the impact of audio description style on presence in visually impaired audiences', *British Journal of Visual Impairment*, 35(1), pp. 6–17.

Walczak, A. (2017b) 'Measuring immersion in audio description with Polish blind and visually impaired audiences', *Rivista Internazionale di Tecnica della Traduzione*, 19, pp. 33–48.

Wilken, N., and Kruger, J. L. (2016) 'Putting the audience in the picture: mise-en-shot and psychological immersion in audio described film', *Across Languages and Cultures*, 17(2), pp. 251–270.

Wollen, P. (2013) *Signs and Meanings in the Cinema*. 5th edn. London: Palgrave Macmillan on behalf of the British Film Institute.

Zabalbeascoa, P. (2008) 'The nature of the audiovisual text and its parameters', in J. Díaz-Cintas (ed.), *The Didactics of Audiovisual Translation*, Amsterdam: John Benjamins, pp. 21–37.

Filmography

Making of Nuit Blanche (2009) Directed by A. Manoukian. [Short film]. Toronto: Stellar Scene Pictures.

Nuit Blanche (2009) Directed by A. Manoukian. [Short film]. Toronto: Stellar Scene Pictures.

Star Wars (1977) Directed by G. Lucas. [Feature film]. San Francisco: Lucasfilm Ltd.

The Mighty Angel (2014) Directed by W. Smarzowski. [Feature film]. Warsaw: Profil Film.

Volver (2006) Directed by P. Almodóvar. [Feature film]. Madrid: El Deseo.

5 Audio description 2.0

Re-versioning audiovisual accessibility to assist emotion recognition

Kim Starr and Sabine Braun

5.1 Introduction

In the colliding worlds of audiovisual research and practice, audio description (AD) has transitioned from being the 'new kid on the block' to a mature and extensively researched commodity focused primarily on audiences experiencing varying degrees of visual impairment. While there remains broad scope to explore the linguistic, stylistic and technological aspects of standard AD creation and delivery, there is growing consensus that the study of multimodal meaning-making by reference to sensory challenges – visual, auditory and cognitive – has much to teach us about the machinations of the human mind. Indeed, it is in unravelling the complexities of human inferential behaviour in the context of multiple and competing streams of data, that the study of audiovisual translation may yet make its most valuable and enduring contribution to knowledge.

Simultaneously iconographic and yet informed by each person's unique life experience, the consumption of audiovisual material and quest to uncover the message contained within places enormous demands on our cognitive processing skills. We are required to mine and assimilate information, ascertain narrative saliency (Kruger, 2012), seek relevance (Sperber and Wilson, 1995) and establish coherence in storytelling (Braun, 2007, 2011), construct mental models which pre-empt a range of possibilities (Johnson-Laird, 2010) and apply rational thinking and common knowledge to arrive at a 'most probable' determination of meaning. The spoils of this rigorous mental boot camp, engagement with and immersion in narrative, are achieved through a series of cognitive processes which are highly individualistic, while underpinning the foundations upon which our social interaction and communication with fellow human beings are built (Looms, 2011: i). Essentially, we all strive to connect through a sense of 'mutual understanding' regardless of any accessibility challenges we may face, and it is shared experiences such as audiovisual entertainment which enrich our lives and help cement our social networks.

Exploring cognitive processing and narrative engagement for the purposes of creating accessible collateral texts (audio descriptions and subtitles), has been shown to shed new light on the nature of meaning-making in multimodal contexts (Kruger, 2012; Kruger and Doherty, 2016). Research into audience 'presence' and AD linguistic styles, as an indication of engagement and immersion (Fryer and Freeman, 2013; Walczak and Fryer, 2017, and Chapter 1 in this volume), has addressed issues such as spatial conceptualisation and environmental verisimilitude. The arrival of virtual and augmented reality gaming applications, and the spectre of audience immersion in an infinite spatial continuum, challenge our narrative processing resources further: non-linear plotlines now have the potential to play out in a three- or even four- dimensional arena. Yet despite the ever-increasing complexity of our narrative worlds, much still remains undiscovered since, as Kruger suggests, we still do not fully understand how the human mind makes narrative sense of a typical two-dimensional audiovisual text (2012: 67).

While audio description research has traditionally been targeted at refining practices to meet the needs of visually challenged individuals, the discipline is becoming ever more diverse, marked by a notable shift towards new audiences and applications. Educational and instructional environments offering opportunities to explore AD in the context of visual learning (Zabalbeascoa, 2013; Cozendey and da Piedade Costa, 2016; Vialard, 2017) have emerged as fertile grounds for cognitive experimentation. Standard AD, of the type adopted for sight-impaired audiences, has also been employed to assist with narrative comprehension in a pilot study involving four individuals affected by learning difficulties and Down's syndrome. In this case it was observed that the AD did not prove 'acoustically efficient' as none of the participants was able to recall the principal character's name despite frequent repetition in the AD script (Franco *et al.*, 2015: 107). Thus, across this broadening research agenda one constant may be observed: while new audiences may be emerging, intermodal transfer strategies and semantic choices currently remain heavily influenced by the traditional AD brief (characters, actions, objects, locations).

This chapter presents a study which challenges the scope of AD, taking it in a new direction. *Bespoke* variants of AD, outside the usual remit of visual accessibility, were modelled for the purpose of assisting audiences overcome cognitive rather than physical barriers to audiovisual accessibility. Targeting individuals with high-functioning autistic spectrum disorders (ASDs), this study trials an audio descriptive intervention designed to address emotion recognition difficulties (ERDs) in relation to characters portrayed in film and television texts. Otherwise known as alexithymia (Bagby *et al.*, 1994), ERDs are frequently observed in those on the autism spectrum, resulting in problems with social communication and interaction; the phenomenon is also associated with a number of other cognitive and neurological conditions, some of which will be discussed further below.

5.2   Emotion recognition difficulties and autism

According to the World Health Organisation (WHO and World Bank, 2011), autism affects 1 in every 100 people internationally. Large-scale studies in the

UK suggest local prevalence sits marginally above 1 per cent of the population (Baird et al., 2006; Brugha *et al.*, 2009). Although sometimes considered a disability for matters of political expediency (Baron-Cohen, 2000: 498), autism is in fact more accurately termed an atypical cognitive framework, with many individuals on the spectrum regarded as having average intelligence or higher ('high-functioning'). Learning difficulties may co-occur with autism, but they are not symptomatic of the condition according to the definition provided by the Diagnostic and Statistical Manual of Mental Disorders, *DSM V*, (APA, 2013).

Autism has been described as a cluster of developmental disorders 'with life-long effects and that have in common a triad of impairments in: social interaction, communication, imagination and behaviour' (Wing, 1997: 1761). Although highly individualistic in nature in terms of characterisation, scope and complexity, ASDs generally manifest as a number of behaviours which impede an individual's social communication and interpersonal skills. These may include atypical conversational pragmatics (Happé, 1993), compromised social reciprocity (Mongillo *et al.,* 2008), non-standard eye gaze (Loth *et al.*, 2011), over-literal communication and interpretation (Kanner, 1943), misjudgements in understanding conversational turn-taking (Happé, 1993; Frith, 2003) and an impaired ability to read prosody, irony and sarcasm in the speech patterns of others (Happé, 1993: 103–104). These non-standard behaviours are most evident in ecologically embedded social situations. However, since they share a common theme of being prerequisites for reading the frequently opaque intentions and motivations of other people, the effect naturally transfers to interpreting character-driven audiovisual (AV) material. There is much still to learn about this aspect of the condition, but current evidence suggests that autistic children engage less effectively with visually sourced markers and human-centric aspects of communication in AV content than their non-ASD counterparts (Mongillo *et al.*, 2008; Balconi *et al.*, 2012). Notably, Mongillo *et al.* concluded that children with ASD underperformed in audiovisual tasks 'involving human faces and voices', by contrast with tasks involving inanimate matter (2008: 1349).

Hobson suggests that for autistic individuals the chief barrier to communication 'is in understanding people and what people think, feel or intend to convey' (2012: 92). This has been addressed under the conceptual framework of 'theory of mind' (ToM), which has been used to explain the social interaction challenges, and difficulties understanding how people think and feel, which can prove problematic for many of those on the autism spectrum (Baron-Cohen, 1995; Frith, 2003).[1] Naturally, one area where accessing the thoughts of others is particularly important, is in the reading of affective behaviours. Emotions are essentially a filter through which we view and interact with the world. Taking a 'temperature reading' on the emotional state of another individual plays a key role in determining how we interpret social situations, allows us to anticipate actions and thought processes, and enables us to extract meaning from words and actions. It also helps us to deliver an appropriate response. This interplay is termed 'social-emotional reciprocity (i.e. the ability to engage with others and share thoughts and feelings)' (APA, 2013: 54). Interpreting emotions in others using cues found in facial expressions, body language, intonation and wordplay is therefore a fundamental life skill. When access to emotions is thwarted, social interaction in a real-life environment, and gaining access to meaningful narrative in simulated or observed scenarios (e.g. on-screen entertainment), become daunting prospects.

In a recent survey of 48 research publications in the field, Uljarevic and Hamilton (2013: 1517) concluded that emotion recognition difficulties (ERDs) are commonplace in ASDs. In support of this finding, Poljac *et al.* (2012: 677) suggested the level of difficulty encountered when attempting to read emotions increases with the extent of an individual's autism. Those who experience fewer problems in this respect tend to be at the 'higher-functioning' end of the autistic spectrum, where simple emotional markers may have been learned in late childhood, although more complex emotions (e.g. jealousy, guilt, feeling criticised) can remain problematic into adult life (Baron-Cohen *et al.*, 2001).

As stated above, difficulty accessing emotions is not the sole preserve of individuals on the autism spectrum. This emotion-related disconnect (Sifneos, 1973) can be found in many neurological, pathological and trauma-related conditions, including attention deficit disorders such as ADHD, post-traumatic stress disorder, and aphasia and dementia (Lane *et al.*, 1997), suggesting interventions explored in this study have the potential to resonate with other cognitively diverse audiences.

With these considerations to the fore, the remodelling of AD for supplementary cognitive needs took a two-phased approach: (i) the development and application of translation strategies for producing bespoke forms of audio description oriented to mitigation of the difficulties in accessing the emotion markers in audiovisual texts amongst audiences with ERDs; and (ii) testing these AD materials with a group of high-functioning ASD children exhibiting alexithymic tendencies ('the reception study'). The latter lies beyond the scope of this chapter and will be the subject of a future publication; the remainder of this chapter therefore pertains to phase (i), the AD remodelling exercise.

5.3 Remodelling AD for new audiences

Our study set out to establish whether, by applying a functionalist framework and purpose-driven approach (Nord, 1997; Vermeer, 2012) to remodelling AD, it would be feasible to derive new variants of AD with the potential to enhance audiovisual cognitive accessibility for individuals experiencing emotion recognition difficulties (Starr, 2018). As such, it represents a fundamental and paradigmatic shift in the nature of AD, reorientating the translation process to a cognitive, rather than physical, accessibility problem. We took as our audience sample a group of high-functioning (average or above IQ) autistic children, between the ages of 9 and 14, all of whom displayed emotion recognition difficulties (Toronto Alexithymia Scale [Bagby *et al.*, 1994] tested). Our source texts were selected extracts from film and television productions considered to have wide appeal to audiences in this demographic, and included audiovisual material both with and without narratively signifi- cant dialogue (e.g. *E.T. the Extra-Terrestrial*, 1982; *Mr Bean: The Ultimate Disaster Movie*, 1997; *Snow White: The Fairest of Them All*, 2002). Each extract represented one emotion or 'state of mind' which was both visually impactful and suitable for isolation (to avoid any confusion) using a face-framing technique during the empirical testing phase. Extracts lacking, or containing minimal, dialogue allowed us to examine the use of longer, inter-pretive AD interjections without having to accommodate lengthy interludes of speech; those with a greater volume of dialogue enabled us to explore the viability of adding AD to a multi-sensory environment which can already be cognitively challenging for those on the autism spectrum.

In the first phase of the project our audiovisual source texts were used to create two *bespoke* variants of emotion-based audio description for our target ASD audience: (a) emotionally descriptive AD, with the aim of detecting and labelling the key emotions displayed by key protagonists (EMO-AD); and (b) interpretive AD, whereby emotions were first labelled and subsequently contextualised by reference to causality or consequence (CXT-AD). For the sake of comparison, and to provide a control in the reception study phase, a third variant of AD was created for the same materials, according to the standards generally applied for blind and visually impaired audiences (BVI-AD).

5.3.1 Re-versioning AD for cognitive diversity

A total of ten extracts[2] were selected from our multimodal corpus, and used as working examples for the purposes of textual analysis and the scripting of visually and cognitively oriented audio descriptions. Each film extract captured the visual representation of one distinct emotion or 'state of mind' depicted by a key protagonist. These ranged from simple emotions which might typically be determined from facial expression alone (e.g. excited, afraid), to compound emotions requiring the application of 'theory of mind' to establish meaning (e.g. criticised, lying, guilty). The choice of emotions was informed by the Golan *et al.* (2008) 'Reading the Mind in Films' study, also conducted with autistic children using similarly isolated emotions in film extracts to determine emotion detection, although in their case without the assistance of audio description.

For practical reasons, a smaller representative sample of emotions and 'states of mind' was chosen for the current study than adopted by Golan *et al.* (2008). The current selection ranged from those that had proved relatively accessible to ASD children in the 2008 study, through several with mid-range accessibility, to those which registered as more problematic in terms of ASD-ERD audience identification. A list of the emotions tested and the source texts from which they were derived is detailed in Table 5.1 below.

Table 5.1 Summary of extracts

Extract and title	Source text	Action summary	Emotion	Identifiability %*
Quite enough	*Snow White: The Fairest of Them All*	Snow White is in a carriage with her Wicked Stepmother. She waves to the local children, but is told off for being too friendly.	'Critcised'	61
Bathroom guest	*Mr Bean: The Animated Series*	Mr Bean has a guest staying at his house. He is losing patience with waiting for the man to finish using the bathroom. He makes a rude face at the man when he exits the bathroom.	'Unfriendly'	48
$20 Bill	*Paper Moon*	Addie buys some goods in a shop and pays with a $5 bill. She later claims a $20 bill already in the till was hers. She pretends to be unhappy at being short-changed.	'Upset'	48
Wet trousers	*Mr Bean: The Ultimate Disaster Movie*	Mr Bean is at an important meeting. He spilt water on his trousers while washing his hands and is hiding the stain by standing very closely behind David.	'Uncomfortable'	70
Nose-blowing	*Mr Bean: The Ultimate Disaster Movie*	Mr Bean is waiting in the secretary's office. He makes a commotion as he repeatedly blows his nose. This irritates the secretary.	'Annoyed'	78
Flying napkin	*The Return of Mr Bean*	It is Mr Bean's birthday. He is celebrating in a restaurant, and playfully allows a napkin to fly onto the adjacent table. He tries to hide his guilt.	'Guilty'	70

Table 5.1 Cont.

Extract and title	Source text	Action summary	Emotion	Identifiability %*
I Want my $200	*Paper Moon*	Addie's accomplice, Moses, has taken $200 from her. She wants it back, but he consistently refuses. Growing increasingly angry, Addie threatens to tell the police unless Moses returns the cash. She is furious.	'Furious'	52
Sick day	*E.T The Extra-Terrestrial*	Elliot is in bed, feigning illness so he can stay home from school and play with E.T., the extra-terrestrial. He warms the thermometer on his bedside lamp, to convince his mother that he has a fever.	'Lying'	35
Credit card	*The Return of Mr Bean*	Mr Bean has a credit card. Walking down the street towards a department store, he notices a sale. He looks excited.	'Excited'	70
Laundrette	*The Return of Mr Bean*	Mr Bean is in the laundrette loading his washing when a man enters. The man intimidates Mr Bean, insisting he use Mr Bean's washing machine. Mr Bean backs away.	'Afraid'	78

Note: * % correctly identified in Golan *et al.* (2008).

5.3.1.1 Form and functionality

Our approach to the remodelling exercise was guided by a functionalist, or 'skopostheorie' (Nord, 1997; Vermeer, 2012; Reiss and Vermeer, 2014) framework, with the needs of the end-user (ERD-ASD individuals) taking precedence when building translation strategies for the transfer of affective content between modalities, audiovisual to verbal.

Since the project lacked an authentic client or *commission* (Vermeer, cited in Nord, 1997: 30) and therefore had no formal translation brief, putative commissions were determined for the AD conditions ('variants'), i.e. (i) standard AD formulated to meet the needs of individuals with sight-impairment (BVI-AD); (ii) AD designed to help individuals with emotion recognition/'theory of mind' (ToM) identification difficulties (EMO-AD); and (iii) AD focused on meeting the requirements of those with emotion recognition/ToM identification issues for whom contextualisation would render the target text more transparent and thus, the intended message potentially more accessible (CXT-AD). In the development of translation strategies which fulfilled these *skopoi*, Vermeer's rule relating to audience coherence was observed, with heed given to whether the resulting target texts were coherent with the receiver's 'culture specific world knowledge, their expectations and their communicative needs' (cited in Nord, 1997: 12).

5.3.1.2 Determining translation strategies

Having established the purpose of each translation stream according to audience needs, Reiss's 'text types' (Nord, 1997: 37) were employed to tease out the key features driving translation strategies. Originally intended to categorise source texts, Reiss suggests that where a change of function is required, text types may be used to determine the nature of the required target text (Nord, 1997: 38). Consequently, for each of the putative commissions outlined above, primary functionality of the target text was established by reference to the most apposite text type classification: informative, expressive or operative. It should also be acknowledged that the source texts, being multimodal in nature, also fall within Reiss's 'audiomedial' text category (Reiss and Vermeer, 2014: 43).

5.3.1.3 BVI-AD: audio description for the blind and visually impaired

In the case of the BVI-AD brief, devised for an audience experiencing sight loss, the *skopos* is visually oriented, with imagery and unexplained audio interjections in the source text relating to 'objects and phenomena' requiring explication in the target text. To this extent, the audio description could be considered chiefly '*informative-expressive*' (Nord, 1997: 37–38) in nature. The naming and labelling of characters, actions and locations were generally prioritised since they constituted an *informative* functionality, representing the key elements upon which a basic understanding of the narrative is founded. Where hiatuses in the original film dialogue allowed, this *informative* function was enhanced by *expressive* elements, e.g. colourful depictions of the visual aesthetic (room décor, scenic views, costume), rich character descriptors (facial features, body language, facial expressions) and more nuanced descriptions of actions by the application of adverbial and adjectival phrases. This approach, as a strategy for deriving functional BVI-AD, may be

Table 5.2 BVI-AD: visual-descriptive

Narrative action	BVI-AD
Mr Bean is in a smart restaurant.	Mr Bean taps the glasses with his knife.* (*over sound-effect)
He plays a tune on his wine glass with a knife. A waiter arrives and places a napkin on Mr Bean's lap with a flourish.	Mr Bean has an 'I'm so clever' face when the waiter arrives. He takes the napkin off the table with a flick, and lays it across Mr Bean's lap.
Mr Bean replicates the napkin 'flourish' several times, until it flies onto a neighbouring table.	Mr Bean picks up the napkin and copies the waiter's flick several times, smiling to himself. The napkin flies out of his hand, onto the next table!
To hide his guilt, he pretends the tablecloth is his napkin. He scans the room to see if anyone noticed it was his fault.	He tucks the tablecloth in his collar, and looks cheekily around the room.

labelled *visual-descriptive*, since the emphasis lies primarily in describing the visual aspects of the source material.

One illustration of the BVI-AD strategy, applied to an extract from the *The Return of Mr Bean* (1990) television series, can be observed in Table 5.2 above. For the sake of streamlining our description of the AD workflow, a scene has been chosen which contains no dialogue, although certain extraneous sounds and non-verbal utterances were intrinsic to the comedic effect of the narrative. In this example, the 'phenomena and objects' which constitute the *informative* aspect of the translation comprise (i) exposition of the physical entities and environments (i.e. cues that suggest Mr Bean is sitting at a table by reference to a knife, glasses, napkin and tablecloth) and (ii) the rendering of key actions (tapping of the glasses with a knife; the ostentatious and repetitious flourish of a napkin from table-top to lap; a napkin flying in the air from one table to another). Semantic constructs are chiefly verb-based or adverbial in nature ('takes the napkin', 'taps the glasses', 'looks cheekily'). Although the short duration of audio hiatuses in the source material prevented elaborate descriptions of the *expressive* elements, these are nevertheless touched upon with phrases such as 'Mr Bean has an "I'm so clever" face when the waiter arrives' (facial expression) and 'He [...] looks cheekily around the room' (verb phrase including an adverb suggesting mood). Had more extensive hiatuses been available, it might have been preferable to incorporate an elaborate description of the interior of the restaurant and table setting at which Mr Bean found himself, and perhaps an indication as to the geography of the room (e.g. the proximity of tables that permitted a 'flying napkin' to travel with ease from one table to another), both of which played a key role in the comedic aspect of the sketch and would not necessarily be available to viewers with sight loss.

5.3.1.4 EMO-AD: audio description for people with emotion recognition difficulties (descriptive)

Turning to the second *skopos*, AD designed to assist ASD individuals experiencing emotion recognition and 'theory of mind' (ToM) identification difficulties, we encounter the first of the experimental AD variants – bespoke in nature, and defined by translation strategies targeted at audiences with cognitive, rather than physical, accessibility requirements. This first bespoke variant, 'EMO-AD', reflects a shift of emphasis away from visually descriptive strategies to labelling emotions, whether they are displayed via imagery, or communicated by other means (non-verbal utterances, sound effects, non-diegetic sound, etc.). In this instance it is the *'operative'* classification that is the most relevant of Reiss's 'text types' (Nord, 1997: 37), since the principal function of EMO-AD is to render the target text in such a way as to evoke the desired 'effect' upon the audience. In other words, the emotion carried in the source text has to be 'operationalised' in the target text in order that the ERD viewer is able to engage with an aspect of the narrative which might otherwise be inaccessible. To this end, 'both content and form are subordinate to the extra-linguistic effect that the text is designed to achieve' (Nord, 1997:3 8). Nevertheless, the purpose of this approach is not to elicit a 'vicarious sharing of emotion' (Smith, 2006: 17) between multimodal text and ERD-ASD audience (emotional empathy); rather, it is to provide a tool for circumnavigating the cognitive barriers that prevent these individuals from reading socio-affective behaviour in others (cognitive empathy). Ultimately, the aim is therefore to enhance the ERD viewer's understanding of subjectivity in storytelling, sometimes described as 'mental perspective taking' (Smith, 2006: 3).

Informing the viewer by 'operationalising' the affective narrative is a matter of identification, attribution and labelling. As a translation strategy, it may be termed *emoto-descriptive*, since the describer need only apply their standard knowledge of social communicative norms, aligned with text-specific knowledge of the characters and situations portrayed in any given film narrative, in order to assign an affective condition or 'state of mind' to the relevant protagonist. The resulting labels are by and large descriptive.

As illustrated by reference to the same audiovisual extract considered in the case of BVI-AD above (*The Return of Mr Bean*, 1990), emotional markers and ToM prompts, both *visual* and *aural*, are the key elements the describer must distil from the source text when creating EMO-AD. Predominantly, these will be drawn from facial expressions, body language and gesture, although musical scoring, ambient audio, special effects and cinematographic references also play a significant role in creating emotional capital during a film or television production.

In this example (Table 5.3), the language transfer takes a somewhat truncated form by contrast with both BVI-AD explored above, and our second bespoke variant (CXT-AD) discussed below. Our *emoto-descriptive* translation strategy requires that affective markers in the source text which

Table 5.3 EMO-AD: emoto-descriptive

Narrative action	EMO-AD
Mr Bean is in a smart restaurant.	Mr Bean's feeling playful.
He plays a tune on his wine glass with a knife. A waiter arrives and places a napkin on Mr Bean's lap with a flourish.	Mr Bean's amused.
Mr Bean replicates the napkin 'flourish' several times, until it flies on to a neighbouring table.	He thinks he's being funny …
To hide his guilt, he pretends the tablecloth is his napkin.	He feels bad but …
He scans the room to see if anyone noticed it was his fault.	… he appears innocent.

either represent emotions or indicate the 'states of mind' of key protagonists are rendered in the EMO-AD text as adjectives, verbs or adverbial phrases. Hence, when Mr Bean begins to sound-out the tune 'Happy Birthday', using his knife to play the glasses on the restaurant table as if they were hand bells, it is apparent that he is 'feeling playful'. The self-satisfied expression on his face as he completes this task suggests that he is 'amused', at least to the extent that he has entertained himself, if not the other diners, at this rather formal restaurant. During the segment in which Mr Bean repeatedly places the napkin on his own lap with an extravagant flourish, mimicking the actions of the waiter earlier in the scene, and chuckling to himself as he does so, we perceive that he thinks he is 'being funny'. The *denouement* occurs when Mr Bean accidentally hurls his napkin into the air, allowing it to land in the vicinity of the diners on the adjacent table. An initial look of horror and contrition ('he feels bad') quickly turns to feigned detachment, as he seeks to cover up this misdemeanour ('he appears innocent') from his fellow diners.

These examples illustrate the strategy of brevity adopted for EMO-AD. Forays into fully interpretive AD were avoided at this juncture in order to explore a variant that imposed minimal additional cognitive processing demands on the ERD-ASD viewer. However, we acknowledge that EMO-AD inevitably requires some degree of affective interpretation on the part of the describer who is first and foremost a regular 'viewer'. She/he must assimilate cues and prompts from across the source text in order to extract meaning and establish 'the impression of continuity of sense and connectivity in a text' (Braun, 2011: 647). To seek coherence in storytelling is to search for the 'glue' which connects the competing strands of narrative. Hence, the describer cannot avoid contextualising affective behaviours within the wider storyline, interpreting fleeting facial expressions or gestures as part of a cohesive whole. It is therefore important to emphasise that the act of creating fully interpretive AD is a conscious choice: the process of coherence-seeking and broader contextualisation/interpretation should be regarded as a describer's 'input', while the 'output' (in this case, EMO-AD) has nevertheless to be confined to a concise, descriptive statement of observed behaviours.

5.3.1.5 CXT-AD: audio description for individuals with emotion recognition difficulties (interpretive)

Our third AD functionality, or *skopos* (CXT-AD), tested the hypothesis that contextualisation prompts, when delivered incrementally to descriptive EMO-AD, have the potential to render the target text more accessible to individuals with emotion recognition and ToM identification issues than descriptive AD alone. Frith (2003: 161) observed that contextualisation, as a means of interpreting emotions and 'states of mind' in others, may be compromised by a latent tendency for weak central coherence in autistic individuals. This suggests that descriptive labelling of the emotions alone would not resolve the need for the viewer to interpret the relevance of such emotions within the wider narrative framework. For example we may appreciate that Mr Bean is 'being funny', but in order to fully immerse ourselves in the plot, we are required to supplement this knowledge with an explanation for his affective state: that he has been mimicking the waiter's actions with his napkin. Our approach in the third AD modality (CXT-AD) was therefore to supplement the descriptive nature of EMO-AD with elements of 'causality' and 'consequence' in relation to each emotion-driven narrative action. As well as easing understanding for ERD audiences, which was the main intention in this instance, the addition of context had the potential to deliver a more robust training model in situations where AD might be used as a pedagogical tool to teach identification and attribution of emotions.

Modelling CXT-AD, as a more lexically sophisticated ERD-AD variant, once again began with an examination of the functionality of the target text based on Reiss's text types. In this case, the desired output was regarded as operative-expressive in orientation: *operative* because, similar to the EMO-AD variant, an 'extra-linguistic effect' (engagement with the emotional subtext) was being sought; and *expressive*, since 'the stylistic choices made by the author contribute to the meaning of the text' (Nord, 1997: 38). In order to create affect-triggered narrative interjections relevant to ERD-ASD viewers, the CXT-AD script utilised *expressive* terms reasoned to be of incremental value in transmitting a story-led appreciation of the socio-affective markers contained in the source text. In effect, the added contribution to meaning provided by CXT-AD took the form of an exposition of the rationale underpinning affective behaviours. Needless to say, this approach assumes a level of interpretive unanimity amongst audience members which might arguably be lacking. Audio description is undoubtedly, by its very nature, a subjective undertaking. The audience is invited to share the describer's perspective, interpretation and preconceptions. Even in instances where the adopted AD strategy is robustly descriptive, prioritisation choices – in terms of which aspects of the audiovisual material are described – generate their own agenda and bias. Hence multiple describers demonstrably deliver divergent AD scripts when presented with identical source material. Yet this rarely produces significant differences in the broader direction of AD narrative. More typically, we observe variations in narrative focus or interest between describers, while the overarching direction remains consistent. Nevertheless, in the development phase of this project, the source texts were pilot-tested with a number of neurotypical adults to evaluate general comprehension. Results of these tests indicated that our interpretations of source text narratives, which were in any case chosen to be relatively simplistic in nature, closely matched those of the general consensus.

Bringing together emotion identification cues and contextualising prompts with a view to promoting affective perceptions in ERD-ASD audiences required a translation strategy which was termed *emoto-interpretive* in orientation. Assuming this strategy could be executed in a manner that would avoid overburdening the ERD-ASD audiences' cognitive load, then it was anticipated the result would be a more coherent and accessible text than either BVI-AD or EMO-AD.

Once again revisiting the same film extract from *The Return of Mr Bean* (1990), the CXT-AD text immediately appears more complete, in the sense that it comes closer in length and complexity to standard BVI-AD. However, the strategy has shifted markedly in the direction of producing an operative statement (emotion exposition) aligned with stylistic choices (e.g. exclamatory phrases) which add narrative colour and enhance meaning:

In this extract (Table 5.4), the AD explicates the reason for Mr Bean playing 'Happy Birthday' on his wine glasses: he is 'feeling playful'. Had there been a longer hiatus before the 'musical' interlude, it might have been preferable to expand the contextual cueing to read, 'Mr Bean is feeling playful *because it's his birthday*', as a way to introduce the significance of the tune before it is

Table 5.4 CXT-AD: emoto-interpretive

Narrative action	*CXT-AD*
Mr Bean is in a smart restaurant. *He plays a tune on his wine glass with a knife. A waiter arrives and places a napkin on Mr Bean's lap with a flourish.*	Mr Bean's feeling playful. He looks to see if anyone was watching. He thinks he's very amusing.
Mr Bean replicates the napkin 'flourish' several times, until it flies on to a neighbouring table.	Mr Bean copies what the waiter did with his napkin because it's funny. Oh no … it flew over to the next table! He pretends it's not his fault.
To hide his guilt, he pretends the tablecloth is his napkin. He scans the room to see if anyone noticed it was his fault.	

played. The reason he glances around the restaurant is described here, i.e. to 'see if anyone was watching' and establish if they are finding his antics equally as 'amusing'. Harnessing the dual aspects of context and intent, Mr Bean's mimicking of the waiter's actions ('Mr Bean copies what the waiter did with his napkin') has been rationalised and captured in the causal phrase 'because it's funny'.

This example illustrates the manner in which the emotion descriptors used in CXT-AD tended to mirror those applied in the EMO-AD variant ('amusing', 'playful', 'funny'). It is simply the addition of causality and consequence that has changed. Furthermore, integration of *emoto-interpretive* language within the CXT-AD script has resulted, rather unexpectedly, in the creation of a relatively cohesive, stand-alone narrative. In the above example, we observe a five-step explanation for the 'faux pas' that occurs with the errant napkin. Perhaps the only item of narrative significance that remains absent is the concept of a solo birthday celebration, which might usefully have been appended to the phrase 'Mr Bean's feeling playful', had there been a sufficient hiatus to make such an insertion possible. The relative completeness of CXT-AD as an abridged storyline differs markedly from standard BVI-AD translation strategies, which generally call for interjections that are complementary to the multimodal source text, rather than being fully explanatory or 'complete' (see also Braun and Starr's Introduction to this volume). However, there are also commonalities between the two variants, which will be considered further below.

5.4 Analysis of texts

The methods described above were applied to a series of ten audiovisual extracts chosen from feature films and television productions, in order to stress-test the robustness of our translation strategies in relation to each *skopos*. As discussed previously (Sections 5.1 and 5.2), formulation of the

Table 5.5 Summary of target text types and features

Target audience	Reiss's text type*	Key features	Translation strategy
BVI-AD	informative-expressive	'phenomena and objects' + stylistic choices contributing to meaning	visual-descriptive
EMO-AD	operative	'extra linguistic effect' over content and form	emoto-descriptive
CXT-AD	operative-expressive	'extra linguistic effect' + stylistic choices contributing to meaning	emoto-interpretative

* Nord, 1997: 37.

ERD strategies was driven by a requirement to provide greater access to emotional cues in audiovisual texts for viewers with autistic spectrum disorders; a standard BVI strategy aimed at assisting viewers with visual accessibility needs was also selected for the purposes of comparison. All AD scripts, including the BVI variant, were created ab initio, in the course of this remodelling exercise.

The present section analyses three worked examples of these comparative AD outputs in greater depth in order to highlight the key differences between the three methods.

5.4.1 Extract 1: Quite enough ('criticised')

5.4.1.1 Narrative description

The first extract (Table 5.6), from *Snow White: The Fairest of Them All* (2002), is centred on the interaction between two characters, Snow White and her Wicked Stepmother, as they ride through a rural hamlet and woodlands in an open-top carriage. Audiovisual semiotics consist of a bucolic scene, with peasants and their children following the carriage and calling out 'Princess' as Snow White passes by. She waves back at them, in response. In sharp contrast to the peasants' rough-hewn clothing, Snow White and the Wicked Stepmother are dressed in courtly finery. The scene is resolved when the Wicked Stepmother imposes her will on Snow White and ensures she conforms with courtly practices by keeping her distance from the townsfolk, with the rebuke 'Snow White! That's quite enough.' Snow White sinks back down into her carriage seat, seemingly dejected. Narrative focus lies in the antagonistic relationship between Snow White and the Wicked Stepmother, the contrast of their lifestyle with that of the peasants, and the humility shown by Snow White as she acknowledges her 'subjects'. Snow White's mood shifts through the scene from one of initial happiness to contrition after she is scolded for being friendly with the local people. The latter sentiment is not overt, however, but implied by the Wicked Stepmother's reaction to Snow White's behaviour. Thus the narrative, whilst short, contains many implicatures and nuances of meaning which require 'decoding' by the audience.

Table 5.6 Criticised

AD1 Emotive (EMO)	AdD2 Contextual (CXT)	AD3 Visually impaired (BVI)
Snow White's very happy.	Snow White's happy to see the children.	Snow White's in a carriage with her Wicked Stepmother.
Snow White feels told off.	She feels told off for being friendly.	She happily waves at the children.

5.4.1.2 Audio descriptions

Hiatuses in this brief extract are not sufficient for a detailed audio description of the action, which would have been preferable in the case of intermodal transfer for BVI audiences. However, there is a sufficient break in the original soundtrack for a perfunctory description of mise-en-scène to be inserted in the BVI-AD modality. Reference is made to the two women being in a carriage and that Snow White waves to the children. The emotional cues, although not overt, are carried by the dialogue and sound effects. In the EMO-AD modality, since non-affective visual markers would be accessible to ERD-ASD audiences, no cinematic scene-setting is necessary. Conversely, Snow White's initial emotional aspect (broadly content, as denoted by a wry smile) and her final mood (contrite) would need to be conveyed through the EMO-AD to address difficulties with facial expression recognition (Golan *et al.*, 2008) and prosodic interpretation (Happé, 1993: 103–104) that are likely to occur in ERD-ASD individuals. Body language is also indicative of mood in this scene (i.e. when scolded, Snow White slides back into the carriage seat, having first stood up to wave at the villagers). Once again, the relevance of this action might be overlooked by ERD-ASD viewers. The EMO-AD (*emoto-descriptive*) variant must therefore deliver labelling for each of the emotions implied by the above actions. Consequently, EMO-AD incorporates the descriptors 'very happy' and 'feels told off'. By contrast, in the CXT-AD modality, where emotion identification is perceived to be context-dependent, causality is incorporated alongside emoto-description. In this case, Snow White is described as feeling 'happy to see the children' as she rides through the village, and later, having been scolded for her actions, as 'feel[ing] told off for being friendly'. Both are interpretations made in relation to the multi-semiotic cues provided by the source text. Interestingly, given that the Snow White character does not engage in dialogue, either with the villagers or the Wicked Stepmother, her mood is carried entirely by facial expressions and body language, neither of which is accessible to the BVI audiences or, potentially, the ERD audience. As a result, this particular intersemiotic transfer from visual to verbal is of equal relevance to both audience groups.

5.4.2 Extract 2: Bathroom guest ('unfriendly')

5.4.2.1 Narrative Description

'Bathroom guest' is a cartoon extract taken from an episode of *Mr Bean: The Animated Series* ('The Visitor', 2002), and contains a complex array of audio-visual semiotic cues interwoven across multiple quick-fire shot changes. In this scene (Table 5.7), Mr Bean waits to use the bathroom while an inconsiderate house-guest procrastinates over his nighttime bathroom routine. As time progresses, Mr Bean's irritation at the house-guest grows, until the point when the guest finally emerges from the bathroom and Mr Bean pulls an

Table 5.7 Unfriendly

AD1 Emotive (EMO)	AD2 Contextual (CXT)	AD3 Visually impaired (BVI)
Mr Bean's getting impatient.	Mr Bean's impatient because he needs to use the bathroom.	Mr Bean's in his pyjamas, waiting to use the bathroom.
He's feeling pretty grumpy.	Mr Bean's guest is STILL in the bathroom. It makes him grumpy.	His guest's still brushing his teeth.
Mr Bean doesn't like the man.	Mr Bean makes a rude face at the silly man.	Mr Bean's grumpy.
		Finally the bathroom door opens ....
		Mr Bean blows a 'raspberry' at the man.

unfriendly face, blowing him a 'raspberry'. The cartoon nature of this extract poses a different set of audiovisual translation issues when compared with Extract 1 above. Essentially, these can be reduced to two key challenges for the audio describer: (i) the extract contains no dialogue, although the rich soundscape plays a key role in carrying narrative, and a number of non-verbal utterances suggest emotional undercurrents (e.g. sighing, 'raspberry' blowing and an ill-tempered nonsense rhyme); (ii) representations of facial expressions in animated material are less nuanced and expressive than real-life facial manifestations. On the one hand, this makes facially expressed emotions easier to read, because they are not complex. On the other hand, it places a heavier burden of cognitive processing on the audience, who must draw on other semiotic channels in order to differentiate between possible readings (e.g. to distinguish between 'angry' and 'annoyed'). Both challenges create problems for BVI and ERD-ASD audiences alike, although BVI viewers may be aided by the ability to interpret audio-affective cues more accurately. Nevertheless, AD scripting requirements also intensify in the case of the BVI modality, since non-affective visual representations must also be incorporated.

5.4.2.2 Audio descriptions

In the BVI-AD variant, the two principal characters are introduced and a sequence of narrative events described: Mr Bean is 'in his pyjamas' (suggesting that it is just before bedtime); he is 'waiting to use the bathroom' (location, situation); his guest is 'still brushing' (suggesting that the house-guest takes too long brushing his teeth in the bathroom); Mr Bean grows increasingly 'grumpy'; when the guest finally emerges, Mr Bean is rude and unfriendly, blowing a 'raspberry' at the selfish man. Thus, BVI-AD supplies the visually derived implicatures (bedtime, duration of wait, building irritation) as well as affective cues. For the sparse EMO-AD variant, Mr Bean's emotions are simply labelled 'impatient' and 'grumpy', ending with the conclusion that he 'doesn't like the man'. The use of multiple shot changes between Mr Bean in his bedroom and the house-guest in the bathroom produces a sizeable stream of narrative cues within a short space of time. These could prove problematic for audiences with ERDs because there is minimal opportunity for the evaluation of facial expressions before the scene cuts to another segment. In isolation, emotion labelling may therefore prove insufficient to promote full access to narrative. By contrast, contextual descriptions (CXT-AD) can be used to signpost cause-and-effect associations at key junctures in the plot: (i) initially, that Mr Bean is impatient because he must wait for the bathroom; (ii) subsequently, Mr Bean's impatience turns to 'grump[iness]'; and (iii) Mr Bean makes an unfriendly gesture ('rude face') directed at the guest when he finally vacates the bathroom. Perhaps somewhat counter-intuitively, CXT-AD *emoto-interpretative* cues may also be of assistance to BVI audiences in this instance, as the interjections coincide with the most narratively critical shot changes. Sight-impaired viewers may find the CXT-AD in combination with the original soundtrack (e.g. echoed vocals defining the bathroom scenes) sufficient to gain full access to the visual narrative, including critical changes in location.

5.4.3 Extract 3: Nose-blowing ('Annoyed')

5.4.3.1 Narrative description

Two characters, Mr Bean and a female personal assistant, feature in this short extract (Table 5.8) from *The Return of Mr Bean* (1990). They are located in a formal corporate office suite, the secretary at her desk, head bent, concentrating on her papers. Mr Bean, who is sitting opposite the assistant, waits nervously to meet with the company boss. The tension manifests itself as fidgeting, when Mr Bean's nose begins to itch. He starts to blow it repeatedly, with immense gusto. This behaviour irritates the secretary and she casts him a series of reproachful glances. The soundtrack is free from dialogue, with the only aural cueing device being the embellished and protracted sound of Mr Bean blowing his nose.

5.4.3.2 Audio descriptions

Three affective states demonstrated in this extract demand the describer's attention: Mr Bean's 'nervous' condition, provoking 'fidgety' mannerisms (hyperbolic nose-blowing); the assistant's response ('grumpy', 'annoyed'); and her closing scowl at Mr Bean ('very irritated'). As the soundtrack consists only of a short musical introduction and the noise of Mr Bean blowing his nose, there is adequate audio hiatus to construct a comprehensive BVI-AD narrative. In order for sight-impaired audiences to access the comedic aspects of the scene, a complex sequence of events must be captured: initial

Table 5.8 Annoyed

AD1 Emotive (EMO)	AD2 Contextual (CXT)	AD3 Visually impaired (BVI)
Mr Bean's nervous and fidgety.	Mr Bean feels nervous and fidgety.	Mr Bean sits nervously in the secretary's office. He starts to rub his nose.
The secretary looks grumpily at Mr Bean.	He has an itchy nose and starts to rub it.	He pulls a handkerchief out of his pocket, carefully unfolds it ... and blows his nose.
Now the secretary is getting very irritated with Mr Bean.	Oh, what a relief! He's found a nice clean hanky in his pocket.	The secretary frowns.
	The secretary looks grumpy ... she doesn't like the noise.	Mr Bean puts the hanky back in his pocket ...
	The secretary is now really irritated with Mr Bean.	.. then takes it straight back out again.
		The secretary looks very irritated.

nose-rubbing and fidgeting; the slow build-up to capitulation and the point of first nose-blowing; a ritualistic unfolding of the handkerchief; replacement of the handkerchief in Mr Bean's pocket; subsequent removal of the handkerchief from the pocket, followed by more ostentatious nose-blowing. Selective use of adverbs in the BVI-AD variant delivers key aspects of the humour such as 'sits nervously' and 'carefully unfolds it' (the handkerchief). Equally, the segment whereby the handkerchief is placed back in a trouser pocket only to be instantaneously taken 'straight back out again', underpins the strangely compulsive nature of the character. Such an exhaustive level of visual description is therefore essential if sight-impaired viewers are to enjoy the brilliantly nuanced humorous aspects of the presentation. Moving on to ERD-centric AD variants, a significant shift away from straightforward action-description now takes place in order to deliver the same comedic impact. In the EMO-AD modality, three principal emotional states require attention: (a) Mr Bean's exaggerated mannerisms ('nervous', 'fidgety'); (b) the assistant's early displeasure with her visitor ('looks grumpily at ...'); and (c) the assistant's growing annoyance ('getting very irritated'). Paired with the visual semiotics surrounding the handkerchief interplay, emotion-labelling of this type should ensure full engagement with the scene by ERD viewers. The more effusive CXT-AD variant is again noteworthy, in that it closely resembles the BVI-AD script and might, with minor exceptions, be directly substituted. Just one narrative marker which occurs in the BVI-AD is omitted from the CXT-AD, and that is the removal and almost instant replacement of the handkerchief in the pocket. This can be explained by the fact that it is one of the few events in the scene that does not correspond directly to a visually expressed emotion. Thus, it is again possible to infer that instances of convergence between CXT- and BVI-AD variants occur where visually expressed emotions are present.

5.5 Discussion

As an exercise in remodelling for the purposes of producing innovative and functional variants of AD for new audiences, we have shown that by exploiting attributes derived from Reiss's 'text types' (Nord, 1997: 37) and developing corresponding translation strategies for the transfer of narrative from film text to AD, a new approach and methodology for AD creation has emerged. Text typologies served to pinpoint a semantic blueprint for each AD variant (BVI: *informative-expressive*; EMO: *operative*; CXT: *operative-expressive*) while the corresponding translation strategies (*visual descriptive* [BVI]; *emoto-descriptive* [EMO'; *emoto-interpretive* [CXT]) guided the selection of elements from across the range of available multimodal markers through which the purpose could be fulfilled. This saliency-based selection process was highly dependent on the putative translation *brief* (Nord, 1997: 30) in each instance, with affective behaviours and their corresponding contextual markers being the primary focus for EMO-AD and CXT-AD respectively. In a sense, saliency-seeking might be considered a process of information 'filtration', since the many layers of meaning-making in film narrative must be examined for relevance to purpose: dialogue, non-verbal utterances, emotional subtext (facial expression, gesture, body language), soundscape and musical scoring, cinematography (perspective, shot selection, scale) and scenography (temporal and spatial, lighting, set design). Although derived from the same source material, BVI-AD was filtered to deliver only visual narrative and therefore required consideration of cues beyond the wholly affective.

As previously stated, a key component of this study was first to model and subsequently prepare AD scripts, ab initio, for a series of film and television extracts in anticipation of a reception study with ERD-ASD individuals. It was projected that the latter would test the efficacy of emotion-centric AD in a socio-ecologically representative environment. Results of this second-phase study will be published in due course. However, a number of key findings from the application of our newly evolved AD model became evident during the pilot study phase of testing. Firstly, BVI-AD proved dysfunctional for some ERD-ASD audiences, leading to comments from participants about the superfluous nature of certain visual descriptions. This bias against a BVI-AD-centric translation strategy presented as a common theme across both the pilot and main ERD reception studies, suggesting standard BVI-AD contained an inherent element of translational redundancy. By contrast, both EMO-AD and the CXT-AD variant, which evolved through a strategy of providing causality and consequence for affective behaviours and thus adhered to the principles of explicitation (i.e.

whereby implicit elements of a source text are made explicit in the target product (Klaudy, 2009), proved more valuable to the ERD-ASD audience.

One further point of interest in relation to the adoption of novel AD translation strategies was a clear point of intersection between descriptions which met the brief for BVI individuals, and those which satisfied the remit established for ERD audiences. This 'crossover' phenomenon could be observed where semantically analogous descriptions were employed as relevant to both BVI and ERD individuals. Such occurrences were illustrated in Extracts 2 and 3 above, and took place where emotions, moods or 'states of mind' were portrayed by visual means in the source material. Since this material was potentially problematic to sight-impaired and emotionally challenged viewers alike, strategies for intermodal transfer in relation to both audiences (BVI and ERD) resulted in significant audio descriptive overlap. For instance, in Extract 3 above, the act of 'nose-rubbing' was referenced in the BVI-AD variant to suggest nervous behaviour, since physical demonstrations of mood would not be available to sight-impaired audiences. Conversely, whilst the 'nose-rubbing' *is* visibly accessible to ERD audiences, it might be overlooked as an emotion-signifier (or incorrectly interpreted), and so demands explicitation to reveal underlying causality in the CXT-AD, i.e. 'nose-rubbing' as a manifestation of 'fidgeting' indicates a state of nervousness. Despite these instances of content crossover, semantic and syntactic elements varied widely between the three AD modalities.

5.6 Concluding remarks

Remodelling AD for audiences presenting with atypical cognitive accessibility requirements posed a novel translation challenge originating from a radical change in AD functionality. *Skopostheorie* (Vermeer, 2012; Reiss and Vermeer, 2014), as a purpose-driven approach to solving translation problems, together with the application of Reiss's text type classifications (Nord, 1997), offered a framework for strategising solutions in order to address this fundamental, functional shift. Through consideration of parallel AD texts, worked examples have been used to illustrate two approaches to delivering the ERD brief, and differences between ERD-AD variants and standard audio description (BVI-AD) have been exemplified.

Modelling and re-versioning AD for individuals with ERDs clearly has the potential to assist autism spectrum audiences requiring help with interpreting emotional cues. As a new approach to AD, it could also open up access to affective behaviours in multimodal narrative for those with other socio-affective conditions, such as post-traumatic stress disorder (Minzenberg *et al.*, 2006). Furthermore, given that evidence of co-occurrence/crossover was demonstrated between ERD and BVI textual renderings, multidimensional AD which meets the needs of both cognitively and physically challenged individuals could be an advantageous avenue to explore in the future.

Notes

1 ToM/SoM: 'theory of mind' (and the reflexive 'state of mind') is used to denote an ability 'to attribute independent mental states to self and others in order to explain and predict behaviour' (Frith and Happé, 1994: 116).
2 Two extracts (*Credit Card* and *Laundrette*) were used as 'warm-up' exercises only, during phase (ii).

References

APA (American Psychiatric Association) (2013) *Diagnostic and Statistical Manual of Mental Disorders, Fifth Edition (DSM-5)*. Washington, DC: American Psychiatric Publishing.

Bagby, R. M., Parker, J. D. A., and Taylor, G. J. (1994) 'The Twenty-Item Toronto Alexithymia Scale, Part I: Item Selection and Cross-Validation of the Factor Structure', *Journal of Psychosomatic Research*, 38, pp. 23–32.

Baird, G., Simonoff, E., Pickles, A., Chandler, S., Loucas, T., Meldrum, D., and Charman, T. (2006) 'Prevalence of Disorders of the Autism Spectrum in a Population Cohort of Children in South Thames: The Special Needs and Autism Project (SNAP)', *Lancet*, 368(9531), pp. 210–215.

Balconi, M., Amenta, S., and Ferrari, C. (2012) 'Emotional Decoding in Facial Expression, Scripts and Videos: A Comparison between Normal, Autistic and Asperger Children', *Research in Autism Spectrum Disorders*, 6, pp. 193–203.

Baron-Cohen, S. (1995) *Mindblindness: An Essay on Autism and Theory of Mind*. Cambridge, MA: MIT Press.

Baron-Cohen, S. (2000) 'Is Asperger Syndrome/High Functioning Autism Necessarily a Disability?', *Development and Psychopathology*, 12, p. 489–500.

Baron-Cohen, S., Wheelwright, S., Hill, J., Raste, Y., and Plum, I. (2001) 'The "Reading the Mind in the Eyes" Test Revised Version: A Study with Normal Adults, and Adults with Asperger Syndrome or High-Functioning Autism', *Journal of. Child Psychology and Psychiatry*, 42(2), pp. 241–251.

Brugha, T., McManus, S., Meltzer, H., Smith, J., Scott, F. J., Purdon, S., Harris, J., and Bankart, J. (2009) *Autism Spectrum Disorders in Adults Living in Households throughout England: Report from the Adult Psychiatric Morbidity Survey, 2007*. Leeds: NHS Information Centre for Health and Social Care. Available at: www. hscic.gov.uk/catalogue/PUB01131.

Braun, S. (2007) 'Audio Description from a Discourse Perspective: A Socially Relevant Framework for Research and Training', *Linguistica Antverpiensia*, 6, pp. 357–369.

Braun, S. (2011) 'Creating Coherence in Audio Description', *Meta*, 56(3), pp. 645–662.

Cozendey, S., and da Piedade Costa, M. (2016) 'The Audio Description as a Physics Teaching Tool', *Journal of Research in Special Educational Needs*, 16(1), pp. 1031–1034.

Franco, E., Silveira, D., and Carneiro, B. (2015) 'Audio Describing for an Audience with Learning Disabilities in Brazil: A Pilot Study', in R. Baños Piñero and J. Dìaz-Cintas (eds.), *Audiovisual Translation in a Global Context: Mapping an Ever Changing Landscape*. Basingstoke: Palgrave Macmillan, pp. 99–109.

Frith, U. (2003) *Autism: Explaining the Enigma*. 2nd edn. Oxford: Blackwell.

Frith, U., and Happé, F. (1994) 'Autism: Beyond "Theory of Mind"', *Cognition*, 50(1–3), pp. 115–132.

Fryer, L., and Freeman, J. (2013) 'Visual Impairment and Presence: Measuring the Effect of Audio Description', Article 4 in *Proceedings of the 2013 Inputs-Outputs Conference: An Interdisciplinary Conference on Engagement in HCI and Performance* New York: ACM.

Golan, O., Baron-Cohen, S., and Golan, Y. (2008) 'The "Reading the Mind in Films" Task [Child Version]: Complex Emotion and Mental State Recognition in Children with and without Autism Spectrum Conditions', *Journal of Autism and Developmental Disorders*, 38, pp. 1534–1541.

Happé, F. (1993) 'Communicative Competence and Theory of Mind in Autism: A Test of Relevance Theory', *Cognition*, 48(2), pp. 101–119.

Hobson, R. P. (2012) 'Emotion as Personal Relatedness', *Emotion Review*, 4(2), pp. 169–175.

Johnson-Laird, P. N. (2010) 'Mental Models and Human Reasoning', *Proceedings of the National Academy of Sciences*, 107, pp. 18243–18250.

Kanner, L. (1943) 'Autistic Disturbances of Affective Contact', *Nervous Child*, 2(3), pp. 217–250.

Klaudy, K. (2009) 'Explicitation', in M. Baker and G. Saldanha (eds.), *Routledge Encyclopedia of Translation Studies*, 2nd edn, Abingdon: Routledge, pp. 104–108.

Kruger, J-L. (2012) 'Making Meaning in AVT: Eye Tracking and Viewer Construction of Narrative', *Perspectives: Studies in Translatology*, 20(1), pp. 67–86.

Kruger, J-L., and Doherty, S. (2016) 'Measuring Cognitive Load in the Presence of Educational Video: Towards a Multimodal Methodology', *Australasian Journal of Educational Technology*, 32(6), pp. 19–31.

Lane, R. D., Ahern, G. L., Schwartz, G. E., and Kaszniak, A. W. (1997) 'Is Alexithymia the Emotional Equivalent of Blindsight?', *Biological Psychiatry*, 42(9), pp. 834–844.

Looms, P. (2011) *Making Television Accessible*. Geneva: International Television Union.

Loth, E., Gómez, J. C., and Happé, F. (2011) 'Do High-Functioning People with Autism Spectrum Disorder Spontaneously Use Event Knowledge to Selectively Attend to and Remember Context-relevant Aspects in Scenes?', *Journal of Autism and Developmental Disorders*, 41, pp. 945–961.

Minzenberg, M. J., Poole , J. H., and Vinogradov, S. (2006) 'Social-emotion Recognition in Borderline Personality Disorder', *Comprehensive Psychiatry*, 47(6), pp. 468–474.

Mongillo, E. A., Irwin, J. R., Whalen, D. H., Klaiman, C., Carter, A. S., and Schultz, R. T. (2008) 'Audiovisual Processing in Children with and without Autism Spectrum Disorders', *Journal of Autism and Developmental Disorders*, 38, pp. 1349–1358.

Nord, C. (1997) *Translating as a Purposeful Activity: Functionalist Approaches Explained.* Manchester: St Jerome.

Poljac, E., Poljac, E., and Wagemans, J. (2012) 'Reduced Accuracy and Sensitivity in the Perception of Emotional Facial Expressions in Individuals with High Autism Spectrum Traits', *Autism*, 17(6), pp. 668–680.

Reiss, K., and Vermeer, H. (2014) *Towards a General Theory of Translational Action: Skopos Theory Explained.* Translated by Christiane Nord. London: Routledge.

Sifneos, P. E. (1973) 'The Prevalence of Alexithymic Characteristics in Psychosomatic Patients', *Psychotherapy and Psychosomatics*, 22, pp. 255–262.

Smith, A. (2006) 'Cognitive Empathy and Emotional Empathy in Human Behaviour and Evolution', *Psychological Record*, 56, pp. 3–21.

Sperber, D., and Wilson, D. (1995) *Relevance: Communication and Cognition.* 2nd edn. Oxford: Blackwell.

Starr, K. (2018) 'Audio Description and Cognitive Diversity: A Bespoke Approach to Facilitating Access to the Emotional Content in Multimodal Narrative Texts for Autistic Audiences.' PhD thesis. University of Surrey. Available at: http://epubs.surrey.ac.uk/848660.

Uljarevic, M., and Hamilton, A. (2013) 'Recognition of Emotions in Autism: A Formal Meta-Analysis', *Journal of Autism and Developmental Disorders*, 43, pp. 1517–1526.

Vermeer, H. (2012) 'Skopos and Commission in Translational Action', in L. Venuti (ed.), *The Translation Studies Reader*, 3rd edn, Abingdon: Routledge, pp. 191–202.

Vialard, D. (2017) 'Audio Description as a Pedagogical Tool in Composition and Writing', *Proceedings of Advanced Research Seminar on Audio Description*, Universitat Autònoma de Barcelona, 16–17 March.

Walczak, A. and Fryer, L. (2017) 'Creative Description: The Impact of Audio Description Style on Presence in Visually Impaired Audiences', *British Journal of Visual Impairment*, 35(1), pp. 6–17.

Wing, L. (1997) 'The Autism Spectrum', *Lancet*, 350, pp. 1761–1766.

WHO (World Health Organization and World Bank) (2011) *World Report on Disability*. Geneva: World Health Organization and World Bank Publications.

Zabalbeascoa, P. (2013) *ClipFlair: Foreign Language Learning through Interactive Revoicing and Captioning of Clips*. Brussels: Education, Audiovisual & Culture Executive Agency.

Filmography

E.T. the Extra-Terrestrial (1982) Directed by Steven Spielberg. [Feature film]. USA: Universal Pictures.

Mr Bean: The Ultimate Disaster Movie (1997) Directed by Mel Smith. [Feature film]. UK: PolyGram Filmed Entertainment.

Snow White: The Fairest of Them All (2002) Directed by Caroline Thompson. [Feature film]. USA: Hallmark.

The Return of Mr Bean (1990) Directed by John Howard Davies [Television]. UK: Tiger Television.

6 Towards a user specification for immersive audio description

Chris Hughes, Pilar Orero and Sonali Rai

6.1 Introduction

The aim of the Immersive Accessibility project is to establish how traditional access tools such as subtitles, audio description, sign language and audio subtitles may be used to transform the experience of consuming immersive content for people with hearing and/or sight loss. In contrast to the controlled environments designed for the delivery of mass media, ImAc will offer a fully customisable platform to present immersive content to users with varying degrees of sensory loss and learning disabilities. A range of open source tools will also be designed for the content production industry and showcased at the final project conference.

The ImAc Consortium brings together stakeholders from organisations across sectors including broadcast, charitable and volunteer organisations, academia, research and development with the aim of combining a range of different yet relevant skills to deliver on this project.

The project aims to create accessible and fully personalised services for all citizens using access features such as subtitles, audio description and sign language to transform the accessibility of immersive content. This will develop novel resources for the broadcasting industry, providing adapted content and ensuring accessibility in immersive environments. In order to ensure content is accessible across platforms, broadcasters need resources and tools which can be integrated with current production workflows and allow the repurposing of existing content whenever possible. ImAc will provide new, and enhance existing, tools to deliver access features for 360-degree content.

The ImAc project will also demonstrate the newly developed tools and platforms through open access pilot testing. The execution and evaluation of pilot studies is crucial to ensure that the developed services, tools and the platform are functional and can be operated in real-world scenarios. Therefore within the project there will be pilot studies in three countries: the UK, Spain and Germany. This will help to standardise accessibility data in immersive content environments. For the inclusion of accessibility services in immersive content, it is important that standardisation bodies acknowledge the need for these services and define requirements for their delivery from an early stage.

Finally, ImAc aims to maximise the impact on society by delivering useful solutions. The project development will be driven by real user needs and will seek to continuously involve users by means of user-centric design methodologies. Tools developed for this purpose should meet the requirements of experienced broadcasters from the start, and tools and services are to be thoroughly tested by means of pilot studies.

6.2 Literature review

Audio description (AD) research is usually conducted within the field of audiovisual translation. Generally, this is because the audio describer has a similar function to that of the language translator, who has to render the work written in a source language (multimodal text) into a target language (AD). The audio describer must provide an account of the visual image and disambiguate any meaningful sound which is not explicit (Szarkowska and Orero, 2014). The image to be described may vary from a movie to a play, an opera or a picture hung in a museum. In the case of a museum picture the AD renders not only the picture, but also where it hangs, the frame, its size and so on. Matching user expectations to existing audio description production and guidelines is an interesting issue with much research (Maszerowska et al., 2014). Classifying AD according to its genre has also been studied, mostly regarding TV (Van der Heijden, 2007), cinema (Fryer and Freeman 2012a, 2014; Fryer et al., 2013; Perego, 2014), comedy (Fels et al., 2006), Bollywood (Rai, 2009) and opera (Matamala and Orero, 2008). Other authors have narrowed down the analysis to film components such as lighting (Maszerowska, 2012), secondary details (Orero and Vilaró, 2012), film credits (Matamala and Orero, 2011), leitmotifs (Vilaró and Orero, 2013) and sound (Szarkowska and Orero, 2014; Orero et al., 2016). Udo and Fels (2009) refined their research to audio describing not only a play but, more specifically, audio describing Shakespeare.

On the other hand authors have studied the creation of AD, this time looking at the adequacy of the target text with the audience, considering general audience engagement (Afonso et al., 2010; Chmiel and Mazur, 2012, 2016; Fryer and Freeman, 2012b, 2014; Wilken and Kruger, 2016; Wissmath and Weibel, 2012; Walczak, 2017). Some authors have limited the audience to children (Schmeidler and Kirchner, 2001; Palomo López, 2008; Orero, 2012; Krejtz et al., 2012; Starr, 2018). Other studies have proposed changes to the target audio described text to aid comprehension (Cabeza-Cáceres, 2013) and engagement (Walczak and Fryer, 2017); and a recent study (Starr, 2018) developed AD as a bespoke accessibility service for a cognitively challenged target audience of autistic individuals needing help with emotion identification.

Regarding the format of the audio description, Walczak (2018) and Knigge and Erkau (2014) looked at the reception of AD on smart phones, but very little research has been performed regarding AD in other formats such as virtual reality or 360-degree scenarios. This can be considered the first publication dealing with such a complex environment, and points to the many lines of research opening in this field. Research to date has focused on many aspects of the technology, reception and production of AD where, until now, an image—or a scene—has been matched by one dedicated audio description oral text with its unidirectional associated soundtrack. The new format developed in the ImAc project will allow for multiple audio descriptions for an image – or scene – according to the end user relative position. The associated soundtrack will also change, offering additional information regarding environmental conditions such as directionality and distance. Finally, user interaction with the new audiovisual content and its audio description will also change, from the traditional passive audience to an interaction where the audience has a choice in what is consumed.

6.3 Research methodology

Following a user-centred design approach (Norman, 2013) enables us to engage with the requirements of the UN Committee on the Rights of Persons with Disabilities (CRPD)[1] where the maxim 'nothing about us without us' was established. It provides the classification of a 'person with disability' by referencing a medical model, defined within the International Classification of Functioning, Disability and Health (WHO, 2001). This provides a classification within health and the health-related domains. As the functioning and disability of an individual occur within a societal context, ICF also includes a list of environmental factors to consider, and these are implemented through a standard questionnaire issued by the UN World Health Organisation's WHODAS 2.0 (WHO, 2001), which is primarily related to clinical issues. The UN approach profiles users through a single health-related marker. Within our research disability is not a health-related issue but a communication condition, i.e. an impairment (Ellis, 2016) not always related to a disability. For example education will have a greater impact on the overall development of a person with sight impairments than a diagnosis of inherited *retinitis pigmentosa*, which will help define the type and level of adjustment that will be needed to achieve the educational goal.

User-centred design (UCD) is a philosophy that seeks to place the end user at the centre of the design process (Orero and Matamala, 2016). From the field of engineering, Norman (2013) provided a set of guidelines that designers could follow in order for their interfaces to achieve good usability outcomes. In addition, the ISO standard 9241-210 (ISO, 2010) deals with UCD to 'address impacts on a number of stakeholders, not just those typically considered as users', referring to the approach as human-centred design. This standard defines human-centred design as 'an approach to systems design and development that aims to make interactive systems more usable by focusing on the use of the system and applying human factors/ergonomics and usability knowledge and techniques'. It also describes the potential benefit of following a design approach that improves usability and human factors: 'Usable systems can provide a number of benefits, including improved productivity, enhanced user well-being, avoidance of stress, increased accessibility and reduced risk of harm.' Putting the user at the core of the design process is also the guiding principle of universal design (Story *et al.*, 1998), where the aim is to create accessible products, environments and services for all users regardless of their physical or cognitive abilities, thereby satisfying the requirements of the United Nations' CRPD.

UCD has four defined activity phases: (i) identify the user and specify the context of use; (ii) specify the user requirements; (iii) produce design solutions; and (iv) evaluate design solutions against requirements. This chapter makes reference to the first phase.

6.4 Focus group

This study focuses on the accessibility of 360-degree video content from an AD perspective, as tested by a focus group of blind and partially sighted people. The aim of the focus group was to gather feedback from regular users of AD on viewing and interacting with 360-degree content within an immersive environment.

A review within the ImAc project of immersive environments highlighted several key areas on which feedback was sought during the focus group. Firstly, we needed to consider the differences between the traditional curated linear approach where the viewer consumes the content that the director wishes to show on the screen, and a non-linear approach where the viewer has control over the content and can choose their own path by interacting with the environment. We also needed to understand how using audio could both enhance the immersive experience and address issues surrounding the creation of a fully accessible interface for 360-degree content.

In the absence of any commercially available audio described 360-degree video content, live description was delivered in a clip available on YouTube in a 360-degree format. We wished to explore how a small group of participants would respond to the material. During the test the participants were first shown each video, followed by a period of discussion. A professional audio describer and a technology expert were both present during the entire focus group session and contributed to steering the discussions.

There were 7 participants within the group split between female (3) and male (4) and ranging in age from 26 to 53 years (average age, 38 years). All of the participants are native English speakers and had achieved a university level of education. Five of the participants described themselves as blind, whereas two participants defined themselves as low-sighted. All of the participants stated that they had experienced the disability from birth.

6.4.1 Technology preferences

A survey of users' technology preferences was undertaken before the trial commenced. All participants responded that they use both a television and a mobile phone on a daily basis. However, when further questioned about computer usage, six of the participants claimed to use a laptop and a tablet each day, whereas only one participant stated that they used a desktop computer.

Before participating in our study, none of the participants had ever had access to VR technology or experienced VR content. In terms of consuming online video content, six of the participants showed a strong preference towards using smartphones and tablets, whereas one participant claimed to prefer using a desktop computer for this purpose.

All participants were asked about their preferences for using assistive technologies such as screen readers (JAWS, VoiceOver, TalkBack) and magnification tools (for instance, Zoomtext). Of the seven participants, five used only screen readers, one used only magnification tools, and one used a combination of both. All participants told us that when interacting with online media they would prefer assistive technology to be able to help them identify content, browse content from a library and switch accessibility services, such as AD and subtitles, on and off. They also indicated that it is essential for the assistive technology to interact with functions such as play, stop, pause, forward and rewind.

6.4.2 Sight level

For this study, it was essential to understand the current level of sight that each of the participants could experience. The study group contained a complete range of abilities. Two of the participants could not see anything at all; five participants could identify the windows in the room based on the light. Three participants could identify the shapes of furniture in a room. One participant was able to identify a friend over a metre away, whereas another participant could only recognise a friend if they were in close proximity to their face.

Further, the participants were asked to describe the barriers they experienced whilst watching television. All of the participants expressed difficulty in seeing the buttons on a remote control. None of the participants was able to see fine detail and text on the television screen and everyone stated that they found it difficult to understand what was happening onscreen. More specifically, six of the participants had difficulty seeing a picture on the screen at all; in fact, five participants could only identify the television screen by the light it emitted; and two participants could see nothing at all.

The sight level had a significant impact on the participants' current ability to watch and follow programmes and films on television. One participant told us that they are able to follow the programme using residual sight, whereas another said that their solution was to sit closer to the screen. Six of the group generally attempt to pick up as much as they can about the programme from the sound alone, but they stressed that this was not a preferred option. They also told us that they regularly rely upon friends or family to explain what is happening, or use AD to work out what is happening, on the screen.

6.5 Results

The participants were given four tasks to complete, designed to help with our understanding of the way AD fits within the context of immersive content. Each participant viewed the 360-degree videos on a laptop connected to a projector. The 360-degree rendering was provided by the ImAc player and the audio recorded in order to be transcribed into the results at a later date. The focus group lasted for about one hour.

6.5.1 AD within linear storytelling

The first task was designed to inform our understanding of AD's role within linear storytelling and the manner in which the interactive aspects of 360-degree videos impact an AD track. In conventional television we assume that the consumers are looking directly at a TV screen and therefore that the AD describes what they are seeing on the screen in front of them. However, within a 360-degree video the viewer can be looking in any direction. Therefore, this task was designed to determine the importance of AD in an environment where the viewer is able to choose the line of vision. In this task the participants were guided along a set path. This meant that the choice of view was predetermined for the participant in a similar way to watching traditional directed television.

The video, available on YouTube (BBC Earth, 2016), is a documentary titled *Attenborough and the Giant Dinosaur*, and was created for BBC One's BBC Earth Unplugged series. The participants were required to watch the entire video (run time, four minutes). The AD was delivered 'live' during our pilot study by a professional audio describer who worked without a script, although prior knowledge was employed, as were notes relating to the video content.

Participants praised the live audio description, and all participants believed that the track gave them enough information to understand the complete picture, even the components which lacked alternative audio cues. During the discussion each participant provided feedback on their experience of the AD, such as:

> *Participant 1*: The important thing is the description complemented the narration, it wasn't repetitive and it wasn't overly descriptive.

> *Participant 3*: I think it managed to describe everything that was on the screen even though there wasn't much time.

It was interesting to observe that even though participant 3 was sight-impaired and therefore could not confirm that everything on the screen had been described, they believed that the AD contained enough information to get an understanding of everything that would be on the screen. Although the description was appreciated in terms of making the story clear, some felt it lacked the elements to build the atmosphere needed for an immersive experience:

> *Participant 4*: What I didn't get from the description was the ambience – you hear the rustling of the foliage, large clomping feet, but what's the weather like, what birds can you see in the sky? This is where your imagination comes in.

> *Participant 5*: I still can't get a proper visual picture of the dinosaur in my head, so the colour, has it got a spiky back?

In relation to these comments the describer, who as an expert was present throughout the focus group, pointed out that the lack of sufficient gaps in narration meant there was a need to prioritise what could be described. It was identified that none of the participants wanted the AD to go over the voice-over of the documentary.

6.5.2 AD within the interactive aspects of 360-degree video

The second task was focused on understanding the impact of AD when the viewer is able to choose their own path through the immersive video. The personalisation facilitated by 360-degree video means that the viewer may choose not to look at the key action and therefore the AD was adapted in the moment ('live') to describe what the viewer was actually looking at. The video from the first task was used again, and the AD was delivered 'live' by the same professional audio describer, who had previously made notes on the video.

In order to simulate a 360-degree environment, a cursor provided within the video was used to allow the participant to choose direction by using the mouse. For example instead of watching the presenter gaze at the dinosaur during the first break in voiceover, the view panned left to the mountains in the distance and consequently the audio description changed as it referred to the on-screen elements now in view. This resulted in participants mostly feeling disconnected with the storyline, finding the description to be repetitive and missing important details.

> *Participant 2*: I thought that sounded disjointed and for me if it is a description of 360 then it would take a lot more than just words. This didn't give me anything really.

While the 360-degree movement seemed to enhance the overall immersive experience visually, it was almost impossible to simulate that experience in audio given the lack of sufficient gaps in voiceover. Some participants commented that it was difficult to comprehend a 360-degree view.

> *Participant 4*: I don't understand, was it vertical now, like a vertical axis, looking down? Was that the view? Was it from the perspective of the dinosaur?

> *Participant 5*: For some people who can't see and never have, it is already a challenge to understand 360.

> *Participant 6*: I don't believe this! Where is the TV screen? I can't get my head around it.

Participants agreed that a lot more information would be needed in addition to AD to make the environment more immersive for people with significant sight loss. In order to be able to navigate the 360-degree video they would need to know more information about the environment and therefore have the cues to tell them where to direct their gaze. Getting the right balance without this information would be difficult.

6.5.3 Spatial audio within 360-degree environment

The third task used spatial audio (binaural sound) to create the illusion of a 360-degree environment by providing sound from all around the participant. There was no video present so the focus was on whether the participants could be fully immersed within a scene using only the sound cues.

The demonstration example used was the *Virtual Barbershop* sound file provided by QSoundLabs (2007), which had been designed as a high-quality demonstration of binaural audio technology. The audio places the participant in the seat at a barbershop, where the barber is making conversation whilst walking around the participant cutting their hair. It is an example which worked well in our focus group, as the participants were all familiar with sitting in a barber's chair, where customers are encouraged not to move their heads. Many of the sound cues would also have been familiar to the focus group participants, such as the snipping of hair.

Two stereo speakers were employed to allow the focus group to participate as a group. Participants responded enthusiastically to the clip:

> *Participant 3*: For me this was immersive!

> *Participant 4*: You're actually in the room!

> *Participant 6*: It was very impressive that last one, I found it very interesting. I know who's around this table because I'm in the room. Felt as if it was happening around me!

> *Participant 7*: Honestly, that's what I need to be completely immersed.

It was noted that the narration in the clip integrated elements of audio description within the soundscape, for example "now I'm moving to the right" and "look at my pair of scissors". These cues, combined with the perception of depth delivered in spatial audio, enhanced the experience for the focus group.

6.5.4 Establishing user preference for tools required to access 360-degree content

Whilst discussing the significance of the headset, which would be needed to track head movements and subsequently trigger specific descriptions, most participants felt that a head-mounted display would be unnecessary as audio would be the key access feature for them.

The issue of integrating immersive AD with assistive technology tools such as speech readers and magnification was briefly discussed. It should be noted here that all participants were regular users of video on-demand services such as Netflix, Amazon Videos and BBC iPlayer, which are configured to work with assistive technology. Individuals in our study reiterated that this was essential in order to enable independent access. However, since the characteristics of immersive environments are such that they may not allow control via traditional tools such as keyboard and mouse, voice control was regarded as most appropriate. Once again, members of the focus group had previously used voice control on smartphones, i.e., VoiceOver on IOS, and Talkback on Android devices.

6.6 Discussion

Overall, the focus group agreed that an audio-led immersive environment was easier to comprehend than an environment described only using AD. It was felt that the visual display of a 360-degree environment was somewhat irrelevant without elements of it figuring in the AD track. Head-mounted displays were regarded as unnecessary by the group with the exception of one participant, who is not a regular AD user.

The participants in our study strongly felt that the description track needed to complement the main narrative, and that any deviation from the primary storyline would lead to unnecessary disorientation. The five key elements of AD – *who*, *what*, *why*, *where* and *when* – were prioritised over the description of 360-degree elements by those in our pilot study. These were considered more acceptable when offered in the immersive audio environment of the *Virtual Barber Shop*, where sound alone was used to create a fully immersive environment but the script followed a single narrative with integral clues to the setting.

Our sight-impaired audience suggested that since 360-degree content was designed to be consumed independently, the AD script could be written in the second person, for example 'you're only a few paces away from the stage where the band is playing', etc. The professional describer added that this may help pull listeners into the scene and enhance the immersive experience in general.

The group discussed various factors that could contribute positively to the immersive experience, including the number of voices that would be considered appropriate in an immersive environment, and whether directionality and placement of the audio description would impact the viewer experience for people with sight loss. For example one of the questions that was debated was whether the audio description should be the voice in the viewer's ear, or alternatively, come from somewhere behind the audience. However, no definite conclusions could be reached in the absence of further examples.

On the subject of accessing content, there was a consensus on using a combination of voice control and integration with assistive technology tools – in particular, magnification and speech readers. It was discussed that traditional interfaces such as a keyboard and mouse might not be appropriate for accessible immersive environments, and that voice control may therefore be the only way to access content. It is important to state here that some participants who had previous experience of using voice-controlled environments such as Amazon Fire TV, Amazon Alexa and Google Home indicated that they would be happy to use voice as a control interface.

Further research, including specially produced content and a wider focus group comprising people with different sight levels, could clarify the importance of sound in an immersive environment.

6.7 Conclusions

It was clear from this study that participants, regardless of their sight level, wanted the opportunity to have the same experiences as consumers with normal sight. However, they were pragmatic in understanding that although they wanted to consume the same immersive media, if they had no vision it was pointless to have a full head-mounted display when only a tracked set of headphones would be needed. However, those with partial sight would still benefit from a head-mounted display as it would provide the same cues they have in the real world.

The most successful experiences were encountered during the first task where participants were taken on a directed path through the immersive content, and during the third task, i.e. the audio-only binaural demonstration. In the first instance, this is likely to be because this is how they are familiar with content, and without being able to fully see and experience the environment, it was very hard to choose to follow the action. Secondly, the *Virtual Barbershop* experience provided the most excitement and immersion as it was developed and designed to be a very specific audio-only demo. Nevertheless, it would be technically difficult to adapt this technique to work with general video content.

We therefore conclude that it is important to make immersive content fully accessible and available to all audiences regardless of vision level; however, it is now clear that providing AD for immersive content is not going to be straightforward. It may be necessary to provide a directed mode, where viewers are taken on a designated route through the visual material and guided through the key action in the media. If it is not possible for sight-impaired audiences to navigate 360-degree content independently, perhaps this raises the question as to their ability to contribute to a user-centred design approach. However, sight loss and visual acuity are clearly defined on a scale with a tipping point prior to which 360-degree content can still be enjoyed. As always, audio description must fit around the existing dialogue, never running simultaneously with the characters speaking. Binaural sound is also key to immersion, and further studies must be conducted to identify whether the virtual location of the audio describer voice is important.

Funding statement or declaration of conflicting interests (mandatory)

This publication is part of the EU-funded project ImAc, grant agreement no. 761974.

Note

1 www.ohchr.org/EN/HRBodies/CRPD/Pages/CRPDIndex.aspx.

References

Afonso, A., Blum, A., Katz, B. F., Tarroux, P., Borst, G., and Denis, M. (2010) 'Structural properties of spatial representations in blind people: scanning images constructed from haptic exploration or from locomotion in a 3-D audio virtual environment', *Memory & Cognition*, 38(5), pp. 591–604.

BBC Earth (2016) *360° Attenborough and the Giant Dinosaur*, Available at: https://www.youtube.com/watch?v=IDkbkvOFxng (accessed 3 September 2019).

Cabeza-Cáceres, C. (2013) 'Audiodescripció i recepció. efecte de la velocitat de narració, l'entonació i l'explicitació en la comprensió fílmica' [Audio description and reception. The effect of speed of narration, intonation and explicitation in film comprehension]. PhD thesis, Universitat Autònoma de Barcelona.

Chmiel, A., and Mazur, I. (2012) 'AD reception research: some methodological considerations', in E. Perego (ed.), *Emerging Topics in Translation: Audio Description*, Trieste: Edizioni Università di Trieste, pp. 57–80.

Chmiel, A., and Mazur, I. (2016) 'Researching preferences of audio description users – limitations and solutions', *Across Languages and Cultures*, 17(2), pp. 271–288.

Ellis, G. (2016) 'Impairment and disability: challenging Conceptscof "normality"', in A. Matamala and P. Orero (eds.), *Researching Audio Description: New Approaches*, London: Palgrave Macmillan, pp. 35–45.

Fels, D., Udo, J. P., Diamond, J. E., and Diamond, J. I. (2006) 'A comparison of alternative narrative approaches to video description for animated comedy', *Journal of Visual Impairment & Blindness*, 100(5), pp. 295–305.

Fryer, L., and Freeman, J. (2012a) 'Cinematic language and the description of film: keeping AD users in the frame', *Perspectives: Studies in Translatology*, 21(3), pp. 412–426.

Fryer, L., and Freeman, J. (2012b) 'Presence in those with and without sight: implications for virtual reality and audio description', *Journal of Cybertherapy and Rehabilitation*, 5(1), pp. 15–23.

Fryer, L., and Freeman, J. (2014) 'Can you feel what I'm saying? The impact of verbal information on emotion elicitation and presence in people with a visual impairment', in A. Felnhofer and O. D. Kothgassner (eds.), *Challenging Presence: Proceedings of the 15th International Conference on Presence*, Vienna, 17–19 March. pp. 99–107.

Fryer, L., Pring, L., and Freeman, J. (2013) 'Audio drama and the imagination: the influence of sound effects on presence in people with and without sight', *Journal of Media Psychology*, 25, pp. 65–71.

ISO (2010) '9241-210 Ergonomics of human-system interaction, Part 210: Human-centred design for interactive systems.' Available at: www.iso.org/standard/52075.html (accessed 3 September 2019).

Knigge, M., and Erkau, J. (2014) 'Cinema and theatre: accessible entertainment, with benefits for all', in H. A. Caltenco, P.O. Hedvall, A. Larsson, K. Rassmus-Gröhn and B. Rydeman (eds.), *Proceedings of the International Conference on Universal Design, UD 2014*, Lund, Sweden, 16–18 June.

Krejtz, I., Szarkowska, A., Krejtz, K., Walczak, A., and Duchowski, A. (2012) 'Audio description as an aural guide of children's visual attention: evidence from an eye-tracking study', *Proceedings of the ACM Symposium on Eye Tracking Research and Applications Conference*, New York, ACM, 28–30 March, pp. 99–106.

Maszerowska, A. (2012) 'Casting the light on cinema – how luminance and contrast patterns create meaning', in R. Agost, E. Di Giovanni and P. Orero (eds.), *Multidisciplinarity in Audiovisual Translation*, Special Issue of *MonTI*, 4, pp. 65–85.

Maszerowska, A., Matamala, A., and Orero, P. (eds.) (2014) '*Audio Description: New Perspectives Illustrated*. Amsterdam: John Benjamins.

Matamala, A., and Orero, P. (2008) 'Opera translation', *The Translator*, 14 (2), pp. 429–453.

Matamala, A., and Orero, P. (2011) 'Opening credit sequences: audio describing films within films', *International Journal of Translation*, 23(2), pp. 35–58.

Norman, D. (2013) *The Design of Everyday Things*. New York: Basic Books.

Orero, P. (2012) 'Film reading for writing audio descriptions: a word is worth a thousand images?', in E. Perego (ed.), *Emerging Topics in Translation: Audio Description*, Trieste: Edizioni Università di Trieste, pp.13–28.

Orero, P., and Vilaró, A. (2012) 'Eye tracking analysis of minor details in films for audio description', *MonTI*, 4, pp. 295–319.

Orero, P., and Matamala, A. (2016) 'User-centric audio description: a topsy-turvy research approach', in A. Manco and A. Mancini (eds.), *Scrittura brevi: segni, testi e contesti [Short writing: signs, texts and contexts]*. Naples: Università degli Studi di Napoli, pp. 376–387.

Orero, P., Maszerowska, A., and Cassacuberta, D. (2016) 'Audio describing silence: lost for words', in A. Jankowska and A. Szarkowska (eds.), *New Points of View in Audiovisual Translation*, Oxford: Peter Lang, pp. 219–236.

Palomo López, A. (2008) 'Audio description as language development and language learning for blind and low vision children', in R. Hyde Parker and K. Guadarrama García (eds.), *Thinking Translation: Perspectives from Within and Without*, Boca Ratón, FL: Brown Walker Press, pp. 113–133.

Perego, E. (2014) 'Film language and tools', in A. Maszerowska, A. Matamala and P. Orero (eds.), *Audio Description: New Perspectives Illustrated*, Amsterdam: John Benjamins, pp. 81–102.

QSoundLabs (2007) *Virtual Barber Shop*. Available at: www.qsound.com/demos/binaural-audio.htm (accessed 3 September 2019).

Rai, S. (2009) 'Bollywood for all'. Available at: www.rnib.org.uk/sites/default/files/2009_09_Bollywood_AD_report.pdf (accessed 3 September 2019).

Szarkowska, A., and Orero, P. (2014) 'The Importance of Sound in Audio Description', in A. Maszerowska, A. Matamala and P. Orero (eds.), *Audio Description: New Perspectives Illustrated*, Amsterdam: John Benjamins, pp. 121–139.

Schmeidler, E., and Kirchner, C. (2001) 'Adding audio description: does it make a difference?', *Journal of Visual Impairment & Blindness*, 95(4), pp. 198–212.

Starr, K. (2018) 'Audio description and cognitive diversity: a bespoke approach to facilitating access to the emotional content in multimodal narrative texts for autistic audiences.' PhD thesis, University of Surrey. Available at: http://epubs.surrey.ac.uk/848660 (accessed 3 September 2019).

Story, M. F., Mueller, J. L., and Mace, R. L. (1998) *The Universal Design File: Designing for People of All Ages and Abilities*. Raleigh, NC: Centre for Universal Design. Available at: www.ncsu.edu/ncsu/design/cud/pubs_p/pudfiletoc.htm (accessed 13 December 2019).

Udo, J. P., and Fels, D. I. (2009) 'Suit the action to the word, the word to the action: an unconventional approach to sescribing Shakespeare's Hamlet', *Journal of Visual Impairment & Blindness*, 103(3), pp. 178–183.

Van der Heijden, M. (2007) 'Making film and television accessible to the blind and visually impaired.' MA thesis, Utrecht School of the Arts. Available at: https://static.aminer.org/pdf/PDF/000/288/838/spoken_subtitles_making_subtitled_tv_programmes_accessible.pdf (accessed 3 September 2019).

Vilaró, A., and Orero, P. (2013) 'The audio description of leitmotifs', *International Journal of Humanities and Social Science*, 3(5), pp. 56–64.

Walczak, A. (2017) 'Creative description: audio describing artistic films for individuals with visual impairments', *Journal of Visual Impairment & Blindness*, 111(4), pp. 387–391.

Walczak, A. (2018) 'Audio description on smartphones: making cinema accessible for visually impaired audiences', *Universal Access in the Information Society*, 17(4), pp. 833–840.

Walczak, A., and Fryer, L. (2017) 'Creative description: the impact of audio description style on presence in visually impaired audiences', *British Journal of Visual Impairment*, 35(1), pp. 6–17.

Wilken, N., and Kruger, J. L. (2016) 'Putting the audience in the picture: mise-en-shot and psychological immersion in audio described film', *Across Languages and Cultures*, 17(2), pp. 251–270.

Wissmath, B., and Weibel, D. (2012) 'Translating movies and the sensation of being there', in E. Perego (ed.), *Eye Tracking in Audiovisual Translation*, Rome: Aracne, pp. 281–298.

WHO (World Health Organisation) (2001) International Classification of Functioning, Disability, and Health. 2nd edn. Geneva: World Health Organisation.

WHO (World Health Organisation) (2001) *World Health Organisation Disability Assessment Schedule 2.0*. Available at: www.who.int/classifications/icf/whodasii/en (accessed 3 September 2019).

7 Mainstreaming audio description through technology

Anna Jankowska

7.1 Introduction

To make the cinema experience accessible to audiences with vision loss, three dimensions of accessibility need to be catered for (Jankowska, 2019b). The first, and the most obvious one, is *access to content*. This is achieved through two additional soundtracks: audio description (AD) that renders visual images into words and audio subtitles (AST) that provide an audible alternative to subtitles of foreign-language dialogue. The other two dimensions are *access to medium* and *access to environment*. The former consists in providing an appropriate and barrier-free technology for delivery and reception, and the latter in ensuring a barrier-less setting.

Access to medium is closely related to research into new technologies, that make them more user-friendly and more economically viable. Research into technologies that facilitate distribution and delivery of audiovisual content to blind audiences started as early as the 1990s when the Audetel consortium designed and tested decoders needed to receive AD for television broadcasts (Rai and Petre, 2011). More recently, initiatives that are based on the 'bring your own device' approach, e.g., mobile applications that make live events (Oncins *et al.*, 2013) or cinemas (Walczak, 2018) more accessible, have emerged. Mobile applications that allow for reproduction of alternative audio tracks (for example, AD, AST, dubbing), subtitles and even sign language interpreting are now available in many countries in Europe and beyond.[1]

This article reports on the usability test of the AudioMovie app – a mobile application created in Poland within the "AudioMovie – Cinema for All" project (2015–2018, www.audiomovie.pl) carried out by a consortium of six partners[2] and financed by the Polish National Centre for Research and Innovations under the 'Social Innovations' funding scheme. AudioMovie is the first, and up to now the only, cinema access app in Poland. The app was developed based on the participatory design approach. During app construction, we conducted a number of studies and consultations with potential users. However, all of these studies tested different app features separately, and were not conducted in its target setting. The main aim of this study was to evaluate how the app is used as a whole in an ecologically valid setting: a cinema. In particular, we wanted to see if the app meets the needs of its target users: persons with sight loss, but also people with dyslexia and intellectual impairments, as well as senior citizens. We wanted to find ways to improve the app before it is launched commercially.

7.2 Cinema accessibility in Poland

Jankowska and Walczak (2019) identified five barriers that obstruct mainstreaming AD in Poland: legislation, infrastructure, delivery and distribution, communication-cooperation-coordination and last, but not least, funding. AudioMovie was a large-scale project carried out to create a holistic solution that could help overcome some of these barriers, that is to say: distribution, infrastructure and legislation. All of them are briefly discussed below, as understanding them, and the complex relationship between them, helps to apprehend the concept behind AudioMovie.

Currently, in Poland, there are no legal provisions that regulate supplying AD and AST in cinemas (see below). For this reason, provision of AD and AST in Poland relies mostly on sporadic inclusive screenings organised by cultural institutions and NGOs that are financed through national or local grant programmes and that sometimes collaborate with film festivals. Inclusive screenings are organised after film premieres in the cinemas and are often one-time events that take place in selected cities. Audio descriptions and audio subtitles created for these screenings are rarely reused or repurposed. So far, as few as five films[3] have been made available with AD through official distribution. What is more, this happened before the change of regulations in 2016 (see below) and was achieved through close collaboration between distributors and NGOs who paid for AD production and distribution. Foreign-language films are available only during inclusive screenings and film festivals. To render foreign films accessible, organisers use dubbing or voice-over tracks embedded in the DVDs or they produce audio subtitles based on the subtitles. The most common practice in Poland is to record AST and AD with two different voices. Due to the longstanding tradition of voice-over, when combined, AST is usually voiced by male voice talents and AD by female voice talents. However, it would be very uncommon for any of the organisers to recognise that they produce AST. While in many countries subtitles that are read out loud are categorised as audio subtitles and are perceived as a modality distinct to voice-over (Braun and Orero, 2010; Remael *et al.*, 2014), for Poles this distinction is ambiguous and purely academic, especially since very often subtitles and voice-over do not differ or the differences are almost non-existent. To give an example, although the AudioMove app technically offers AST, it was necessary to refer to them as VO. Otherwise, neither the end-users nor film producers would understand what we actually want to offer.

High hopes for a change arose in 2016, when the Polish Film Institute (PISF) changed its policy regarding subsidies. According to those regulations, anyone who received funding from PISF was obliged to 'produce audio description and subtitles for the deaf and hard of hearing' (PISF, 2020). However, since the regulations were ambiguous, many film producers 'produced' what they were required to produce, added AD and ADH to the answer copy but did not make AD and SDH available in distribution (Jankowska and Walczak, 2019).

Infrastructure is another burning issue as only 10.2 per cent of cinemas in Poland have the infrastructure that is needed to provide AD (Statistical Office in Kraków, 2014). The reason for this is quite simple – the costs of buying or even renting the necessary infrastructure (e.g., infrared headsets) is higher than the expected box office and is not expected to amortise over time, especially since the number of films distributed with AD is very limited.

When it comes to legislation – apart from the lack of legislation that regulates AD provision, which is beyond the scope of this article and the project itself – the legal status of AD in Poland seems to remain unclear. Since accessibility services are a relatively new phenomenon, there seem to be many doubts about the relationship between AD and intellectual property rights. It is unclear what conditions need to be met to create and distribute AD in legally compliant ways.

Having the above in mind, the three main goals of the project were: (1) designing an alternative distribution system based on a cloud-based service for storing and sharing of alternative audio tracks, such as AD and AST; (2) developing an alternative and less costly infrastructure solution, based on an application for mobile devices allowing users to play alternative soundtracks; and (3) analysing the legal status of AD in order to set the ground-rules for legal AD production and sharing.

7.3 The AudioMovie app

AudioMovie is a mobile application which allows users to listen to alternative soundtracks (e.g., AD, AST, dubbing) on their smartphones or tablets in cinemas. While playing the soundtracks, the application synchronises with the film. It functions on both IOS and Android operating systems, and is currently only available in the Polish language. The app was developed following the co-design approach (Sanders and Stappers, 2008) with end-users included in the design process and also in the final usability tests on which we report in this chapter.

There are two launching modes. Both of them require the users to scan a QR code. The QR code is used as a security mechanism and unlocks the downloaded soundtracks on the user's mobile device. In other words, soundtracks can be downloaded prior to the screening but they will not play unless the QR code has been scanned. Soundtrack protection was introduced into AudioMovie after consultations with producers and distributors due to copyright issues. The QR code can be provided in the cinemas (for example, printed on tickets or displayed at the ticket office, entrance door or on the screen prior to a screening) or sent to the users via email.

In the first mode, users open the 'Cinema' (*kino* in Polish) tab and select the screening they plan to access (see Figure 7.1). The next step is to download (*pobierz* in Polish) the additional soundtracks (see Figure 7.2). However, as pointed out above, before being able to play any tracks, the users are required to scan (*skanuj* in Polish) a QR code provided in the cinema (see Figure 7.3).

Alternatively, users can launch the app by scanning the QR code (see Fig. 7.4). In this mode they are automatically redirected to the download screen and they can download the additional soundtracks. In this mode the users do not need to browse through the app to find the screening they are planning to attend.

After scanning the QR code (see Figure 7.4) the users are automatically taken to the correct screening and they can download the additional soundtracks.

Once the QR code is scanned, the app is ready to be used and the soundtrack starts playing automatically as soon as the screening begins. Users can adjust the settings (for example, enable/disable individual soundtracks, set balance between the soundtracks) individually for each screening.

7.4 Overview of the current study

The main goal of this study was to assess how the AudioMovie application is used in a real-life setting, i.e. in a cinema. We were particularly interested in finding out if the app caters for the needs of its primary users – persons with vision loss. We also wanted to see if the app is attractive to potential secondary users, i.e. senior citizens and persons with dyslexia and intellectual impairments. Following the co-design approach (Sanders and Stappers, 2008), we hoped to identify ways of improving the app so that future iterations matched the needs of target users even more closely. Given the large amount of data collected, this chapter reports only the results of the study undertaken with the app's primary users, persons with vision loss.

7.4.1 Research method

The study was designed and conducted to test the AudioMovie application in natural settings, that is to say during a bona fide cinema screening. The study took place in three different locations and on four separate dates: (1) Nowe Horyzonty – a multiplex in Wrocław, Poland (19 November 2017); (2) Kino Pod Baranami – an art-house cinema in Kraków, Poland (19 and 20 December 2017); and (3) Helios – a multiplex in Sosnowiec, Poland (24 January 2018).

Research procedure was similar in each of the venues and it consisted of five steps: (1) app presentation, (2) app training session, (3) film viewing,

Figure 7.1 The AudioMovie app – film selection launch mode.

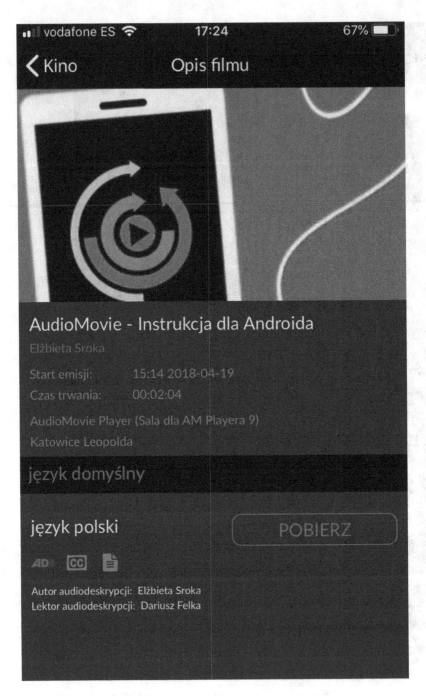

Figure 7.2 The AudioMovie app – soundtrack download tab.

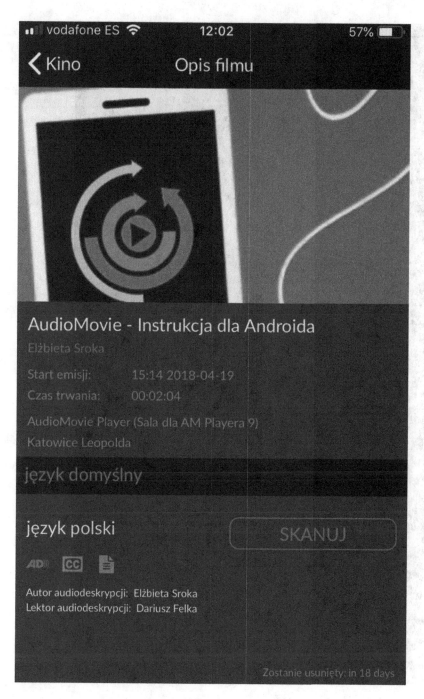

Figure 7.3 The AudioMovie app – QR code scanning tab.

Figure 7.4 The AudioMovie app – QR code scanning launch mode.

(4) questionnaire and (5) focus group interview. Each stage is described in detail below.

1. App presentation: each experiment started with a short presentation of the AudioMovie project and app. The experimental procedure was subsequently explained, after which informed consent forms were signed and collected. Assistance was provided by AudioMovie partners in each of the venues.

2. App training session: following the presentation all participants were asked to open the app and scan the QR codes they received upon arriving at the venue. All participants were asked to install the app and download the AD and AST files prior to the experiment. Those who had not pre-prepared in this manner were permitted to make the downloads at the time of the experiment. Assistance was provided to anyone who needed it.

3. Film screening: two films were used to test the AudioMovie app. In Kraków and Wrocław we used a short film called *What Happens While* (dir. N. Nia, 15 minutes). The film was presented in English without subtitles with AD and AST available through the AudioMovie app. AST tracks were prepared based on subtitles created for the film. The subtitles were not shown in order to make sure that sighted participants used the AST track. In Sosnowiec we used an animated feature film titled *Loving Vincent* (dir. D. Kobiela, H. Welchman, 91 minutes) which was presented with Polish dubbing. AD was available through the AudioMovie app. Although two different film stimuli were used for the experiment, we do not consider the film productions to be dependent variables as we were interested in testing the app itself, irrespective of the length of the film it is used for and its original language. We aimed at creating an ecologically valid setting, which for cinemas in Poland is dubbed and subtitled films.

4. Questionnaire: after watching the film, participants were asked to stay in the screening room and to complete a questionnaire. The questionnaire consisted of 17 closed questions (single choice, multiple choice, 1–5 Likert scale) that enabled us to gather data about participants' demography (gender, age, vision loss, hearing loss, dyslexia, intellectual impairment[4]), internet and technology consumption habits (devices used to browse the internet, use of smartphone, frequency of smartphone use, smartphone operating system), cinema-going habits (frequency, company, alternative track preference) and to evaluate the app (easiness, naturalness, pleasure, difficulty, willingness to use). The questionnaire was based on questionnaires used previously for testing of an accessibility app (Jankowska *et al.*, 2017).

    The questionnaire was created and hosted on Survey Monkey (www.surveymonkey), an online tool for the production and dissemination of polls. Participants were able to access the questionnaire via mobile devices using a link embedded in the application menu. The accessibility of the questionnaire had been tested prior to the experiment with consultants experiencing vision loss. The use of the mobile questionnaire proved to be important for two reasons. First of all, it enabled the participants with vision loss to complete the questionnaire unaided, which we felt was particularly important as participants tend to abstain from expressing criticism if their answers are not deemed private. Secondly, since most participants were able to complete the questionnaire on their own the entire process was much smoother, whilst anyone who did not want to fill out the mobile questionnaire was given the alternative of completing a traditional, paper version with the support of assistants. Participation in this part of the study was not remunerated.

5. Focus group: focus groups (one in Wrocław and two in Kraków) were conducted directly after the previous part of the study. Participants who had registered to take part in the focus groups were invited to separate rooms within the cinemas. The focus groups were semi-structured, with the matters discussed covering topics related to the usability of the applications. We concentrated our efforts on those issues which, according to the participants, would benefit from some improvement. All focus groups were recorded with a dictaphone and later transcribed. Additionally, notes were taken by assistant moderators. Participants who engaged in focus groups received a gift card for Empik, a major Polish chain store selling multimedia and books.

The quantitative data obtained during the study were considered alongside the qualitative analysis of interview answers and observed behaviours. The statistical analyses were conducted with the use of SPSS Statistics 24.0.0 and Microsoft Office 2016.

7.4.2 Participants

Overall 55 (N=55) participants (25 female and 28 male), aged between 19 and 60+, took part in the questionnaire aspects of the study. All participants experience vision loss, with 26 participants declared to be blind and a further 29 partially sighted. There were more male participants among the blind subjects (N=16) compared to the female (N=9) participants in that group. In the group of partially sighted participants there were more female (N=16) than male (N=12) participants. 49 participants stated that they had no hearing impairment, 5 claimed that they were hard-of-hearing and one participant claimed to be deaf. Four participants declared to have been diagnosed with dyslexia. None of the participants declared to have an intellectual impairment.

In total, 21 individuals participated in the focus groups: 8 in Wrocław (19.11.2018) and 13 in Kraków (7 during the first session, 19 December 2018; and 6 in the second session, 20 December 2018).

The study followed ethical rules of empirical research with human participants. Before taking part in the study all participants received (via email) detailed information about the project and the experimental procedure.

They also signed an informed consent form and were informed that they could withdraw from the study at any point without providing any reasons for their decision. All the data collected during the study were anonymised. Participants were recruited by two NGOs that provide access services – the Seventh Sense Foundation and Katarynka Foundation – through advertising on their social media platforms and in newsletters.

7.5 Results and discussion

Below we present the results of the usability study carried out to test the AudioMovie app. First we present and discuss the quantitative results from the questionnaires and then the qualitative data from the focus groups.

7.5.1 Digital profile of the participants

One of the core issues for an app's future success is the digital literacy of its users. Consequently, the survey included questions regarding the use of new technologies and the internet. When asked 'What devices do you use to go online?', the participants said they mostly use desktop computers and laptops (85.19 per cent). Nearly as many participants (74.07 per cent) said they use smartphones, and only one person does not use the internet. Tablets seem to be the least popular device among participants (22.22 per cent). We also asked the participants about how often they use the smartphones. A clear majority (75 per cent) said they use smartphones on an everyday basis and only one person said they use a smartphone 2–3 times a week. However, it should be noted that 23.08 per cent of participants declared not to use a smartphone at all. This is a clear sign that the app is not a solution for all users and that steps need to be taken in order to prevent further exclusion of those who do not use smartphones. One possibility is to provide smartphones in the cinemas as well as the help of trained assistants, since someone who does not have a smartphone, or use one on a daily basis, might experience difficulties with navigation. At the same time, AudioMovie should be introduced gradually and as an alternative system, working alongside the currently used headsets.

An interesting observation was made regarding the use of mobile operating systems. According to study participants, 51.28 per cent said they use IOS and 48.72 per cent prefer Android. These results are in considerable contrast with each operating system's market share both in Poland and globally. In December of 2018 Android commanded 95.25 per cent of the market share in Poland and 75.16 per cent globally. IOS reached 2.96 per cent in Poland and 21.98 per cent globally (StatCounter 2018a; StatCounter, 2018b. This appears to be a very clear message to anyone who is planning to design mobile applications for users with vision loss in Poland, or indeed, in many other territories. However, based on general data from Poland, while it is tempting to create Android-based apps, it has to be considered that IOS could be equally popular among the population with vision loss.

7.5.2 Cinema profile of the participants

To establish participants' cinema-going habits we asked them about the frequency with which they go to the cinema. Nearly one quarter (24.1 per cent) declared that they visit cinemas once a year, however quite a few participants said they visit a cinema only once every few years (16.7 per cent). The most participants (38.9 per cent) said they visit cinemas several times a year, however some go as often as once a month (14.8 per cent) or even several times per month (5.5 per cent). None of the participants said that they had never been to a cinema. These results might be surprising when compared with data on cinema-going habits in Poland. According to the Public Opinion Research Center (2018) 27 per cent of Poles went to the cinema several times per year, 11 per cent many times per year and 11 per cent only once a year.

When asked 'Who do you go to the cinema with?', most participants chose friends (81.13 per cent), followed by family (37.74 per cent). Some participants (7.55 per cent) declare to go to the cinema alone. This means that participants primarily perceive going to the cinema as a social activity, which points to two important consequences. On the one hand it could imply that AudioMovie will fulfil its ultimate purpose, that is, to enable audiences with various access needs to enjoy the cinema experience together. On the other, it could also mean that the introduction of AudioMovie in the cinemas would be financially beneficial for the cinema and film industry, prompting larger audiences, and better box-office figures. This way, providing access services could move from being perceived as a costly obligation to an audience-building technique.

7.5.3 Usability

Study participants were asked to evaluate the app based on five usability questions that examined easiness, naturalness, pleasure, difficulty and willingness to use the app in the future (see Table 7.1 below). They were asked to agree with statements regarding the above-mentioned dimensions on a scale from 1 (strongly disagree) to 5 (strongly agree). Participants most strongly agreed with two of the statements, i.e. 'I would like to use the app in the cinema' (Mdn = 5; Mo = 5; SD = 1.03) and 'I found the app pleasant to use' (Mdn = 5; Mo = 5; SD = 0.85). Slightly lower ratings were obtained for the following questions: 'I found the app natural to use' (Mdn = 4; Mo = 5; SD = 1.12) and 'I found the app easy to use' (Mdn = 4; Mo = 5; SD = 1.26). Respondents agreed with the statement 'I found the app difficult to use' to a much lesser extent (Mdn = 2; Mo = 1; SD = 1.48).

The distribution of responses in all statements, excluding the statement 'I found the app difficult to use', was skewed left (see Figure 7.5). Additionally, as compared to the other statements, the distribution of responses in 'I

Table 7.1 Evaluation of app's usability

	I found the app easy to use (N = 54)	I found the app natural to use (N = 54)	I found the app pleasant to use (N = 54)	I found the app difficult to use (N = 54)	I would like to use the app in the cinema (N = 53)
Median	4.00	4.00	5.00	2.00	5.00
Mode	5.00	5.00	5.00	1.00	5.00
Standard deviation	1.26	1.12	.85	1.48	1.03
Minimum	1.00	1.00	1.00	1.00	1.00
Maximum	5.00	5.00	5.00	5.00	5.00
Skewness	−1.054	−.777	−1.715	.574	−2.052
Kurtosis	.302	−.121	3.915	−1.200	3.101
Shapiro-Wilk	W = 0.817 p < 0.001	W = 0.863 p < 0.001	W = 0.733 p < 0.001	W = 0.807 p < 0.001	W = 0.547 p < 0.001

found the app pleasant to use' and 'I would like to use the app in the cinema' was characterised by a greater concentration around the central value than in normal distribution. The values of the Shapiro-Wilk test indicate that agreements levels for all the statements are non-normally distributed (see Table 7.1 above).

We did not observe a significant correlation ($p < 0.05$) between the operating systems on participants' smartphones and participants' agreement with any of the statements. This allows us to conclude that the app's design for both Android and IOS was acceptable.

Spearman rank correlation (see Table 7.2) showed significant positive correlations between the frequency of smartphone use and participants' agreement with the following statements: 'I found the app easy to use' ($r = 0.445$; $p = 0.001$), 'I found the app natural to use' ($r = 0.403$; $p = 0.003$), and 'I would like to use the app in the cinema' ($r = 0.332$; $p = 0.017$). Those participants who use smartphones most frequently seemed to find the app easier and more natural to use and are more willing to use it in the future. Spearman rank correlation also showed a significant negative correlation between the frequency of smartphone use and the perception of the app's difficulty ($r = -0.285$; $p = 0.045$). This suggests that the more often the participants use smartphones, the smaller the difficulty in managing the app. However, this again shows that when implementing the AudioMovie app measures should be taken so that those who are not used to using smartphones are not doubly excluded (from both access to content and access to medium).

Spearman rank correlation did not show any significant correlations ($p <$ .05) between the frequency with which the participants go to the cinema and their agreement with any of the statements.

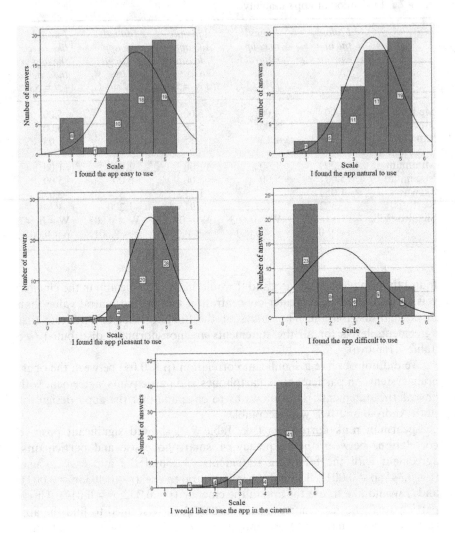

Figure 7.5 Distribution of responses.

7.5.4 App's evaluation

In this section we present the app's evaluation based on the focus groups interviews. Given the scope of this chapter we do not present all the topics covered during the interview. For example, app-specific issues such as menu distribution, buttons, labels, QR code scanning, volume settings, etc. are only briefly discussed. They will be addressed in more detail in a separate, more technical paper. In this chapter, we discuss those issues that in our opinion might be of interest and use to non-technical audiences and those who are

Table 7.2 Evaluation according to smartphone use frequency

		Frequency of smartphone use
I found the app easy to use	Rho Spearman	.445
	Significance	.001
I found the app natural to use	Rho Spearman	.403
	Significance	.003
I found the app pleasant to use	Rho Spearman	.150
	Significance	.290
I found the app difficult to use	Rho Spearman	−.285
	Significance	.045
I would like to use the app in the cinema	Rho Spearman	.332
	Significance	.017

Table 7.3 Evaluation according to cinema-going frequency

		Frequency of going to the cinema
I found the app easy to use	Rho Spearman	.166
	Significance	.231
I found the app natural to use	Rho Spearman	−.044
	Significance	.751
I found the app pleasant to use	Rho Spearman	−.258
	Significance	.059
I found the app difficult to use	Rho Spearman	.111
	Significance	.432
I would like to use the app in the cinema	Rho Spearman	−.120
	Significance	.392

thinking about commissioning or implementing mobile technologies for accessibility, especially with audio description in mind.

7.5.4.1 General evaluation

Overall evaluation of the 'bring your own device' approach was very positive. Participants underlined that the simplicity of the idea based on the 'bring your own device' approach makes it very attractive. One of the arguments that was commented on most often was the independence this solution offers to users with vision loss. As two of the participants said:[5]

> *Participant 1*: It's very cool and comfortable. And let me put it this way – you don't need to go around and ask for help or equipment. You can just come to the cinema, turn it on and you are all set. It's an excellent thing.

Participant 2: It's completely different when you come in with your own equipment. One that you know well. It gives you more independence. I think it's really great.

The participants were very enthusiastic about the possibility of using the app both in cinemas and at home while watching television. We did not include the issue of home use in the interview plan since this option was and still is disabled; however, the users in all groups brought it up themselves after noting that it is included in the app's menu. Participants were so enthusiastic about it that one of them even said that they would be willing to buy themselves a television. Others noticed that turning on the AD for television broadcasts seems to be a complicated process, not only for them, but also for their sighted family members. Being able to use the app instead would not only make it simpler but, again, would give them a sense of independence. As one of the participants pointed out:

Participant 3: Another issue is that it's nearly impossible to turn on the AD on the telly. My mother can't do it and me even less. So, the app could be a solution. We could turn it on on our own, without asking anyone for help.

What seemed to be even more appealing to the participants was the fact that the app could allow them to enjoy television with their friends and family without disturbing those who do not need description. This observation was particularly important to us, since one of the reasons for creating the AudioMovie app was to create a solution that would enable users with various needs to enjoy cinema and television together. As one of the participants said:

Participant 4: We can sit down at home with the entire family. They watch the film and we have AD in the phone. This way we are not disturbing anyone.

One of the participants was even more enthusiastic about this:

Participant 5: Thanks to the app we could all watch together. It's fantastic and genial!

Also, the mobile application itself was evaluated positively. Participants said that it was easy to manage and that it worked well. As one of the participants noted:

Participant 6: If I were to talk about the cons of the app, there is nothing to talk about. It's one giant pro. The fact that it exists is a pro. And I think that the project should be developed, because it's a fantastic thing.

However, it should be noted that some participants argued against introducing the app as the only option available. As one of the participants highlighted:

> *Participant 7*: I think that the application is great. And it is a fantastic alternative for people who have smartphones. But I think that the solution used until now is good for all those people who for various reasons cannot use smartphones. Some of our friends have old phones with Symbian and they do not want to get rid of them. And in my opinion, it could happen that people who don't have a smartphone are being excluded.

This is a very important observation especially in light of the results obtained from the questionnaire, which show that a significant group of the audiences with vision loss do not use smartphones. As stated above, this should be taken into account when implementing the app in cinemas to avoid further exclusion caused by the digital divide.

7.5.4.2 Audio subtitles

In this chapter we use 'audio subtitles' and 'voice-over' interchangeably to refer to subtitles read out loud. Audio subtitles are used in the body of the article and voice-over in direct quotations from the interviews, since this is the term the participants were using. Voice-over is widely used in Polish television and the distinction between the two types of AVT is ambiguous to many Poles. Availability of audio subtitles in the AudioMovie app was an issue that drew particular attention from the participants, probably because most films available with AD in Poland are domestic productions. An interesting discussion arose when some of the participants claimed that since Poland is a subtitling country, at least when it comes to the cinema, it is even more important to provide AST than AD. As one of the participants noted:

> *Participant 5*: I actually think that it is more important for blind people to have voice-over. Audio description is also important, but ... if I may be honest, I really want to go to the cinema. And if I had to choose, for now, I would choose to have voice-over over audio description.

This spurred a heated discussion, because other participants emphasised that AD is very important to them and that they would not be able to follow many films without it, even if AST were provided. In the end participants agreed that it is impossible to decide whether either of the two tracks is more important, but this discussion led them to interesting conclusions regarding the availability of AST through the app. As argued by a number of participants, the app could be used to repurpose the existing subtitle files using text-to-speech technology. Even though the participants were not entirely convinced by the use of text-to-speech technology, they stated that they would be willing to accept this solution for the creation of audio subtitles since it seems feasible, especially as it would not imply additional costs for the distributors. As two of the participants stated:

> *Participant 8*: The subtitles could be available in the app and read by the screen-reader. Then we wouldn't need to depend on the distributor to provide voice-over. Because right now we can't go to the cinema, because of subtitles. We must wait for the film to appear on DVD, because then it has voice-over.

> *Participant 9*: We should adapt our technology to the reality. They already have the subtitle files. So, if it's text-to-speech or nothing I would be willing to accept [text-to-speech]. Because at least then I feel equal to my friends and we could go to the cinema together.

7.5.4.3 Some technical considerations

When it comes to the more technical aspects, participants especially appreciated the fact that additional soundtracks could be downloaded prior to the screening (e.g., at home) giving them a feeling of being well prepared. At the same time, those who downloaded both the app and the additional soundtracks during the screening were positively surprised that this process did not take long. On a more negative note, participants complained about QR code scanning, sound quality and volume. These issues will be briefly addressed in this final section and will be discussed in more detail in future work.

One of the most controversial and problematic technical issues was the QR code scanning. Most participants commented that scanning was challenging for them. The solution we provided – top left corner of the tickets was trimmed to indicate QR code position (see Figure 7.6 below) – did not prove to be sufficient. While one of the participants suggested that in future the code could be marketed with embossed or raised print, some of the participants

Figure 7.6 AudioMovie QR code ticket.

were very sceptical about having to scan the code at all and suggested introducing a pin code instead.

With regard to sound quality some participants suggested that the AudioMovie app could offer a better quality as compared to the solutions that are currently most commonly used (i.e. infrared hearing systems or radio systems). Participants emphasised that the headsets used in current systems often do not work properly due to connection failure and that the headphones are of poor quality. Nevertheless, app sound proved to be the issue participants complained about the most. They emphasised that the quality and volume of the soundtrack were too low. Neither of these problems was caused directly by the app. Low volume was due to the poor quality of the soundtrack provided and low sound quality to high file compression and low bitrate. Nevertheless, we feel it is important to understand, discuss and solve problems related to volume and quality, regardless of their source, if AudioMovie is to be used comfortably by its target users. This is why sound quality should be taken into account when accepting content for the AudioMovie system. Production guidelines and quality control measures should be introduced.

Finally, some participants noticed sound jamming. This might be caused by synchronisation. While the app checks and adjusts the synchronisation every 20 seconds, it may sometimes cut or repeat words to resynchronise the soundtrack. However, this can be solved by making sure that synchronisation only takes place when the AD or AST are not playing.

7.6 Users' awareness

Many participants raised issues that were not foreseen in our list of discussion topics. The issues that the participants raised were financial viability of the AudioMovie system, legal regulations regarding accessibility, and finally the perception of audiences with visual impairment by the cinema industry.

With regard to the financial viability of the new system, participants showed familiarity with the current situation, that is to say, that cinemas frequently cannot afford to buy or rent the necessary equipment. They repeatedly inquired about the costs of implementing AudioMovie both for the cinemas and for those who would like to organise a screening on their own. As two of the participants articulated:

> *Participant 5*: I wonder what is the cost of AudioMovie? Will cinemas be able to afford it? Is it cheaper than the headsets? Because if it is, maybe it would be possible to make it widely available? Not only in selected cinemas, but to convince for example big cinema chains to have it?

> *Participant 4*: How expensive is it? Would it be possible for someone, for example an organisation that wants to organise a screening with AD, to come to the cinema, install it for a one-time screening? I mean in case the cinema doesn't have it installed.

The experience of many organisations involved in accessibility provision in Poland shows that the cinema industry does not perceive audiences with vision loss as a potential target group (Mariusz Trzeciakiewicz, personal communication, 9 December 2018; Agata Psiuk, personal communication, 15 November 2018). This seems to stand in stark contrast to the views of participants in our experiment. Most participants made it very clear that in their opinion audiences with vision loss are an important target group that could add to the box-office earnings. One of the participants suggested that, if AD were available in the cinemas, she would spend more money on the cinema than on restaurant dining. As other participants stated:

> *Participant 10*: Cinemas should have it and they should advertise it. In the end it's also about them making profit. I mean, we are quite numerous. I am sure that if there was a cinema that had AD for all the screenings, the tickets would be booked for at least half a year in advance.

> *Participant 11*: Even in Kraków alone there are many blind people. And we want to go to the cinema. And we can pay. But we will go and pay only if we are able to enjoy the films like everyone else. And we will take our families too. Because right now it's ridiculous. I'm going with my family and they are not enjoying the film, because they must describe it to me.

What is even more important, participants noticed the potential that AudioMovie has for secondary users, that is to say persons without vision loss. They particularly referred to the fact that since, when it comes to the cinema, Poland is a subtitling country, AST might be an attractive service to some audiences. They also stated that secondary (non-sight-impaired) users could make the solution more attractive to the cinema industry. As one of the participants said:

> *Participant 3*: I wanted to add that many new clients could be gained through the app. Since it's possible to turn on voice-over, people who do not have vision loss could use it. Many people don't like to read subtitles. They prefer voice-over.

This observation is in fact in line with the app creator's idea and also with the results of two other studies carried out within the AudioMovie project. An audience preferences study suggested audiences aged 60 or over would like to listen to voice-over (96.55 per cent) and dubbing (96 per cent) in cinemas if these options were to be made available (Jankowska, 2019a). At the same time this usability study conducted among senior citizens without vision loss showed that 81 per cent of participants aged 60 or over would like to use the app in cinemas.

When it comes to mainstreaming AD, participants were aware that the Polish Film Institute requires AD to be produced for films that are funded through their grant system. Nonetheless, most participants expressed serious doubts about the influence that legal provisions will have. As one of the participants said:

> Participant 5: We already have regulations about accessible internet sites. And how did that work for us? The truth is that there are many pages that are totally inaccessible. So, even if there is a legal obligation to prepare AD for films... will that really change anything?

Unfortunately, this disbelief in the effectiveness of legal provisions is not unfounded. As previous experience shows, television broadcasters resort to many strategies to comply with the law while providing as little AD as possible (see Jankowska and Walczak, 2019). As discussed previously, the case of film producers is very similar. To comply with PISF regulations, AD and SDH are produced but not distributed.

In summary, we believe that the issues raised by study participants show their awareness of the current situation of AD availability in Poland and consciousness of the challenges that need to be faced. This, in our opinion, means that many of them are not just mere users of access services, but are also willing to be proactive co-creators of the accessibility scene.

7.7 Conclusions

This chapter reports on the results of a usability study on the AudioMovie mobile application conducted in cinemas with participants with vision loss. In general, the app was evaluated positively, as most participants were satisfied with it and declared that they would like to use it in the future, both in the cinemas and at home. More importantly, it seems that most participants agree with the 'bring your own device' approach and consider AudioMovie as an opportunity to provide wider access to both domestic and foreign films. We also detected some aspects that should be improved in the future, if the app is to serve its purpose and end-users. These are, for example, the QR scanning, sound quality and volume. Some of these suggestions would require further research and consultations both with the app users as well as with the film and cinema industry.

However, we believe that the most important conclusion of this study is that new technologies have to be introduced with consideration for the digital divide. While mainstreaming accessibility through information and communication technology (ICT) is most probably a reasonable solution, it is clear that if it is done in the wrong way, it can exclude those who for a variety of reasons – be it lack of money or skills – are unable to use it.

To conclude, we would like to quote one of the participants who said, 'unfortunately many great initiatives have failed because of lack of good will'.

AudioMovie proved to be a successful tool. The technology behind it works, even though there is room for improvement. Yet technology is not all. There are other issues that need to be solved if AudioMovie, or any app for that matter, is to work to the benefit of viewers with specific needs. Most importantly, apps need to be filled with content, otherwise they are just a piece of fine, but useless technology. Unless the film industry is willing to participate actively in producing and sharing access services, not much will change. The same applies to the cinema industry, legislators and regulatory bodies – as long as they are not on board to cater for viewers with specific needs, there will be no improvement in the current situation. Finally, and perhaps most relevant to the accessibility cause, there is an awareness-raising exercise to be undertaken by researchers, organisations providing access services and most importantly the users. Otherwise accessibility services will continue to be perceived as a 'strange idea' made up by some clerk in some office and not a life-changing experience for so many people.

Acknowledgements

I would like to thank Agata Psiuk and Regina Mynarska from the Seventh Sense Foundation, Mariusz Trzeciakiewicz and Justyna Mańkowska from the Katarynka Foundation, Adam Piasecki from the Institute of Innovative Technologies EMAG, and students from the Jagiellonian University in Kraków: Katarzyna Chwast, Magdalena Samonis, Paulina Zawadzka, Sandra Brochocka, Zofia Kania and Radosław Sterna. Without their help it would have been impossible to organise and carry out the experiment.

This work was supported by the Polish National Centre for Research and Development under the Social Innovations II programme, research grant 'AudioMovie – Cinema for All' (no. /IS2-110/NCBR/2015).

Notes

1 Australia, Brazil, Finland, Italy, Norway and Sweden: MovieReading (www. moviereading.com). Spain: AudescMobile(http://cidat.once.es/home.cfm?id=1516& nivel=2), Whatscine (www.whatscine.es) and Artaccés (https://sdos.es/blog/exitosa-presentacion-de-la-aplicacion-artacces). Sweden: Movie Talk (www.movietalk.nu). Germany, Austria and Switzerland: Greta & Starks (www.gretaundstarks.de/greta/home). Holland: EarCatch (https://earcatch.nl). USA: Actiview (https://actiview.co/en).

2 Seventh Sense Foundation, Foundation for Audio Description Progress 'Katarynka', Jagiellonian University in Kraków, Institute of Innovative Technologies EMAG, cinema Kino Pod Baranami and Centre of Technology Transfer EMAG.

3 *Imagine* (2012, dir. Andrzej Jakimowski), *Życie jest piękne* [*Life Feels Good*] (2013, dir. Maciej Pieprzyca), *Warszawa 44* [*Warsaw 44*] (2014, dir. Jan Komasa), *Carte Blanche* (2015, dir. Jacek Lusiński) and *Ostatnia rodzina* [*The Last Family*] (2016, dir. Jan P. Matuszyński).

4 Participants with dyslexia and intellectual impairment were recruited from a pool of people with an official disability certificate.
5 All quotations are my translations from Polish.

References

Braun, S., and Orero, P. (2010) 'Audio description with audio subtitling – an emergent modality of audiovisual localisation', *Perspectives: Studies in Translatology*, 18, pp. 173–188.

Jankowska, A. (2019a) 'Accessibility mainstreaming and beyond – senior citizens as secondary users of audio subtitles in cinemas', *International Journal of Language, Translation and Intercultural Communication*, 8, pp. 28–47.

Jankowska, A. (2019b) 'Audiovisual media accessibility', in E. Angelone, M. Ehrensberger-Dow and G. Massey (eds.), *The Bloomsbury Companion to Language Industry Studies*. London: Bloomsbury Academic Publishing. pp. 231–260

Jankowska, A., Szarkowska, A., Krejtz, K., Fidyka, A., Kowalski, J., and Wichrowski, M. (2017) 'Smartphone app as a museum guide: testing the Open Art application with blind, deaf, and sighted users', *International Journal of Translation*, 19, pp. 113–130.

Jankowska, A., and Walczak, A. (2019) 'Audio description for films in Poland: history, present state and future prospects', *Journal of Specialised Translation*, 32, pp. 236–261. Available at: www.jostrans.org/issue32/art_jankowska.php (accessed 13 December 2019).

Oncins, E., Lopes, O., Orero, P., and Serrano, J. (2013) 'All together now: a multi-language and multi-system mobile application to make live performing arts accessible', *Journal of Specialised Translation*, 20, 147–164. Available at: www.jostrans.org/issue20/art_oncins.pdf (accessed 14 December 2019).

StatCounter (2018a) *Mobile Operating System Market Share Worldwide*. Available at: https://gs.statcounter.com/os-market-share/mobile/worldwide/2018 (acccessed 30 April 2020).

StatCounter (2018b) *Mobile Operating System Market Share Poland*. Available at: https://gs.statcounter.com/os-market-share/mobile/poland/2018 (acccessed 30 April 2020).

PISF (Polski Instytut Sztuki Filmowej) (2020) *Programy Operacyjne Polskiego Instytutu Sztuki Filmowej na rok 2020*. Available at: www.pisf.pl/wp-content/uploads/2020/02/Programy_Operacyjne_2020.pdf (acccessed 30 April 2020).

Public Opinion Research Center (2018) *Aktywności i doświadczenia Polaków w 2017 roku*. Available at: www.cbos.pl/SPISKOM.POL/2018/K_017_18.PDF (acccessed 30 April 2020).

Rai, S., and Petre, L. (2011) 'International toolkit on providing, delivering and campaigning for audio description on television and film commissioned by the World Blind Union.' Available at: https://www.itu.int/en/ITU-D/Digital-Inclusion/Persons-with-Disabilities/Documents/International. (acccessed 30 April 2020).

Remael, A., Reviers, N., and Vercauteren, G. (eds.) (2014) 'Pictures Painted in Words: ADLAB Audio Description guidelines'. Available at: www.adlabproject.eu/Docs/adlab book/index.html#index (accessed 14 December 2019).

Sanders, E. B.-N., and Stappers, P. J. (2008) 'Co-creation and the new landscapes of design', *CoDesign*, 4(1), pp. 5–18.

Statistical Office in Kraków (2014) *Urząd Statystyczny w Krakowie Działalność instytucji kultury w Polsce w 2013 r.* Available at: http://stat.gov.pl/obszary-tematyczne/kultura-turystyka-sport/kultura/dzialalnosc-instytucji-kultury-w-polsce-w-2013-r-,3,5.html (acccessed 30 April 2020).

Walczak, A. (2018) 'Audio description on smartphones: making cinema accessible for visually impaired audiences', *Universal Access in the Information Society*, 4, pp. 1–8.

8 Comparing human and automated approaches to visual storytelling

Sabine Braun, Kim Starr and Jorma Laaksonen

8.1 Introduction

In recent years, there has been a noticeable surge of interest in methods for describing audiovisual content, whether for automatic image search and retrieval, for advanced audiovisual storytelling, or because of an increasing demand for audio description (AD) following changes in national and European broadcasting legislation to meet the needs of visually impaired audiences. Approaches to creating AD for audiovisual content such as TV programmes and feature films are well established in some countries and can serve as models for other countries. However, the production of AD relies heavily on the specialised skills of audio describers and is therefore expensive. Attempts to automate visual content description, on the other hand, come with their own challenges. Although the computer vision and natural language processing communities have intensified research on automating image descriptions (Bernardi *et al.*, 2016), even the automatic description of *still* images remains challenging in terms of accuracy, completeness and robustness (Husain and Bober, 2016). Descriptions of *moving* images and audiovisual content where visual and auditory channels combine for the purposes of audiovisual storytelling pose additional challenges linked to temporality, including co-referencing (Rohrbach *et al.*, 2017), and other features of narrative continuity (Huang *et al.*, 2016). Machine-generated descriptions are currently at best more semantically and syntactically naïve than their human equivalents; but they are often also incoherent or incorrect.

By contrast, human-made AD, which is the product of a highly creative process of intersemiotic translation (Braun 2016), provides one of the most elaborate and reliable types of content description currently available for (still and) moving images. Audio descriptions of audiovisual content such as TV programmes are not intended to be stand-alone texts. They are created and processed/consumed in conjunction with those elements of the audiovisual narrative that remain accessible for visually impaired audiences, i.e. the dialogue, narration, sound effects, music and song lyrics. However, when combined with these elements, AD is not only an effective means of making audiovisual content accessible but potentially also a source of information about visual, auditory and verbal elements in audiovisual narrative that can be exploited for research and machine training.

Against such a backdrop, this chapter reports on a study comprising a systematic comparison of human- and machine-generated descriptions of audiovisual content, with the aim of identifying key characteristics of human descriptions that can inform and guide the development of (semi-)automated solutions. In line with the wider objectives of the project from which this study emanates, i.e. the EU-funded H2020 project 'Methods for Managing Audiovisual Data: Combining Automatic Efficiency with Human Accuracy' (MeMAD), the aim is that these solutions can be applied to different contexts of use, especially content retrieval from broadcasting archives and content description for the benefit of sight-impaired people.

As pointed out above, the most relevant type of audiovisual content description for automation is AD. A further type of visual description that would benefit from AI intervention is content description for broadcasting archives. Anecdotal evidence suggests that this type of description is currently created to varying levels of detail, ranging from keywords to more elaborate descriptions of what an image or visual scene depicts. The main driver for producing content descriptions is the likelihood of reuse/resale of the content, i.e. the insertion of the content into another programme. Broadcasters therefore prioritise the description of content for which they own or have cleared or established the rights, to support reuse internally or sale to other media companies. In contrast to AD, content descriptions for archival purposes are used in written form only, as an ancillary text to the audiovisual content, obviating the need for the descriptions to fit in audio hiatuses. Content descriptions also tend to be more 'literal' or factual than AD, especially AD for filmic drama and movies, which can at times be 'narrative' or figurative (Table 8.1). A model for machine-generated content description is therefore likely to be a more achievable goal in the shorter term than a model for generating elaborate audio descriptions. However, as pointed out above, AD can be used to derive guidance for automation. AD is also more widely and systematically accessible than content descriptions, which are an internal resource for broadcasters. Although the availability of AD varies in quantity, depth/detail and quality between countries and audiovisual genres, it is a rich source of information about the visual elements in audiovisual content and a relatively well-studied source of insight into how both human understanding and human description of audiovisual content works. On balance, it therefore appears to be a suitable basis for modelling audiovisual comprehension and description.

As our first excursion into considering the merits of using human-made AD for the purposes of modelling (semi-)automation, this chapter will begin by summarising key points from the study of human AD and human assimilation of audiovisual content (Section 8.2) that are pertinent for the present study. This is followed by an overview of computer vision and machine-based

Table 8.1 Key features of different types of visual content description

Audio description for visually impaired people – surrogate text; provides media access	Content descriptions for broadcasting archives – ancillary text; retrieval aid
• Scripted and then voiced and inserted into hiatuses in audio track so as not to overlap with the audio track	• Scripted and time-aligned, used in written form; no problems of overlap with the audio track
• High demands for coherence with other elements in the audio track (e.g. dialogue) due to shared use of audio track	• Lower demand for coherence with audio track, due to independent use of descriptions
• Time/space restrictions entail incompleteness, but complementarity and human ability to infer 'missing' information mitigate against information loss	• Fewer space/time restrictions facilitate a higher level of completeness where required, due to stand-alone use of the descriptions
• Less factual/literal, i.e. narrative rather than descriptive	• More factual/literal, i.e. descriptive rather than narrative

approaches to audiovisual narrative and storytelling (Section 8.3). Together these sections provide the foundations for the core of this chapter, i.e. a discussion of the methodological approach that we have adopted for this study (Section 8.4). Although the focus of this chapter is on methodological considerations for this uncharted area of study, i.e. the elicitation and exploitation of human knowledge of audiovisual content description to advance automated solutions, we include a summary of observations from our pilot stage (Section 8.5). We conclude by outlining what the piloting phase has highlighted and how this is shaping future steps (Section 8.6).

8.2 Human understanding and description of audiovisual content

The study of (human) AD is mostly situated within the field of translation studies, where AD is characterised as a modality of intersemiotic translation, and more specifically as a practice of translating visual images or visual elements (and occasionally sounds that are incomprehensible without seeing the associated visuals) of audiovisual material into verbal descriptions. As we have shown in our research overview (Introduction to this volume), irrespective of specific outcomes of individual studies, research on AD highlights the complexity of this type of translation, including the complexity of information selection, prioritisation and verbalisation strategies; the advantages and drawbacks of different description styles; and the insight that whilst AD cannot be entirely objective, a degree of interpretation and subjectivity may lead to more successful AD. Given the relatively low level of sophistication that machine-generated descriptions of audiovisual content can currently achieve, the key characteristics of human-made audiovisual content description are likely to create challenges for machine-generated descriptions. However, the MeMAD project aim to advance the automation of audiovisual content description makes it necessary to tackle these challenges. Arguably, an important prerequisite for this is to understand in more detail how human meaning-making works. This will be the focus of the remaining sections in this part of the chapter.

8.2.1 *Cognitive-pragmatic frameworks of human storytelling*

Among the plethora of theoretical models developed to study human communication, cognitive and pragmatic models of discourse processing offer great potential in the context of audiovisual content description, as they focus on explaining how we process monomodal verbal and/or multimodal (including audiovisual) content and retrieve the underlying story. Three particularly pertinent frameworks will be explored in more detail here, namely Mental Model Theory (Johnson-Laird, 1983, 2006), Relevance Theory (Sperber and Wilson, 1995) and Cognitive Narratology (Herman 2002, 2013).

Mental Model Theory (MMT) is essentially a theory of human reasoning. One of its basic postulates is that communication and understanding work on the basis of mental representations of what is being communicated, by virtue of combining perceptual input and prior knowledge. Mental models represent possibilities of how things could be in any given situation. In the process of reasoning and understanding, we draw conclusions about the plausibility of different possibilities based on what we know.

MMT has been used to model (verbal) discourse processing, i.e. to explain how we create mental models of situations described in texts (Van Dijk and Kintsch, 1983; Brown and Yule, 1983; Herman, 2002). The beginning of a story (news item, text, novel, etc.) normally gives rise to several possibilities, i.e. mental models. As the story unfolds, we normally settle on one of these in our interpretation of the textual cues (bottom-up processing) in light of the socio-cultural context of reception and common knowledge, including knowledge about places, activities and/or events (top-down processing). Mental modelling thus constitutes a process of hypothesis formation, confirmation and/or revision. Through its focus on the different sources of input, MMT provides a useful starting point for analysing how we process discourse or tell and understand stories, including in the context of audio description. Relevance Theory is complementary in that it elaborates on some of the details of this process.

Relevance Theory (RT) focuses on the human ability to derive meaning through inferential processes. It provides a detailed account of how we understand individual and conjoined utterances in a text. It postulates that utterances are normally under-specified (e.g. by omitting information that can be retrieved from common knowledge) and that as recipients we develop them into full-blown semantic representations (propositions) as a basis for deriving the intended meaning (Sperber and Wilson, 1995). According to RT, we achieve this by retrieving the explicit and implicit assumptions (i.e. *explicatures* and *implicatures*) that a speaker is making. The retrieval of explicatures involves working out the meaning of the key lexical items in an utterance (reference assignment), disambiguating words (e.g. pronouns) and pragmatically enriching what is said (e.g. working out temporal references or links between utterances), resulting in a basic level of utterance understanding. This is followed or complemented by the retrieval of implicatures to uncover a speaker's communicative message or intention.

RT asserts that these processes are highly inferential, drawing on common knowledge and cultural experience, and that they are guided by the human tendency to maximise relevance (*Cognitive Principle of Relevance*) and our assumption that speakers/storytellers normally choose the optimally relevant way of communicating their intentions (*Communicative Principle of Relevance*) (Sperber and Wilson, 1995). In accordance with this, we stop processing an utterance as soon as we derive an interpretation that we find sufficiently relevant, regarding this interpretation as the optimally relevant interpretation as it provides the best balance between processing effort and effect. RT's detailed account of how we work out utterance meaning 'step-by-step' highlights the human 'effort after meaning' (Bartlett, 1932), i.e. our ability and perhaps conditioning to fill in unsaid details and supply links in the pursuit of making sense of someone's utterances and, more broadly, the world around us. However, to fully explain our ability to process *stories*, i.e. entire narratives, which normally have a beginning, a main part (problem and resolution) and an ending, it is useful to consider the main tenets of Cognitive Narratology as a complementary framework.

The emergent field of Cognitive Narratology (CN) has been defined as 'the study of mind-relevant aspects of storytelling practices' (Herman, 2013). It builds on earlier models of Schema Theory, which postulate that our knowledge about the world—including knowledge about different types of events and situations—is organised through (stereotypical) schemata of these events or situations, which we derive from our experience (Bartlett, 1932; Shank and Abelson, 1977; Mandler, 1984). Schemata are thought to be part of our cognitive system. They include story schemata, i.e. knowledge about how different genres of stories are normally constructed. These schemata have become known as story grammars (Mandler and Johnson, 1977; Mandler, 1984; see also Appose and Karuppali, 1980). They provide a 'skeleton' onto which cues from the story can be mapped. As a theoretical construct, they can explain how we derive complex interpretations of stories based on a small number of cues, and the way we recall and structure salient narrative during the act of story retelling (Mandler and Johnson, 1977).

An important question for narratology is how we achieve coherence in narrative exposition, i.e. the impression of temporal and causal continuity of meaning and connectivity across the story arc. In a seminal work in text linguistics, Halliday and Hasan (1976) have analysed coherence from a semantic point of view, as a product of textual cohesion. This has led them to emphasise the role of lexico-grammatical cues on the text surface ('cohesive ties') in the creation of textual coherence. Further research has demonstrated that coherence is in fact a much more complex concept (e.g. Blakemore, 1992; De Beaugrande and Dressler, 1981; Brown and Yule, 1983; Bublitz and Lenk, 1999; Gernsbacher and Givón, 1995) and that the links needed to create continuity of meaning are supplied by text recipients whilst formal cohesion is neither a necessary nor a sufficient condition for coherence. However, a human storyteller will normally select appropriate means of expression to support the creation of temporal or causal coherence in the recipient's mind, including temporal, causal and other link words; coreference chains; bridging inferences (Myers *et al.*, 2010); and motion verbs to create a sense of 'fictive motion' in a story (Talmy, 1983). Furthermore, focalisation (Bal and Lewin, 1983; Bal, 2009) as a function of both story and storyteller, and often formulated by means of pronominalisation, creates an intermediate layer of narrative perspective (or 'bias') from which events are described and interpreted, and which also impacts our understanding of story worlds.

8.2.2 *Visual storytelling through the cognitive-pragmatic lens*

Cognitive-pragmatic frameworks have traditionally focused on monomodal and monolingual communication, but MMT claims that mental models can be created on the basis of visual perception as well as verbal discourse, emphasising that 'Models of the propositions expressed in language are rudimentary in comparison with perceptual models of the world, which contain much more information— many more referents, properties, and relations' (Johnson-Laird, 2006: 234). Sperber and Wilson (1995) do not discuss visual or multimodal discourse, but various suggestions have been made to adapt RT to the analysis of multimodal discourse, arguing that visual images may give rise to both explicatures and implicatures (e.g. Braun, 2007; Yus, 2008; Forceville, 2014). CN has been applied to both monomodal and multimodal storytelling, especially in filmic narrative (Herman, 2002). Furthermore, there is a growing body of research using these frameworks to investigate multimodal translation (e.g. Dicerto, 2018), audiovisual translation (e.g. Kovačič, 1993; Desilla, 2012, 2014) and audio description (Braun, 2007, 2011, 2016; Fresno, 2014; Vercauteren and Remael, 2014).

One question investigated in this body of work is how, according to the cognitive-pragmatic models, meaning arises from multimodal and/or audiovisual content. Although Johnson-Laird (2006: 233) maintains that the cognitive processes involved in integrating cues from different sources into mental models are not well understood yet, there is consensus that in audiovisual co-narration, where different modes of expression are combined, their meanings are not simply added to each other but contextualise, specify and modify each other (Lemke, 2006).

Table 8.2 Frida – taking a family photograph, old style[1]

Guillermo: And concentrate, everybody.

Christina: Wait. Where is Frida?

Mathilda: Adriana, go tell your sister to hurry up.

Plain-featured <u>Adriana</u> goes off <u>to look for Frida</u>, who appears <u>in a man's grey suit</u>, her black hair combed back.

<u>Christina</u> grins at Frida

who fixes a red rose into her lapel.

<u>Mathilda</u> sighs with exasperation.

<u>Guillermo's</u> eyes twinkle. He stands behind the camera, waiting to take the family photo.

Guillermo: I always wanted <u>a son</u>.

Guillermo: and, Mathilda, everyone, eyes to the camera, …and…[Click of camera]

In the black and white snap, Frida stands with her hand thrust into her <u>trouser</u> pocket.

Table 8.2, taken from *Frida* (2002), illustrates this effect. The first dialogue turn in this extract ('And concentrate everybody') is invested with meaning by the accompanying visuals, which show Guillermo and his family getting ready to take a family photograph. Conversely, the two subsequent dialogue turns, which indicate that one family member—namely Frida—is missing, serve to frame the unfolding visual actions, namely Arianna getting up and walking off, and Frida entering the scene. The visual reactions of Frida's mother and sisters as Frida appears in a man's suit tell a story about their relationship with Frida. Together with the inferable knowledge that there are no male siblings in the family, these visual cues enable us to create a mental model about the family relationships that ultimately enables us to retrieve the ironic spin on Guillermo's penultimate utterance ('I always wanted a son') in this extract.

The AD for this extract captures many of these salient visual cues, providing a good example of how human audio describers enable visually impaired audiences to make sense of the dialogue/audio track. The description generally follows the main characters and describes their actions, using simple sentences in which the characters in focus are the agents ('Christina grins at Frida', 'Mathilda sighs with exasperation'). Whilst most characters are only referred to by name, Adriana and Frida are assigned brief descriptions of their appearances ('plain featured' and 'in a man's grey suit' respectively). Guillermo's joke ('I always wanted a son') explains why the detail of Frida's appearance, which is further reinforced by the reference to her trouser pocket, is crucial in the AD. The reason for describing Adriana's appearance is less obvious, but her appearance ('plain featured') contrasts with the more intriguing appearance of Frida, highlighting Frida's avant-gardist character. The other women's reactions to Frida's appearance ('Christina grins', 'Mathilda sighs with exasperation') support this further.

At the same time the extract also illustrates that audio describers add aspects that are only inferable rather than being visible. This corroborates Gutt's (2000) observation that translation involves not only identifying the explicatures and implicatures in the source discourse but replacing and/or 'redistributing' them in the target discourse to provide for differences in the source and target recipients' cognitive environments. Here, for example, an assumption that is implicit in the visual narrative, namely that Adriana goes off to look *for Frida* (3), is made explicit in the verbal description. There is no visual element that provides the reason why Adriana walks away; we infer the reason from the preceding dialogue turn (2). Similarly, the assumption that Christina's grinning is directed *at Frida* (4) is only inferable from the direction of Christina's gaze and our understanding of the preceding and subsequent shots (3 and 5), in which Frida enters the scene, as Christina and Frida are not shown together in shot 4.

Furthermore, the richness of visual images raises the question of the most efficient way of describing, i.e. whether it is more efficient to state the explicatures arising from the images, leaving it to the audience to derive appropriate implicatures, or whether the description should verbalise the implicatures to save time. In Table 8.3, taken from the opening scenes of *The Hours* (2003), the AD relating to 1–3 spells out some of the explicatures first, by taking us through the physical details of the woman's attempt to fasten the buttons and belt of her coat (note that we do not see the woman in full) while leaving us to infer that she is getting ready to go out. By contrast, the AD relating to 4–5 focuses on a simple implicature from the images, namely that the woman is sitting down and is writing something. The further-reaching implicature, that she may be writing a suicide note, is not spelt out as the audience can retrieve this from the narrator who is reading out what she is writing, and from further visual cues reinforcing the suicide note hypothesis (e.g. a note being left on the mantelpiece as the woman walks to a nearby river and begins to put small rocks in her coat pockets). All of these cues are

Table 8.3 The Hours: describing at different levels

A woman's slender hands tremble as she fastens the buttons and ties the belt of her tweed coat.

Earlier she sits writing.

selected for description, in line with the goal of the AD, this being to create a coherent story.

As these two examples highlight, the complexity of human processing of audiovisual content means that *human description* of such content is a highly complex task. The complexity of the processes involved in deriving good and meaningful descriptions of audiovisual content may also serve to explain current limitations in the efforts to automate such descriptions. At the same time, the prospect that different levels of granularity in AD may return useful descriptions, by exploiting the human ability to create mental models and derive meaningful inferences, may mitigate against some of the current problems with automatically producing elaborate video scene descriptions.

The current state of the art of computer-generated machine description and automated visual storytelling will be outlined in the next section. The system of annotation that we have developed for the comparison of human- and machine-generated content descriptions (Section 8.4) is sufficiently agile to accommodate the anticipated evolution of the machine-generated descriptions.

8.3 Computer vision and automated description of audiovisual content

Until recently, automatic audiovisual content description has consisted of techniques that detect visual and auditory elements from audiovisual content, and label them with predefined keywords or indexing concepts. Such keywords can be words derived from visual and aural categories and/or words recognised with a speech recogniser from the spoken utterances. This approach has severe limitations as, for example, accurate description of actions and the inherent properties of visible objects has not been possible because the

Table 8.4 Image and video training datasets

Name	Content	# Objects	# Captions	Reference
Flickr30k	images	31,783	158,925	(Plummer *et al.*, 2015)
MS-COCO	images	123,287	616,767	(Lin *et al.*, 2015)
Conceptual Captions	images	3,178,371	3,178,371	(Sharma *et al.*, 2018)
VisualGenome	images + graphs	108,249	5,408,689	(Krishna *et al.*, 2017)
VIST	image sequences	20,080	100,400	(Huang *et al.*, 2016)
TGIF	video w/o audio	125,713	125,713	(Li et al., 2016)
MSVD	video	1,969	80,800	(Chen and Dolan, 2011)
LSMDC	video	108,536	108,536	(Rohrbach et al., 2015)
MSR-VTT	video	6,513	130,260	(Xu et al., 2015)

existing sets of labelled training data, on which all methods of automatic image recognition rely, have focused more on nouns as object classes and less on adjectives and verbs.

As a more recent trend, large image and video datasets, such as Microsoft Research's COCO (Lin *et al.*, 2015) and MSR-VTT (Xu *et al.*, 2015), respectively, have emerged. These datasets contain multiple human-written full-sentence annotations (captions) in unrestricted natural English for each image or video object. Moreover, some image datasets, such as the *Visual Genome* (Krishna *et al.*, 2017), provide both sentence-based and scene-graph-based annotations. In the latter case, the natural language annotations can be localised to specific parts of the images. These developments in the availability of training and testing data have opened up new avenues for devising more accurate and efficient methods for automatic visual data description. The most important computer vision datasets available for media captioning research are listed and characterised in Table 8.4.

Furthermore, deep neural networks have been found to provide superior performance in many visual machine learning and media analysis tasks. The success stories of deep neural methods include visual feature extraction and classification, and the implementation of recurrent encoder-decoder language models for translation from the visual domain to natural language. The modern approach to automatic image and video captioning is based on using deep convolutional neural networks for feature extraction or visual input encoding (Krizhevsky *et al.*, 2012; Szegedy *et al.*, 2015; He *et al.*, 2016). This representation is then fed to a recurrent neural network, typically a long short-term memory (LSTM) network (Hochreiter and Schmidhuber, 1997), that decodes this visual encoding to an output sequence of words, a sentence or a caption that describes the audiovisual content.

Training the word sequence decoders for image and video content description has conventionally been based on minimising the discrepancy (cross-entropy) between the sentences generated by the model and the desired output. This approach is well motivated theoretically, but does not aim to directly optimise any automatic performance measure used in practice such as BLEU, METEOR or CIDEr evaluation mechanisms. In order to improve the captioning performance with respect to these measures, researchers have started to use reinforcement learning (Ren *et al.*, 2017) in training the captioning models. This has led to better results when measured by the automatically obtainable scores. Despite significant recent progress, current image and video description techniques are still unreliable, producing different textual descriptions for visually very similar contents.

As a step beyond the automation of descriptions of individual visual images, the automation of *sequenced descriptions within a static image* environment (Huang *et al.*, 2016; Smilevski *et al.*, 2018) has developed apace, most notably in relation to the description of object inter-relatedness within single-frame images (Krishna *et al.*, 2017). Meanwhile, progress in machine-generated *descriptions for moving image sequences* has moved at a more modest speed (Xu *et al.*, 2015; Rohrbach *et al.*, 2017) due, in large part, to the dearth of sufficiently sizeable training and test datasets required to assist machine learning. Nevertheless, a range of innovative approaches has been trialled: the exploitation of temporal structures (Yao *et al.*, 2015), question–answer techniques (Wu *et al.*, 2016), video–sentence pairing (Venugopalan *et al.*, 2015) and visual attention strategies (Xu *et al.*, 2015; Kim *et al.*, 2018).

Regardless of whether the data adopted for the purposes of training computer vision models comprise still or moving imagery, however, the holy grail for the automated description of audiovisual content remains to produce a model for creating intuitive and coherent storytelling across multiple images read in sequence.

One of the challenges is that, while sequences of images frequently contain persons or objects that recur across the piece, and should therefore be regarded as prime candidates for conveying information of narrative saliency (see also Table 8.2, from *Frida*, above), variations in scale or placement may confound the automatic identification of continuity cues. Initially, this impacts the identification of key protagonists and action-relevant objects, subsequently inducing a knock-on effect where abstract concepts associated with these entities are also disregarded (e.g. failure to identify an image as relating to a group of 'friends' may also impact the visual-semantic association that cross-references a social gathering). Secondly, backward- and forward-referencing of objects and concepts between connected images ('inferential bridging') is still in its infancy, and consequently a consistent means of establishing coherence between frames within sequential moving imagery remains, as yet, largely out of reach.

Issues of inter-relatedness between people and objects in sequential imagery, both moving and still, represent a major milestone in automating descriptions, with the 'who did what to whom' question (who is talking to whom?) still posing a significant challenge which remains unresolved. Hypothetically, the addition of audio cue isolation to the computer vision model should assist in the disambiguation process. One avenue worth exploring is whether audio event detection and speaker diarisation could assist in the identification of characters and sound-associated objects. Audio events comprise audible data attributable to specific actions, including elements such as speech, non-verbal utterances, animal noises, vehicle sounds, doorbell and telephone rings, and so forth. Automatic classification of these sound artefacts is referred to as audio event detection (AED) and can be applied to a range of practical applications, such as speech and speaker recognition (Babaee *et al.*, 2018). Current methods for achieving AED include audio 'preprocessing, feature extraction and classification methods' (Babaee *et al.*, 2018: 661). Within the spectrum of opportunities this affords is the determination of specific prosodic features capturing pitch, volume and duration.

Automatic speaker diarisation, on the other hand, 'is the process of partitioning an input audio stream into homogeneous segments according to the speakers' identities' (Vallet *et al.*, 2013), promoting the identification of speech events and turn-taking between individuals in a shared audio event (e.g. a talk show), such that each speaker's entry and exit points are recorded (speech repartition) and data, including cumulative speaking times, is captured. Work combining speaker diarisation with visual data cues, notably changes in camera shot which focus on the current speaker, has refined the concept of a correlation between those who are speaking and those who are featured in the visual content. This link extends to the automatic identification of persons featured across multiple frames.

Pairing automated audio event extraction and speaker diarisation with image sequencing models could exponentially improve continuous character identification between frames, eased by the extraction of a speaker's combined vocal and visual 'DNA'. Audio tagging of principal characters would likewise mitigate computer vision confounds arising where abstruse camera angles or abrupt changes of scale impede the machine in identifying reoccurring characters (or audio-defined objects, such as a barking dog). Combining audio and visual cues to infer continuity would therefore contribute significantly to creating narrative coherence in automatic descriptions. Currently, however, automated approaches to video scene description remain largely confined to the description of individual frames within video scenes, thereby eliminating the possibility of cohesion and coherence between descriptions of subsequent frames. Initial analysis of automatically generated description needs to be adjusted to this state of affairs while remaining open to a comparative analysis between more advanced combined sound-image machine-generated descriptions and their human-generated equivalents. This would ensure that the further development of automated solutions can be informed by insights into human approaches to description in the future. We believe that the methodological approach outlined in the next section is sufficiently flexible to accommodate this.

8.4 Methodological approach

The initial phase of the present study has focused on three principal components. The first was the construction of a corpus of audiovisual materials consisting of human AD and original film dialogue (in English), the MeMAD Video Corpus (MVC), and the subsequent identification of short extracts within the corpus which lend themselves to human vs. machine-generated description comparisons. The second component was the annotation of this audiovisual content in a manner which facilitates a comparative study featuring human and computer-generated video description, while the third component was a preliminary analysis of parallel datasets (human annotations, AD and a first iteration of experimental machine-generated video descriptions) to pilot the methodological design and initiate first improvements in automated descriptions. Each of these items was a key step in the preparation of more comprehensive comparative analyses between human-generated and machine-generated audiovisual content descriptions in the later phases of the study. This section elaborates on the first two components. Observations of the preliminary analysis are reported in Section 8.5.

8.4.1 Materials

Selection of materials

While audio described content is more readily available than other types of audiovisual content description (Section 8.1), being used by some broadcasters and content producers to enhance accessibility for sight-impaired audiences, the sourcing of audio described broadcast and digital media content is not without challenges, regardless of host territory. The availability and quantity of audio described content varies widely according to the legislative frameworks in operation in each country, with many territories remaining unregulated despite moves by EU legislators to encourage wider participation and equal access to broadcast media for citizens (European Council, 2010).

In addition, stylistic factors, in terms both of the density of audio insertions and their granularity in relation to the narratively salient details, mean much current television production content is of limited use in the context of our study. An example of the type of issues encountered was highlighted during the pilot phase, when the serial drama genre was explored as a potential source of audiovisual data for the purposes of investigating human- vs. machine-generated video descriptions. Episodes of *EastEnders*, a serial drama/'soap' produced by the BBC in the UK, were examined for quality and quantity of human AD. While this material contained useful examples of the kinds of narrative action which could theoretically inform human meaning-making in storytelling, the extent of the AD was constrained by quick-fire direction (multiple very short scenes and rapid shot-changes) and a shortage of audio hiatuses. Hampered by these technical parameters, the corresponding AD was minimal, largely becoming a vehicle for announcing changes of location ('in the pub…') or for introducing new characters ('Bernadette and Tiffany arrive'). Documentaries, as an alternative genre of programming containing AD, also proved problematic. With the exception of flagship programmes such as the BBC's *Blue Planet* (BBC, 2017), where worldwide distribution rights positively impact production budgets, documentaries generally contain minimal AD, even in circumstances where the material naturally lends itself to colourful descriptions. Documentaries may also lack a clear narrative, with isolated segments failing to deliver 'intact', self-contained, micro-plots.

By contrast film productions, due to their long-form narrative exposition, lend themselves to more elaborate and narratively sophisticated storytelling and AD scripting, with opportunities for the describers to paint an audio picture which does more than merely label the characters and their locations. Poetic and evocative descriptions of cinematographic elements, as well as interpretive commentary on the narrative importance of key actions and events, elevate film AD from a mechanism for streaming basic information to a rich and colourful art form. This greater emphasis on explication in film storytelling is frequently matched by a richer lexicon and more complete descriptions than would be found in a standard television production. Our pilot study suggested these dual aspects, rich descriptions and contextualisation of content, distinguished feature film AD as the most comprehensive source of audiovisual data available for informing the creation of machine-generated descriptions. In theory, at least, film AD should facilitate visual information extraction, serving as a ready-made comparator for evaluating computer outputs.

However, while AD has a perceived value in the context of informing machine-generated video descriptions, our pilot stages also show that extracting *comprehensive* visual information from AD can prove problematic. As discussed in Section 8.2, approaches to AD vary considerably in terms of style and granularity, and are ultimately subject to the audio describer's personal filter and individual interpretation, life experience and intuition, all of which are tested against the benchmarks of redundancy and saliency. Perhaps not surprisingly therefore, the application of rule-based methodologies for arriving at audio described outputs (ITC, 2000; AENOR, 2005) has proved largely untenable, with a lack of consensus between describers about what should be included or omitted in a narratively complementary script (Vercauteren, 2007: 139; Yeung, 2007: 241; Ibanez, 2010: 144). This lack of standardisation naturally impacts objectivity, with considerable variation between describers in the way they choose to prioritise visual cues for inclusion in the AD, and the lexical breadth with which they choose to describe the selected elements (Matamala, 2018).

In addition to these constraints, the absence of suitable hiatuses in the audio track, due either to inopportune timing or a density of dialogue (or both), often shackle the describer, limiting the extent to which any supplementary

Table 8.5 Advantages and disadvantages of AD for informing machine-generated descriptions

Advantages of film AD	Disadvantages of film AD
Focused on visual imagery	Not a complete narrative, but rather a 'constrained' supplementary text
May contain cues for key narrative events: characters, actions and locations	Key narrative events may alternatively be relayed via other audio channels (dialogue, sound effects, original music score, etc.)
and eclectic	Choice of lexicon may be too sophisticated or subjective for direct comparison with machine descriptions
Where sufficient hiatuses occur in the original audio, evocative descriptions can inform deeper immersion in film text	Paucity of hiatuses in the original audio may limit the extent of, or preclude, AD
More reliable source of narrative cues than subtitles/dialogue alone	Personal 'take' on plot interpretation and therefore not 'definitive'
Subjectivity may be at the heart of 'human touch' AD	Not objective

visual information can be inserted into the source material. As was highlighted in Section 8.2.1, this is not such a sizeable problem for AD recipients, usually blind and partially sighted audiences, as omissions in the AD will often be mitigated by the use of inferencing strategies, resulting in a more or less complete comprehension of narrative. Computer vision algorithms, on the other hand, currently lack complex inferential capacity, which means that AD alone cannot provide sufficient data to serve as a 'complete solution' for training machines to produce human-like descriptions. In summary, while it is unquestionably a useful source of visually descriptive information, closer inspection during the pilot stage has revealed that AD taken in isolation cannot offer a 'one-stop-shop' solution for informing the development of human-like machine-generated descriptions of moving images. A summary of key issues can be found in Table 8.5.

As highlighted above, AD for motion picture (movie) productions remains the most complete audio descriptive data resource available in respect of the visual content of moving images, and for this reason it is possible to make a compelling argument for using audio described films as a point of departure for analysing and comparing human- and machine-generated descriptions of audiovisual content. However, our pilot work and the human models of communication reviewed above also make it clear that additional information would be necessary to compensate for the 'shortcomings' of AD in our context. The textual surface of AD serves as a starting point for creating a comprehensive mental representation of the audiovisual content, but it cannot be regarded as the sole source of narrative saliency. For this reason, we rejected the idea of a direct comparison between AD and machine-generated video descriptions, which we determined to be methodologically flawed. Instead, we decided to compile a corpus of audiovisual content with AD, which we would use as one source of information about the content, and to create different sets of annotations to complement the audio descriptive texts in this corpus.

Compiling the audiovisual corpus and identifying 'story arcs'

Our primary experimental corpus, numbering 45 feature-length films, was drawn from a limited catalogue of audio described productions currently available on commercial release in DVD format through online retailers. Five movie genres, representing a diversity of cinematic styles, were chosen for analysis: comedy, action, thriller, 'romcom' and drama. Historical dramas containing anachronistic references, e.g. period costume, and animated productions featuring cartoon characters, were intentionally excluded in the knowledge that they were likely to confound computer vision applications which rely heavily on training data compiled from contemporary still and moving image datasets, paired with crowd-sourced captioning (e.g. the Microsoft COCO dataset, detailed in Lin *et al.*, 2015).

Acknowledging the important role of story schemata in the comprehension of multimodal discourse (Section 2.1), our first step in data preparation was to identify a series of 'story arcs' within each feature film. These took the form of short stories-within-a-story (micro-narratives), containing clear, narratively significant beginning and end points, and illustrated elements of crisis and resolution. Extracts were drawn from full-length feature films due to the availability of high-quality AD; however, it has not been the intention that they would be treated as part of a narrative with greater reach than the parameters of the extracts themselves.

Mindful of the lack of sophistication in current machine-generated video descriptions, we selected examples of basic social interaction as the focus for our data-mining exercise. Uniform parameters were applied to the selection of 'story arcs' in order to standardise the dataset, and facilitate meaningful comparison and evaluation between human descriptions and those produced by machine-learning techniques (Table 8.6).

Thus, in order to avoid a level of narrative complexity likely to defy current machine-generated description capabilities, scenes were selected on the basis that they contained one or two principal characters only, behaving or interacting in a naturalistic, socio-representational manner. Simple actions such as sitting, walking, talking, running, hugging and kissing occur frequently in film material (Salway, 2007) and for this reason are especially relevant to the improvement of simple, machine-generated video descriptions which currently fail to register these basic movements consistently and accurately.

Table 8.6 Criteria for selecting 'story arc' extracts

Category	Criteria	Observations
Source text	Must contain audio description	Required to explore value of AD for informing computer-generated descriptions
Persons	1 or 2 principal characters	Incidental characters and small groups of people in the background of shots also permitted.
Actions	Minimum of 4 or 5 simple, common actions	E.g. sitting, running, talking, walking, hugging, kissing
Duration	10 seconds – 3 minutes	Limited-duration story arcs should simplify sequence modelling
Storyline	Self-contained micro-narrative	E.g. initiating action/crisis, proposed solution, action based on solution, consequence, result
Objects	Unlimited	Although no limitation was put on the number of objects in an extract, only those objects regarded as key to the action were included in our annotations

While film presentations typically have a duration of between one and a half and two and half hours, the number of 'story arcs' available within each production varies according to narrative composition, directorial choices and cinematographic presentation. For this reason, and in order to set an achievable goal, our target was to identify between 10 and 20 'story arcs' which met our selection criteria per film. We set a ceiling of 20 extracts per film in order to avoid over-representation by any one audio description style, production house or describer. This approach resulted in a corpus of approximately 500 extracts for annotation and analysis.

Selected 'story arcs' take the form of short micro-narratives occurring within the context of a full feature-length film. Essentially, each 'story arc' represents both a dramatic episode salient to interpretation of the wider narrative (although this was not our research focus, as noted above), and a self-contained mini-plot in its own right. The duration of 'story arcs' was maintained between 10 seconds and 3 minutes in order to ease the application of sequence modelling techniques during later machine iterations.

An example of one such 'story arc' ('Boy in a field') is provided in Table 8.7, and is taken from the film *Little Miss Sunshine (2006)*. At the beginning of the extract a dispute arises between a teenage boy and his family. The dispute is subsequently resolved by the intervention of a young family member.

Table 8.7 'Boy in a field' (*Little Miss Sunshine*)

On a family road trip, a teenage boy (Dwayne) discovers he can no longer follow his dream of becoming a fighter pilot. He demands the campervan the family are travelling in be stopped, and he jumps out. Refusing words of comfort from his mother, he runs into an empty field, and sits down alone, to contemplate his future.

Dwayne's young sister (Olive) offers to talk to him. She leaves the rest of the family back at the roadside and walks down a grassy slope towards her brother.

Olive crouches down behind Dwayne, and without speaking …

… puts an arm around him, leaning her head tenderly on his shoulder.

Comforted by her presence and the knowledge that she truly understands his despair, Dwayne relinquishes his anger. They both rise …

… and walk back towards the roadside where the rest of the family is waiting for them.

In a sentimental, reciprocal declaration of affection, Dwayne resumes his role as 'big brother', carrying his little sister up the sharp incline near the road.

Screenshots of narratively key frames from the scene are shown alongside a brief description of the action, provided in linear fashion.

In the above extract, we observe a typical film crisis-resolution scenario, in which the crisis (boy learns bad news) precipitates action (the boy leaves a parked van and sits alone in a field), followed by crisis resolution (his little sister comforts him), through consequences of action (boy returns to van). The scene contains only minimal dialogue, allowing the AD to 'breathe' and deliver a relatively unhindered audio guide to the action. Although the majority of 'story arcs' selected for inclusion in our corpus contain dialogue in addition to AD, this example illustrates the type of short narrative sequence we sought to isolate. As stated above, our criteria for selecting story arcs (duration, complexity, number of characters present, classes of action, etc.) were driven by the current evolutionary state of automated video descriptions.

8.4.2 Data processing and annotation

Annotation models and levels

In parallel with determining the nature of our experimental data, resources were initially focused on exploring multimodal annotation frameworks. The uncharted nature of future machine description iterations, as the basis of human vs. computer description analyses, required that our annotation methodology be sufficiently flexible to be able to accommodate machine-generated descriptions of varying complexity over the course of the project. Hierarchical multimodal taxonomies (Jiménez and Seibel, 2012) for tagging audiovisual material (narratological, grammatical and imagery-based), and storytelling ontologies for broadcast news (e.g. BBC, 2018) were considered as frameworks for annotating semantic and narrative content. However, the former applied tagging protocols that were considerably more granular than was required for our purposes (for instance, tagging characters' ages); while the latter, derived from news production workflows, incorporated elements that had no correspondence with feature film analysis (e.g. logging multiple story sources). Hence it became apparent that a bespoke methodology would have to be developed.

Based on the theoretical frameworks of discourse processing/storytelling outlined in Section 3 and in order to overcome the 'shortcomings' of AD in our context, as explained above, we have therefore derived a bespoke annotation model. The starting point in considering the types of annotation that would be required was to conceptualise the highly complex process of multimodal engagement, breaking it down into layers of meaning-making which generally co-occur in the human viewing experience. These are represented in the pyramid featured in Figure 8.1, whereby in a reading from bottom to

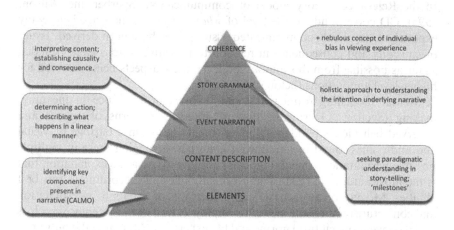

Figure 8.1 Accessing multimedia content – levels of complexity.

top, the level of meaning-making becomes increasingly sophisticated and requires greater cognitive resources in order to retrieve results. Clearly, human understanding transcends a simplistic explanation of the type denoted by a simple 'climbing the ladder' to greater comprehension, but these multiple layers of engagement typify the kinds of human endeavour undertaken in an unspecified and most likely highly individualistic order, in the quest to make sense of complex narrative themes.

Our annotations have therefore been designed to address each of these levels of narrative immersion and can be described as follows.

(i) **Key elements (KE)**: At the most fundamental level of meaning-making, our model assumes that viewers identify the building blocks of plot exposition, including main characters, actions, locations, the emotional temperature or mood of the piece, and salient objects, ('CALMO' in Figure 8.1). Establishing the nature of these important cues is generally the first task of the viewer, since without a gauge of mood, characterisation and the setting of narrative action, the viewer's inferential skills cannot be fully engaged. In accordance with this, we identified the KEs of each video scene as an entry point to the annotation and analysis process, using the following categories: *character* (e.g. man, woman, young girl, small boy), *action* (e.g. sitting, walking, talking, eating), *location* (e.g. at the office, in the kitchen, on a road), *mood* (e.g. happy, sad), *action-relevant object* (e.g. car, desk, bed) and optionally, *gestural/body language* (e.g. a shrug, a pointing finger). Although not all of these elements may be present at any given juncture, a combination of two or more will generally be critical to plot development and exposition and can therefore be regarded as narratively important.

(ii) **Content description (CD)**: This annotation stream represents a 'ground truth' summary of the action taking place on screen. Constructed as a factual description while avoiding incursions into interpretation, CD captures the scene as it would be superficially perceived by the average audience member. In the Relevance Theory model of communication (Sperber and Wilson, 1995), CD corresponds to the level of *what is said*, i.e. the stage before any explicitly or implicitly communicated assumptions have been derived. Issues of causality and consequence in relation to narrative actions were excluded as far as possible from this annotation level, these aspects being reserved for higher-level annotations (below).

Mental modelling frameworks and theories of relevance in meaning-making (Section 2.1) suggest that we interpret patterns of speech and observed behaviours by identifying pertinent cues from a barrage of visual and audio cues found in multimedia materials, arranging these in multiple possible permutations (mental models) until we arrive at an explanation that is the most natural and plausible (optimally relevant) according to our best abilities. Moving on from basic comprehension of events to interpretation and conjecture requires the viewer to employ 'extradiegetic' references such as social convention, cultural norms and life experience. Matching the output of this task requires a different approach to annotation, involving interpretation and narrative mapping. These elements are mirrored in two further levels of annotation which we have termed 'event narration' and 'story grammar' (Mandler and Johnson, 1977; Mandler, 1984; Appose and Karuppali, 1980).

(iii) Event narration (EN): This level captures a deeper pass of contextual cues, which we assume is conducted and applied by the viewer within the wider film context. EN reflects the viewer's attempt to establish relevance in relation to particular actions and construct context, which in turn informs understanding. In Relevance Theory, this corresponds, by and large, to deriving the *explicature*, i.e. the explicitly communicated assumptions. EN seeks to contextualise events within the micro-narrative at the centre of the story arc, cross-referencing possible inferences from outside the story arc, and yet not, at this stage, attempting to construct an 'aerial view' of the entire plot.

(iv) Story grammar (SG): This may be considered the highest level of narrative immersion, in which key dramatic 'signposts' are assimilated to construct an overarching plot which contains not only points of entry and departure, but also elements of crisis, resolution, failed resolution, and perhaps, conclusion. Referencing theoretical frameworks and the impact of Relevance Theory, this path to story resolution produces one or several implicatures derived from a summary of audio and visual cues. Accordingly, this layer of annotation corresponds to deriving the *implicature(s)*, i.e. the implicitly communicated assumptions, seen through the eyes of a sentient being endowed with pragmatic world knowledge.

These four layers will be used – along with the audio descriptions and film dialogue – as sources of data to evaluate comparable levels of sophistication in machine-generated video descriptions. The flexible nature of the annotation schema means that we are equipped to match any machine description iterations that are developed and generated in the MeMAD project. We can also adapt them in order to inform future computer vision models.

Transcription and annotation workflow

The initial transcription and annotation process was undertaken by doctoral and post-doctoral researchers at the University of Surrey who are experienced in multimodal analysis and/or audio description. Annotators began by viewing each film in its entirety, in order to gain an appreciation of the broad narrative structure of the piece. This initial viewing was combined with 'spotting' for story arcs (noting time-in and time-out) which met the criteria described above. In order that future machine descriptions could be fairly compared with their human annotation counterparts, these short extracts were selected to stand alone in terms of narrative completeness. However, it is acknowledged that access to the wider narrative significance of these brief 'story arcs' may be found in cues which lie outside the extract, occurring either earlier, or indeed later, in the exposition of the film. Attempts to mitigate any insights lost to this effect were addressed in the construction of 'event narration' annotations, where the interpretation of micro-plots by reference to wider narrative strategies was captured (see above). In 'spotting' mode, our annotators simply identified suitable story arcs, continuing to watch the film in a linear fashion throughout this process. This ensured that the holistic viewing experience was not compromised by a need to pause and complete annotations after each 'story arc' had been selected. Having completed this task, our annotators returned to the first of the selected extracts and began the annotation activity. At this point, extracts were revisited in order of occurrence in the film presentation, transcribing dialogue and AD as well as adding KE, CD and EN in one pass.

SG has not yet been added to our audiovisual corpus. However, if machine-based audiovisual coherence descriptors prove sufficiently robust, and there is evidence of computer-generated story arc exposition, we envisage revisiting our human-annotated corpus and selecting a representative sample of video extracts in order to apply 'story grammar' tagging (Mandler and Johnson, 1977; Mandler, 1978). These annotations would be appended to critical intersections in the exposition of narrative, flagging up key milestones such as initiating event, internal response, plan, attempt to enact plan, consequence and reaction (Appose and Karuppali, 1980: 4; see also Section 2.1).

In the event that automated audiovisual cue extraction fails to produce narratively coherent machine descriptions at a macrostructural level during the life of the project, 'story grammar' annotations can be analysed from within the human-generated film corpus, as a means of determining the manner in which human understanding of plot extends beyond that of the most advanced computer vision models.

Validity of human annotations

Human beings make sense of the world from their own unique perspective. Following Mental Model Theory, we apply individual life experience, personal prejudice and bias, lessons adapted from formal education, an innate and personal moral compass, the results of earlier 'trial and error' approaches in problem-solving, and intuition to navigate the innumerable cues that require decoding for the purposes of meaning-making. Naturally, this highly individualistic perspective can prove problematic where human operatives are required to perform a qualitative task in a standardised and uniform manner. Accepting that absolute standardisation in these circumstances is realistically beyond reach, we established a set of parameters to minimise variation in our human-generated annotations. These guidelines captured the description of 'mood', the treatment of 'location' and the selection of narratively salient 'objects', for instance.

Levels of granularity in description-writing also call for a uniform approach, with the example of whether one sees, for example, an animal, a dog or a Scottish terrier as being pertinent both to the human annotation schema, and in setting expectations for our comparisons with the machine descriptions. Future work exploring acceptable tolerance levels across related words will be required to resolve this issue.

Example of annotation

To illustrate the annotation levels, this section presents an example of the annotation we have created to date, i.e. all levels outlined above with the exception of the SG layer. As is evident from the example shown here (Table 8.5), which is the 'Boy in a field' scene from *Little Miss Sunshine* introduced in Section 3.1, the KEs capture the sine qua non of the dramatic text. CD is based on a 'say what you see' strategy, offering a means of extracting elements which a human viewer would recognise as story-sensitive, while affording those elements minimal narrative context. The EN annotations record the 'why' for events occurring in the narrative and explicate cohesive links across the wider storyline.

The example also highlights the difference between the professional AD and our CD layer. The former strives to be complementary to the primary audio channels (dialogue and sound) and concise to keep pace with the film. As explained in Section 3.1, the example contains very little dialogue, enabling a maximum amount of AD to be included, and yet, in the interest of striking a balance between AD and the other elements in the audio channel, the audio describer has left a range of visual cues for the audience to infer. By contrast, our CD annotation layer aims to give a systematic account of what can be seen on screen, irrespective of the time needed to read or perform the descriptions and of their placement in relation to other elements in the audio channel. Another point to note is that the AD does not introduce the characters. This is typical of our micro-narratives, where relevant information may have been introduced in the AD prior to the beginning of the video clip.

8.5 Initial observations

In addition to creating the audiovisual corpus and the annotations as described above, we have also explored different ways of analysing the data. Mirroring the multi-layered approach to creating annotations for the film corpus extracts, our analysis has taken a similarly stratified path. Drawing on the theoretical frameworks of human meaning-making (Section 2), the analytical process is designed with inherent agility in order to handle expected increments in the convolution of computer-generated descriptions. While reflecting the complex strategies for plot understanding and interpretation adopted by human audiences of film narrative, it enables us to compare the machine descriptions with each level of human description that was added to the corpus in the annotation process. The first example, i.e. the 'Boy in a field' scene repeated from above, but now including the first iteration of

Table 8.8 Example of annotation – *Little Miss Sunshine* ('Boy in a field')

Key elements:
CHARACTER(S): a boy; a little girl
ACTION(S): sitting, walking, hugging, climbing
LOCATION(S): field (road)
OBJECT(S): field, grass
MOOD: sad
OTHER: (gesture) hug

Frame	*Audio description (AD) / Dialogue*	*Content description (CD)*	*Event narration (EN)*
		Dwayne is sitting on the grass in a field, hugging his knees. He is sitting with his back to us.	Dwayne is upset.
	He is sitting with his back to her, arms resting on his knees, gazing at the rocky soil at his feet, and doesn't turn as she comes near.	Olive walks towards Dwayne, who is sitting on the ground, staring at the grass. Sheryl, Frank and Richard are at the top of the slope, standing next to the van, looking down at them.	Dwayne is very upset: his dreams have been shattered ... he just discovered that he is colour-blind and cannot fly fighter jets.
	Dressed in her red T-shirt, pink shorts and red cowboy boots, her long hair tied back, her huge glasses perched on her nose, Olive squats at Dwayne's side.	Once she has reached Dwayne, Olive slows down and bends her knees to sit next to Dwayne. Dwayne does not react.	Olive is sad for her brother and wishes to reassure him. She looks slightly worried at how he might react to her presence and touch.
	She puts her arm around him and rests her head on his shoulder. His head turns slightly towards her.	Olive looks at Dwayne and then puts her arm around him, resting her head on his shoulder. Dwayne is trying not to cry.	

Table 8.8 Cont.

Key elements:
CHARACTER(S): a boy; a little girl
ACTION(S): sitting, walking, hugging, climbing
LOCATION(S): field (road)
OBJECT(S): field, grass
MOOD: sad
OTHER: (gesture) hug

Frame	Audio description (AD) / Dialogue	Content description (CD)	Event narration (EN)
	Dwayne: I'm OK... let's go.	Dwayne turns towards Olive. Dwayne reassures Olive that he is okay, and she looks at him and smiles.	Dwayne understands that Olive really cares about him and that she is genuinely upset for him.
	Olive stands up and Dwayne gets to his feet and goes with her to the bottom of the slope.	Olive and Dwayne stand up and slowly walk towards the bottom of the slope.	
	Olive starts to climb, putting out her hand for support. Dwayne lifts her up underneath her arms and carries her to the top of the slope.	Olive climbs the slope but she wobbles. Dwayne helps her by carrying her up. Olive seems to be smiling.	Dwayne helping his little sister appears to be a sign of him growing up and starting to care about his family. Olive looks proud for having helped her brother.

machine descriptions, is presented to illustrate the insights that can be drawn from comparing the machine descriptions with the different types and levels of human description (Table 8.9).

The comparison of the machine descriptions with the key elements (KE) points to the first problem. With KEs covered in the machine descriptions in bold text, it is evident that the machine descriptions are rather incomplete. In the example below, the computer algorithms miss several key actions such as walking and hugging and the mood of the scene. In some frames, they also miss one of the two main characters. Furthermore, the repeated reference to the main characters as man and woman instead of referring to them

Table 8.9 Example of analysis – *Little Miss Sunshine* ('Boy in a field')

Key elements:
CHARACTER(S): A boy; a little girl.
ACTION(S): Sitting, walking, hugging, climbing.
LOCATION(S): Field (road)
OBJECT(S): Field, grass

MOOD: Sad
OTHER: (Gesture) Hug.

Frame/time codes	Audio description (AD) / Dialogue	Content description (CD)	Event narration (EN)	Machine description (MD)
		Dwayne is sitting on the grass in a field, hugging his knees. He is sitting with his back to us.	Dwayne is upset.	**a man** is **sitting** in a **field**
	He is sitting with his back to her, arms resting on his knees, gazing at the rocky soil at his feet, and doesn't turn as she comes near.	Olive walks towards Dwayne, who is sitting on the ground, staring at the grass. Sheryl, Frank and Richard are at the top of the slope, standing next to the van, looking down at them.	Dwayne is very upset: his dreams have been shattered … he just discovered that he is colour-blind and cannot fly fighter jets.	**a man** and a **woman** are talking to each other
	Dressed in her red T-shirt, pink shorts and red cowboy boots, her long hair tied back, her huge glasses perched on her nose, Olive squats at Dwayne's side.	Once she has reached Dwayne, Olive slows down and bends her knees to sit next to Dwayne. Dwayne does not react.	Olive is sad for her brother and wishes to reassure him. She looks slightly worried at how he might react to her presence and touch.	a group of people are singing and dancing

Table 8.9 Cont.

Key elements:
CHARACTER(S): A boy; a little girl.
ACTION(S): Sitting, walking, hugging, climbing.
LOCATION(S): Field (road)
OBJECT(S): Field, grass

MOOD: Sad
OTHER: (Gesture) Hug.

Frame/time codes	Audio description (AD) / Dialogue	Content description (CD)	Event narration (EN)	Machine description (MD)
	She puts her arm around him and rests her head on his shoulder. His head turns slightly towards her.	Olive looks at Dwayne and then puts her arm around him, resting her head on his shoulder. Dwayne is trying not to cry.		a group of people are in a **field**
	Dwayne: I'm OK... let's go.	Dwayne turns towards Olive. Dwayne reassures Olive that he is okay, and she looks at him and smiles.	Dwayne understands that Olive really cares about him and that she is genuinely upset for him.	a **man** is running
	Olive stands up and Dwayne gets to his feet and goes with her to the bottom of the slope.	Olive and Dwayne stand up and slowly walk towards the bottom of the slope.		a **man** and a **woman** are **walking** in a **field**
	Olive starts to climb, putting out her hand for support. Dwayne lifts her up underneath her arms and carries her to the top of the slope.	Olive climbs the slope but she wobbles. Dwayne helps her by carrying her up. Olive seems to be smiling.	Dwayne helping his little sister appears to be a sign of him growing up and starting to care about his family. Olive looks proud for having helped her brother.	a **woman** is **walking** down the road

more appropriately as boy and a girl is indicative for the lack of precision in current machine descriptions. A further noteworthy problem with regard to accuracy is the change from identifying the two characters as a man and a woman in segment 2 to identifying them incorrectly as a group of people in segments 3 or 4. This is difficult to explain other than by noting, as pointed out in Section 3, that the production of very different textual descriptions of what is similar content to the human eye is a common phenomenon in current machine descriptions. In addition to the problems with character identification, several actions are also described incorrectly (e.g. in the final segment).

Another notable problem, which distinguishes the machine descriptions from all of the human descriptions and annotations, is the lack of relevance in several machine-generated descriptions. Although it is understood, as explained above, that the machine descriptions within one clip do not form a coherent narrative, as only individual frames are currently described, it is noteworthy that the computer vision algorithms often do not select the most salient actions even within individual frames. This is exemplified in the penultimate segment, where the MD reads 'a man and a woman are walking in a field', suggesting an aimless action. Whilst the conclusion that they are in fact *returning* to the van after resolving the problem will only be possible when the algorithms become aware of how this frame is linked to previous frames/actions, a description to the effect that they are walking *towards the van*, which would create a more accurate and relevant description, may be achievable without sequential awareness.

The second example, drawn from *Saving Mr Banks* (2013), highlights further problems, especially the different ways in which the human descriptions and the machine descriptions approach cohesion and coherence across the descriptive segments, and the influence of the training data on the MD. In the selected scene the main character, *Mary Poppins* author Pamela Travers, is angry with Walt Disney for filling her room with Disney-branded toys in an attempt to seduce her into signing over the film rights for *Mary Poppins* to his corporation.

In this example (Table 8.10), the AD is clearly less 'complete' than our CD, as the dialogue leaves little room for AD to be inserted. However, when processed along with the primary sound track (dialogue, non-speech sound), the AD provides the key information. The main character is correctly introduced (in this case, before the selected scene occurs in the film) and then correctly identified as the same person throughout the scene through third person pronoun use. Furthermore, the audience can form an understanding (a mental model) of the character's main action, i.e. collecting stuffed toys from across the room and putting them in a cupboard, in a rather angry fashion, although some of the detail has to be inferred. For example no explicit reference is made to the toys being scattered around the room but the AD segment 'She picks up Disney's "Winnie the Pooh"' (7), Pamela's emphatic comment 'Duck, dog, out!' (10), the sound of objects being moved, jazzy music imitating steps, and the subsequent AD segment 'She stuffs every single one of

Table 8.10 Example of analysis – *Saving Mr Banks*

Key elements:
CHARARCTER(S): woman
ACTION(S): walking, talking, carrying
LOCATION(S): bedroom
MOOD: angry
OBJECT(S): toys, sofa, cupboard
OTHER: gestures (sigh, hand dusting)

Frame/time codes	Dialogue	Audio description (AD)	Content description (CD)	Machine description (MD)
1. 00:00	P: Good riddance!		A woman with short hair wearing a brown suit closes the balcony doors.	A picture of a woman in a room
2. 00:03	P: Now	She dusts off her hands and steps out of her brown court shoes.	She kicks off her shoes ...	
3. 00:05		She picks up a basket of Disney toys ... and stuffs them into a wardrobe.	... and picks up a basket of stuffed toys from a sofa in the hotel room	
4. 00:10	P: Kids.		... carrying them to a cupboard	
5. 00:11	P: How old do they think I am?		... next to the hotel room door.	A room with a bed and pictures on the wall.
6. 00:16	P: Five years old or something?		She walks back across to the corner of the room ...	
7. 00:18		She picks up Disney's 'Winnie the Pooh'.	... looks at another basket of toys ...	A man standing in front of a mirror.

(*continued*)

Table 8.10 Cont.

Key elements:
CHARARCTER(S): woman
ACTION(S): walking, talking, carrying
LOCATION(S): bedroom
MOOD: angry
OBJECT(S): toys, sofa, cupboard
OTHER: gestures (sigh, hand dusting)

Frame/time codes	Dialogue	Audio description (AD)	Content description (CD)	Machine description (MD)
8. 00:19	P: Poor A.A.Milne …		… and picks up both the basket and Winnie the Pooh teddy bear.	A man holding a teddy bear in front of a mirror.
9. 00:22	P: Ghastly business!		She carries the baskets to the cupboard.	
10. 00:24	P: Duck, dog, out!		She picks up Donald Duck and Pluto from the sofa …	A man is cutting a banana in a room.
11. 00:25		She stuffs every single one of the toys into the wardrobe.	… and crams them into the top of the cupboard.	A woman is taking a picture of herself in the mirror.
12. 00:32			She slams the cupboard door shut.	
13. 00:34	P: [Sighs]			

the toys into the wardrobe' (11) paint a picture of Pamela picking up a range of stuffed toy animals from across the entire room.

Our CD verbalises more of the visual detail and also demonstrates the process of character grounding more clearly than the AD: the character is introduced as new through the indefinite noun phrase 'a woman' (1) and then repeatedly co-referenced through the third person pronoun ('she'), creating a simple cohesive chain. By contrast, the MD fails with regard to character grounding and creating of a coherent sequence of action. It first introduces the main and only character in this scene correctly as a woman (1), but later—when only part of the character is visible—the MD wrongly identifies her several times as a man. (Whether this points to a bias in the training data is impossible to say from this one example, but it is an interesting question for further research.)

From the composition of the MD segments it is obvious again that they are unrelated, i.e. that they do not form a coherent whole. Each segment introduces a character or an object as new, using indefinite noun phrase constructions. This appears to be a reflection of the way the descriptions were composed in the training data, i.e. individual images described in a single sentence, by crowd-sourced pieceworkers. Similarly, the first MD segment 'a picture of a woman in a room' points to further problems with the training data: the captioners were instructed not to refer to the images they described as 'pictures' or 'images' but to focus on their content. However, this instruction seems to have been violated in several instances (Braun and Starr, 2019).

Other aspects that stand out in the MD are the poor lexicon, the very restricted repertoire of syntactic structures and the striking errors in action identification (e.g. 'cutting a banana', 10). The combination of the problems with the MD outlined in this section means that it would be difficult to create a coherent story from the MD. More broadly, the problems point to the differences between human audiovisual perception and machine perception, which are summarised in Table 8.11. The problems identified in this initial observation have informed the next steps of our analysis, which are outlined in the final section of this chapter.

8.6 Conclusions and next steps

The aim of this chapter was to outline an analytical procedure that supports a systematic comparison of human- and machine-generated descriptions of audiovisual content with a view to using insights from this comparison to inform and advance the automation of visual or multimodal storytelling.

The theoretical models outlined at the beginning of this chapter make it clear that *human* visual or multimodal storytelling is a complex process with a

Table 8.11 Differences between human and machine perception of audiovisual content

Human perception	Machine perception
Moving images	Still images (single frames)
Character, action, location, mood recognition …	Object recognition
Narrative coherence	Neural networks
Relevance in meaning-making	Crowd-sourced captions
Life experience	Availability of training datasets

range of uncertainties. The models explain why we draw different conclusions from the same premises and can give insight into why storytelling may be unsuccessful. Whilst, by emphasising the subjectivity of discourse interpretation, these models allude to the potential for creativity (which can, e.g., be exploited in making sense of art works), the complexity and subjectivity of human discourse processing and storytelling also mean that they have to date largely eschewed systematisation and formalisation. By extrapolation, the same applies to audiovisual content description, including AD.

Similarly, progress in machine-generated descriptions of audiovisual content, i.e. descriptions of moving image sequences, has so far been modest, mainly because of a dearth of sufficiently large training and test datasets to assist machine learning. Models for creating coherent storytelling across multiple images read in sequence have yet to be developed.

Story grammar approaches, which first emerged in the late 1970s and have seen a recent surge in popularity, appear to be a promising avenue for explaining and analysing (visual and multimodal) storytelling. As a schematised representation of events, processes and similar entities, story grammar lends itself to be formalised and may have a role to play in the development of computer models.

Given the current state of affairs, however, a more immediate step in our analysis will be a comparative lexical analysis of the human- and machine-generated descriptions, seeking out differences in patterns of word use, informativeness values, omissions and misrepresentations. This analysis will be used to identify areas of interest, and examples subsequently selected for qualitative analysis on a case-by-case basis. As moving image descriptions focus on the actions at the heart of each narrative, our intention is to concentrate, initially, on verbs and verbal phrases, drawing out evidence of differences in approach and outputs between corpora. In addition, we expect to extend the corpus-based lexical analyses to the material comprising the machine-generated training data from which the computer outputs are drawn, since this may inform certain expected anomalies within our results.

Further iterations of machine descriptions are expected to introduce sequence modelling techniques to mimic visual coherence between film frames, drawing on the work outlined in the VIST (Huang *et al.*, 2016) and LSMDC (Rohrbach *et al.*, 2015) studies and the addition of audio segmentation and diarisation techniques, i.e. extraction of sound features to measure impact, if any, on increasing inter-frame coherence. Combining audio and visual cues to infer continuity would contribute significantly to creating narrative coherence in automatic descriptions. If this approach proves tenable, we believe our human annotation and analytical methods are sufficiently agile to accommodate a comparative analysis between the combined sound–image machine-generated descriptions and their human-generated equivalents.

More broadly speaking, the increasingly complex association of ideas between frames presented in machine description outputs will allow for a more sophisticated level of analysis and interpretive comparison to be undertaken with human annotations. We anticipate that a smaller sample of human-generated annotations would be revisited in this case, and story grammar 'milestones' (Appose and Karuppali, 1980) added to our original annotations schemata, to denote key moments of narrative storytelling and action-based inter-relatedness between contiguous image frames. This would enable a comparison between machine sequence-modelled story arcs and their human-annotated parallel texts. Narratively intentional words and phrases in the machine-derived lexicon ('next', 'because', 'then', 'due to', etc.) and repetition of key iconographical indicators (e.g. 'meeting', 'birthday', 'holiday', 'graduation') should point to evidence of a predetermined story 'macrostructure' (Appose and Karuppali, 1980: 1). These concepts elide with Mandler's notion of cognitive schemata, upon which the comprehension of narrative is contingent, and which subsume storyline expectations, episode schemata and plot units (Rumelhart, 1977; Lehnert, 1982), the sequencing of narrative and the interconnectivity between story components.

The agility of the annotation system we have adopted lends itself to adaptation for any complexity level of machine outputs envisaged during the life of the project. However, in the event that the level of sophistication achieved by the machine descriptions fails to deliver internally coherent storytelling, an investigation of computer shortcomings would be used to inform future iterations, assessing key differences between human and machine recognition of intertextual referencing via the 'milestones' approach cited above.

Furthermore, different styles of audiovisual content description and different levels of granularity may return useful descriptions, by exploiting human inferencing and mental modelling powers. This may mitigate some of the current problems with producing elaborate video scene descriptions, for instance the overuse of generic vocabulary, lack of continuity and linkage between individual shots/images and so forth. In other words, existing machine-generated descriptions will at least provide a starting point for an analysis that can identify recurrent patterns of problems and thus highlight where the main issues arise. This will generate insights into how their potential for meaning-making can be improved.

Note

1 Images 1–8 were presented in full colour in the original film material, while frame 9 was rendered in black and white for narrative effect.

References

AENOR (2005) *Audiodescripción para personas con discapacidad visual: requisitos para la audiodescripción y elaboración de audioguías*. Madrid: AENOR.

Appose, A., and Karuppali, S. (1980) 'Decoding the Macrostructural Form of Oral Narratives in Typically Developing Children between 6–11 Years of Age: Using

Story Grammar Analysis', *Online Journal of Health and Allied Services*, 17(1), article 12. Available at: www.scopus.com/record/display.uri?eid=2-s2.0-85047524895&origin=inward&txGid=979609e35b955680098849bcea1fd82a (accessed 17 December 2018).

Babaee, M., Dinh, D. T., and Rigoll, G. (2018) 'A Deep Convolutional Neural Network for Video Sequence Background Subtraction', *Pattern Recognition*, 76, pp. 635–649.

Bal, M. (2009) *Narratology: Introduction to the Theory of Narrative*. 3rd edn. Toronto: University of Toronto Press.

Bal, M., and Lewin, J. (1983) 'The Narrating and the Focalizing: A Theory of Agents in Narrative', *Style*, 17(2), pp. 234–269.

Bartlett, F. C. (1932) *Remembering: A Study in Experimental and Social Psychology*. New York: Cambridge University Press.

Bernardi, R., Cakici, R., Elliott, D., Erdem, A., Erdem, E., Ikizler-Cinbis, N., Keller, F., Muscat, A., and Plank, B. (2016) 'Automatic Description Generation from Images: A Survey', *Journal of Artificial Intelligence Research*, 55(1), pp. 409–442.

Blakemore, D. (1992) *Understanding Utterances*. Oxford: Blackwell.

Braun, S. (2007) 'Audio Description from a Discourse Perspective: A Socially Relevant Framework for Research and Training', *Linguistica Antverpiensia, New Series – Themes in Translation Studies*, 6, pp. 357–369.

Braun, S. (2011) 'Creating Coherence in Audio Description', *Meta*, 56(3), pp. 645–662.

Braun, S. (2016) 'The Importance of Being Relevant? A Cognitive-pragmatic Framework for Conceptualising Audiovisual Translation', *Target: International Journal of Translation Studies*, 28(2), pp. 302–313.

Braun, S., and Starr, K. (2019) 'Finding the Right Words: Investigating Machine-Generated Video Description Quality Using a Human-derived Corpus-based Approach', *Journal of Audiovisual Translation*, 2(2), pp. 11–35.

BBC (2017) *Blue Planet II*. Available at: BBC iPlayer (accessed 11 December 2019).

BBC (2018) 'Storyline Ontology.' Available at: www.bbc.co.uk/ontologies/storyline (accessed 19 December 2018).

Brown, G., and Yule, G. (1983) *Discourse Analysis*. Cambridge: Cambridge University Press.

Bublitz, W., and Lenk, U. (1999) 'Disturbed coherence: "Fill me in"', in W. Bublitz, U. Lenk and E. Ventola (eds.), *Coherence in Spoken and Written Discourse*, Amsterdam and Philadelphia: John Benjamins, pp. 153–174.

Chen, D., and Dolan, W. (2011) 'Collecting Highly Parallel Data for Paraphrase Evaluation', *Proceedings of the 49th Annual Meeting of the Association for Computational Linguistics: Human Language Technologies*, 1, Oregon, 19 June, pp. 190–200.

De Beaugrande, R., and Dressler, W. (1981) *Introduction to Text Linguistics*. London: Longman.

Desilla, L. (2012) 'Implicatures in Film: Construal and Functions in Bridget Jones romantic comedies', *Journal of Pragmatics*, 44(1), pp. 30–53.

Desilla, L. (2014) 'Reading between the Lines, Seeing beyond the Images: An Empirical Study on the Comprehension of Implicit Film Dialogue Meaning across Cultures', *The Translator*, 20(2), pp. 194–214.

Dicerto, S. (2018) *Multimodal Pragmatics and Translation: A New Model for Source Text Analysis*. London: Palgrave Macmillan.

European Council (2010) 'Council Directive 2010/13/EC of the European Parliament and of the Council of 10 March 2010 on the Coordination of Certain Provisions Laid Down by Law, Regulation or Administrative Action in Member States Concerning the Provision of Audiovisual Media Services (Audiovisual Media Services)', *Official Journal of the European Communities*, L 95/1–24. Available at: http://eur-lex.europa.eu/legal-content/EN/ALL/?uri=CELEX%3A32010L0013 (accessed 11 December 2019).

Forceville, C. (2014) 'Relevance Theory as a Model for Multimodal Communication', in D. Machin (ed.), *Visual Communication*, Berlin: De Gruyter Mouton, pp. 51–70.

Fresno, N. (2014) 'La (re)construcción de los personajes fílmicos en la audiodescripción.' PhD thesis, Universitat Autònoma de Barcelona. Available at: www.tdx.cat/bitstream/handle/10803/285420/nfc1de1.pdf (accessed 17 December 2018).

Gernsbacher, M. A., and Givón, T. (1995) *Coherence in Spontaneous Text*. Amsterdam: John Benjamins.

Gutt, E-A. (2000) *Translation and Relevance: Cognition and Context*. Manchester: St Jerome.

Halliday, M. A. K., and Hasan, R. (1976) *Cohesion in English*. London: Longman.

He, K., Zhang, X., Ren, S., and Sun, J. (2016) 'Deep Residual Learning for Image Recognition', in *Proceedings of IEEE Conference on Computer Vision and Pattern Recognition*. Available at: https://arxiv.org/abs/1512.03385 (accessed 14 December 2018).

Herman, D. (2002) *Story Logic*. Lincoln: University of Nebraska Press.

Herman, D. (2013) 'Cognitive Narratology', in P. Hühn *et al.* (eds.), The Living Handbook of Narratology. Hamburg: Hamburg University Press. Available at: http://www.lhn.uni-hamburg.de/article/cognitive-narratology-revised-version-uploaded-22-september-2013 (accessed 19 December 2018).

Hochreiter, S., and Schmidhuber, J. (1997) 'Long Short Term Memory', *Neural Computation*, 9(8), pp. 1735–1780.

Huang, T. H., Ferraro, F., Mostafazadeh, N., Misra, I., Agrawal, A., Devlin, J., Girshick, R., He, X., Kohli, P., Dhruv, B., Zitnick, C., Parikh, D., Vanderwende, L., Galley, M., and Mitchell, M. (2016) 'Visual Storytelling', *Proceedings of NAACL-HLT*, San Diego, California, 12–17 June, pp. 1233–1239.

Husain, S.S., and Bober, M. (2016) 'Improving Large-scale Image Retrieval through Robust Aggregation of Local Descriptors', *IEEE Transactions on Pattern Analysis and Machine Intelligence*, 39(9), pp. 1783–1796.

Ibanez, A. (2010) 'Evaluation Criteria and Film Narrative: A Frame to Teaching Relevance in Audio Description', *Perspectives: Studies in Translatology*, 18(3), pp. 143–153.

Independent Television Commission (2000) 'Guidance on Standards for Audio Description.' Available at: www.audiodescription.co.uk/uploads/general/itcguide_sds_audio_desc_word3.pdf (accessed 18 December 2018).

Jiménez, C., and Seibel, C. (2012) 'Multisemiotic and Multimodal Corpus Analysis in Audio Description: TRACCE', in A. Remael, P. Orero and M. Carroll (eds.), *Audiovisual Translation and Media Accessibility at the Crossroads*, Amsterdam: Rodopi, pp. 409–425.

Johnson-Laird, P. (1983) *Mental Models: Towards a Cognitive Science of Language, Inference, and Consciousness*. Cambridge, MA.: Harvard University Press.

Johnson-Laird, P. (2006) *How We Reason*. Oxford: Oxford University Press.

Kim, T., Heo, M-O., Son, S., Park, K-W., and Zhang, B-T. (2018) 'GLAC Net: GLocal Attention Cascading Networks for Multi-image Cued Story Generation.' Available at: https://arxiv.org/abs/1805.10973 (accessed 18 December 2018).

Kovačič, I. (1993) 'Relevance as a Factor in Subtitling Reduction', in C. Dollerup and A. Lindegaard (eds.), *Teaching Translation and Interpretation 2: Insights, Aims, Visions*, Amsterdam: John Benjamins, pp. 245–251.

Krishna, R., Zhu, Y.,Groth, O., Johnson, J., Hata, K., Kravitz, J., Chen, S., Kalantidis, Y., Li, L-J., Shamma, D., Bernstein, M. S., and Li, F-F. (2017) 'Visual Genome: Connecting Language and Vision Using Crowdsourced Dense Image Annotations', *International Journal of Computer Vision*, 123, pp. 32–73.

Krizhevsky, A., Sutskever, I., and Hinton, G. E. (2012) 'Imagenet Classification with Deep Convolutional Neural Networks', *Advances in Neural Information Processing Systems*, 25, pp. 1097–1105.

Lehnert, W. G. (1982) 'Plot units: a narrative summarization strategy', in W. G. Lehnert and M. H. Ringle (eds.), Strategies for Natural Language Processing. Hillsdale, NJ: Erlbaum, pp. 375–414.

Lemke, J. (2006) 'Toward Critical Multimedia Literacy: Technology, Research, and Politics', in M. McKenna (ed.), *International Handbook of Literacy and Technology*, 2, Mahwah, NJ: Lawrence Erlbaum, pp. 3–14.

Li, Y., Song, Y., Cao, L., Tetreault, J., Goldberg, L., Jaimes, A., and Luo, J. (2016). 'TGIF: A new dataset and benchmark on animated GIF description', Proceedings of the IEEE Computer Society Conference on Computer Vision and Pattern Recognition, vol. 2016 (December), pp. 4641–4650.

Lin, T.-Y., Maire, M., Belongie, S., Bourdev, L., Girshick, R., Hays, J., Perona, P., Ramanan, D., Zitnick, C. L., and Dollar, P. (2015) 'Microsoft COCO: Common Objects in Context', in A. Lourdes, M. M. Bronstein and C. Rother (eds.), Computer Vision – ECCV *2014* Workshops, Cham: Springer, pp. 740–755.

Mandler, J. (1978) 'A Code in the Node', *Discourse Processes*, 1(1), pp. 14–35.

Mandler, J. (1984) *Stories, Scripts, and Scenes: Aspects of Schema Theory*. Hillsdale, NJ: Lawrence Erlbaum.

Mandler, J., and Johnson, N. (1977) 'Remembrance of Things Parsed: Story Structure and Recall', *Cognitive Psychology*, 9, pp. 111–151.

Matamala, A. (2018) 'One Short Film, Different Audio Descriptions: Analysing the Language of Audio Descriptions Created by Students and Professionals', *Onomazein*, 41, pp. 186–207.

Myers, J. L., Cook, A., Kambe, G., Mason, R., and O'Brien, E. (2010) 'Semantic and Episodic Effects on Bridging Inferences', *Discourse Processes*, 29(3), pp. 179–199.

Plummer, B. A., Wang, L., Cervantes, C. M., Caicedo, J. C., Hockenmaier, J., and Lazebnik, S. (2015) 'Flickr30k Entities: Collecting Region-to-Phrase Correspondences for Richer Image-to-Sentence Models', *Proceedings of the IEEE International Conference on Computer Vision and Pattern Recognition*, Washington, DC: IEEE Computer Society, pp. 2641–2649.

Ren, Z., Wang, X., Zhang, N., Lv, X., and Li, L-J. (2017) 'Deep Reinforcement Learning-based Image Captioning with Embedding Reward'. Available at: https://arxiv.org/abs/1704.03899 (accessed 18 December 2018).

Rohrbach, A., Rohrbach, M., Tandon, N., and Schiele, B. (2015) 'A Dataset for Movie Description', *Proceedings of the IEEE Conference on Computer Vision and Pattern Recognition*, Washington, DC: IEEE Computer Society, 3202–3212. Available

at: www.cv-foundation.org/openaccess/content_cvpr_2015/papers/Rohrbach_A_
Dataset_for_2015_CVPR_paper.pdf (accessed 14 December 2018).

Rohrbach, A., Rohrbach, M., Tang, S., Oh, S. J., and Schiele, B. (2017) 'Generating
Descriptions with Grounded and Co-referenced People', *Proceedings of the IEEE
Conference on Computer Vision and Pattern Recognition*, Washington, DC: IEEE
Computer Society. Available at: https://arxiv.org/abs/1704.01518 (accessed 20
December 2018).

Rumelhart, D. E. (1977) 'Understanding and summarising brief stories', in D.
Laberge and S. Samuels (eds.), Basic Processing in Reading, Perception, and
Comprehension. Hillsdale, NJ: Lawrence Erlbaum Associates.

Salway, A. (2007) 'A Corpus-based Analysis of the Language of Audio Description',
in J. Diaz Cintas, P. Orero and A. Remael (eds.), *Media for All: Subtitling for the
Deaf, Audio Description and Sign Language*, Amsterdam and New York: Rodopi,
pp. 151–174.

Shank, R. C., and Abelson, R. (1977) *Plans, Scripts, Goals and Understanding.*
Hillsdale, NJ: Lawrence Erlbaum.

Sharma, P., Ding, N., Goodman, S., and Soricut, R. (2018) 'Conceptual Captions: A
Cleaned, Hypernymed, Image Alt-text Dataset for Automatic Image Captioning',
*Proceedings of the 56th Annual Meeting of the Association for Computational
Linguistics*, Melbourne: ACL, vol. 1, pp. 2556–2565.

Smilevski, M., Lalkovski, I., and Madjarov, G. (2018) 'Stories for Images-in-Sequence
by using Visual and Narrative Components', *Communications in Computer and
Information Science*, 940, pp. 148–159.

Sperber, D., and Wilson, D. (1995) *Relevance: Communication and Cognition.* 2nd edn.
Oxford: Blackwell.

Szegedy, C., Liu, W., Jia, Y., Sermanet, P., Reed, S., Anguelov, D., Erhan, D.,
Vanhoucke, V., and Rabinovich, A. (2015) 'Going Deeper with Convolutions',
Proceedings of the IEEE Conference on Computer Vision and Pattern Recognition,
Washington, DC: IEEE Computer Society. Available at: https://arxiv.org/abs/
1409.4842 (accessed 20 December 2018).

Talmy, L. (1983) *How Language Structures Space.* New York: Plenum Press.

Vallet, F., Essid, S., and Carrive, J. (2013) 'A Multimodal Approach to Speaker
Diarization on TV Talk-Shows', *IEEE Transactions on Multimedia*, 15(3),
pp. 503–520.

Van Dijk, T., and Kintsch, W. (1983) *Strategies of Discourse Comprehension.*
New York: Academic Press.

Venugopalan, S., Rohrbach, M., Donahue, J., Mooney, R., Darrell, T., and Saenko, K.
(2015) 'Sequence to Sequence – Video to Text', *Proceedings of the IEEE Conference
on Computer Vision and Pattern Recognition*, Washington, DC: IEEE Computer
Society. Available at: https://arxiv.org/abs/1505.00487 (accessed 18 December 2018).

Vercauteren, G. (2007) 'Towards a European Guideline for Audio Description', in
J. Diaz-Cintas, P. Orero and A. Remael (eds.), *Media for All: Subtitling for the Deaf,
Audio Description, and Sign Language*, Amsterdam: Rodopi, pp. 139–150.

Vercauteren, G., and Remael, A. (2014) 'Audio-describing Spatio-temporal Settings',
in P. Orero, A. Matamala and A. Maszerowska (eds.), *Audio Description: New
Perspectives Illustrated*, Amsterdam: John Benjamins, pp. 61–80.

Wu, Y., Schuster, M., Chen, Z., Le, Q. V., Norouzi, M., Macherey, W., Krikun, M.,
Cao, Y., Gao, Q., Gao, Q., and Macherey, K. (2016) 'Google's Neural Machine

Translation System: Bridging the Gap between Human and Machine Translation.'
Available at: https://arxiv.org/abs/1609.08144v2 (accessed 18 December 2018).

Xu, J., Mei, T., Yao, T., and Rui, Y. (2015) 'MSR-VTT: A Large Video Description
Dataset for Bridging Video and Language', *Proceedings of the IEEE Conference
on Computer Vision and Pattern Recognition*, Washington, DC: IEEE Computer
Society, pp. 5288–5296.

Yao, L., Torabi, A., Cho, K., Ballas, N., Pal, C. Larochelle, H., and Courville, A.
(2015) 'Describing Videos by Exploiting Temporal Structure.' Available at: https://
arxiv.org/abs/1502.08029v5 (accessed 18 December 2018).

Yeung, J. (2007) 'Audio Description in the Chinese World', in J. Dìaz-Cintas, P. Orero
and A. Remael (eds.), *Media for All: Subtitling for the Deaf, Audio Description and
Sign Language*, Amsterdam: Rodopi, pp. 231–244.

Yus, F. (2008) 'Inferring from Comics: A Multi-Stage Account', *Quaderns de
Filologia: Estudis de Comunicació*, 3, pp. 223–249.

Filmography

Frida (2002) Directed by Julie Taymor. [Feature film]. United States: Miramax films.

The Hours (2003) Directed by Stephen Daldry. [Feature film]. USA: Paramount
Pictures.

Little Miss Sunshine (2006) Directed by Jonathon Dayton and Valerie Faris. [Feature
film]. USA: Fox Searchlight Pictures.

Saving Mr Banks (2013) Directed by John Lee Hancock. [Feature film]. UK: Walt
Disney Studios Motion Pictures.

Index

Note: Page numbers in *italics* indicate figures and in **bold** indicate tables on the corresponding pages.

access to content 135
access to environment 135
access features 121, 129
access to medium 135
accessibility: cinema, in Poland 136–137; media 4, 13, 101–112, 117; in museum environments 35–36; *see also* AudioMovie app
accessible digital content 80, 101
accessible interface 7, 124
accessible media 4, 13, 101–112, 117
ADLAB PRO 19, 34, 51
Advanced Research Seminar on Audio Description (ARSAD) 34
affective disorders 99, 103, 106–109, 112–117
Algorithmic Automated Description (AAD) 61–62
Amazon Alexa 130
Amazon Fire TV 130
Amazon Video 129
Armstrong, G. 14
Arnone, M. P. 21
art 25–27, 34–41
artificial intelligence (AI) 160
ASD *see* autism spectrum disorders
'Atalanta and Hippomenes' exhibit 45, *46–47*
Attenborough, D. 24
Attenborough and the Giant Dinosaur 126
audience experience 5, 15–27
audiences 34–35, 56–57; for cognitive diversity 101, **102–103**; remodelling AD for new 100–110, **102–103**, **105**, **107**, **109**

audio description (AD): audiences and functions of 56–57; defined 1, 76; easy-to-listen 59–62; of emotions 97–110, **102–103**, **105**, **107**, **109**; engagement and 18–20, 21, 98; experimental groups and procedure in studying 82–83, **83**, *84*; immersion and 20, 21–22, 90, **90**, 98; within the interactive aspects of 360-degree video 127–128; interactivity and 24–25; within linear storytelling 126–127; presence and 16–18; quality in 13–16; remodelled for new audiences 100–110, **102–103**, **105**, **107**, **109**; research on 1–5, *2*, 55–56; styles of 78–82, **81**, 93–94; virtual art gallery case study in 25–27; *see also* Easy-to-Read (E2R) approach; emotion recognition; museum environments; visual storytelling
audio description style 78, 90, 175
audio event detection (AED) 170
Audio for All 45
AudioMovie app 135, 136, 137–156; cinema profile of users of 146; digital profile of participants in 145; evaluation of 148–153, **149**, *152*; usability of 146–147, **147**, *148*; users' awareness of 153–155
audio subtitling 151, 154
audiovisual accessibility 97–98, 116–117; emotion difficulties and autism and 98–100; remodelling AD for 100–110; text analysis for 110–116
audiovisual transcription 16, 126, 144, 179–180

audiovisual translation 97, 113, 122, 164
autism, autistic spectrum disorders
    98–100, 117
automated approaches to storytelling
    167–170, **168**; data processing
    and annotation in *177*, 177–181;
    methodological approach to
    understanding 171–181; *see also* visual
    storytelling
automatic speaker diarisation 170
automating AD 7, 159, 161, 167–170

Ballester, A. 61
Bazin, A. 16
BBC iPlayer 129
Bernabé, R. 59
Bianchi-Berthouze, N. 21
Bilandzic, H. 19
blind and partially sighted participants
    (BPSP): AD evaluation by *92*, 92–93;
    comprehension issue with 90–91, **91**;
    emotional reception by **89**, 89–90;
    experimental groups and procedure
    with 82–84, *84*; film language
    reception by 87–89, **88**; immersion and
    90, **90**; narrative space and time and
    84–86, **85**; narrative theme 86–87, **87**;
    results with 84–93, **85**, **87–92**
blind and visually impaired, AD for
    (BVI-AD), emotion recognition and
    104–105, **105**
Blue Planet 172
Branje, C. J. 14
Braun, S. 14, 55, 63
Busselle, R. 19
BVI-AD 104–105, **105**; text analysis and
    110–111, 110–116, **113**, **115**

Cabeza-Cáceres, C. 61, 78
Carroll, N. 77
cinematic AD style (AD2) 79, **81**
Cognitive Narratology (CN) 163–164
cognitive-pragmatic lens: human
    storytelling through 162–164; visual
    storytelling through 164–167, **165**, **167**
computer vision 159–160, 167–170, **168**
content description 159–162, **161**,
    167–168, 171, **182–188**, 190–191
conventional AD style (AD1) 79, 80, **81**
curiosity and engagement 21
CXT-AD 108–110, **109**, **110**; discussion
    of 116–117; text analysis and **110–111**,
    110–116, **113**, **115**

denotative audio description 80
Denver Art Museum 34, 35
*Diagnostic and Statistical Manual of
    Mental Disorders, DSM V* 99
Disney company 186
Ditton, T. B. 16–17, 22
Douglas, Y. 20

Eardley, A. F. 36
EASIT (Easy Access for Social Inclusion
    Training) 50, 51
EastEnders 171
easy audio description 63–64, 67–68
Easy-to-listen audio descriptions 59–62;
    language adaptation for 67–68; steps
    in creation of 63–67
Easy-to-Read (E2R) approach 49–51,
    65–66, 68–69; defined 58; text
    simplification and 57–59, *59*
EMO-AD 106–108, **107**, **110**; discussion
    of 116–117; text analysis and **110–111**,
    110–116, **113**, **115**
emotion 21
emotion recognition: autism and
    difficulties in 98–100; blind and
    visually impaired AD and 104–105,
    105; concluding remarks on
    remodelling for 117; discussion of
    strategies for 116; introduction to AD
    and 97–98; remodelling AD for new
    audiences and 100–110, **102–103**, **105**,
    107, **109**; text analysis and **110–111**,
    110–116, **113**, **115**
emotion recognition difficulties (ERDs)
    98–100, 116–117; AD for people
    with 106–108, **107**; target text types
    and features and **110–111**, 110–116,
    113, **115**
emoto-descriptive translation strategy
    106–107, **107**
engagement 18–20, 98; curiosity and 21;
    movement, emotion, and 21; systems
    of measurement of 22–24
Erkau, J. 122
ethnographic museums 37–40

Fan Museum 40–41
Fels, D. I. 14–15, 55, 122
Fernández-Torné, A. 62, 78
Fidyka, A. 24
film 55–56, 76–78; accessibility to,
    in Poland 136–137; human versus
    automated approaches to AD and

171–181; interpretation in watching 77; methodology for analysis of AD and 78–83; story arcs of 174–176, **175**, **176**; styles of AD and 78–82, **81**; *see also* AudioMovie app; *Nuit Blanche* film experience 80–82, 84, 93
focalisation 164
Freeman, J. 16, 36, 77, 94
Fresno N. 15, 18–19
Frida **165**, 165–166
Fryer, L. 14, 16, 36, 62, 77, 94

Goffman, I. 16
Google Home 130
Greco, G. M. 13
Guidelines for Easy-to-Read Materials 58
Guillamon, C. 80
Gutt, E.-A. 166

Halliday, M. A. K. 163–164
Hamilton, A. 100
Hamlet 15–16, 20
Hargadon, A. 20
Hasan, R. 163–164
Hobson, R. P. 99
Hours, The 166–167, **167**
human storytelling: annotations in 180–181; cognitive-pragmatic frameworks of 162–164; methodological approach to studying 171–181
Hutchinson, R. S. 36

IFLA (International Federation of Library Associations and Institutions) 58–59, 63, 66
immersion 20, 21–22, 90, **90**, 98; systems of measurement of 22–24
Immersive Accessibility (ImAc) project: conclusions 130–131; discussion on 129–130; focus group for 124–126; introduction to 121–122; literature review on 122–123; research methodology on 123–124; results on 126–129
Inclusion Europe 63, 66, 67
Independent Television Commission (ITC) 14; Sense of Presence Inventory (ITC-SOPI) 17–18; systems of measurement 22–24
Inglourious Basterds 3
installed interpretives 34

intellectual disabilities 6, 50–51
interactivity 24–25
interlingual translation 1
intersemiotic translation 1, *2*
intralingual translation 1

Jakobson, R. 1
Jankowska, A. 61, 62
Jennett, C. 19, 22, 23
Johnson-Laird, P. 164
Jones, M. T. 16

Kintsch, W. 63, 65
Knigge, M. 122
Kotler, P. 14
Kruger, J. 22, 23, 90
Kurz, I. 14

Lessiter, J. 19
lexico-grammatical cues 164
linear storytelling 126–127
Little Miss Sunshine 175–176, **176**, 181–189, **182–185**, **187–188**
Lombard, M. 16–17, 18, 22
Lopez, M. 19

machine learning 168–169, 174, 190
Mary Poppins 186
Maszerowska, A. 3
Matamala, A. 3–4, 13, 24, 62, 78
Maximilian of Austria, Miramare Castle exhibition 36–37
McGonigle, F. 61
McShane, M. 19
media 4, 7
media accessibility (MA) 4, 13
MeMAD (Methods for Managing Audiovisual Data: Combining Automatic Efficiency with Human Accuracy) 160
MeMAD Video Corpus (MVC) 171
Mental Model Theory (MMT) 162, 164
Michaelson, M. 34
Mighty Angel, The 78
Minsky, M. 16
Miramare Castle 36–37, 41–43
mobile applications 135, 137, 143–145, 149–150
Mr Bean: The Animated Series 112–114, **113**
Murray, J. 21–22
museum environments: accessibility in 35–36; concluding remarks on 51–52;

easy-to-read language to enhance accessibility in 49–51; ethnographic 37–40; Fan Museum 40–41; introduction to 33–34; Maximilian of Austria, Miramare Castle exhibition 36–37; National Angkor Museum 43–44; new audiences in 34–35; new forms of access in 36–51; outdoor areas of 41–44; university 44–49

narrative AD style (AD3) 79, 80–81, **81**
narrative storytelling 191
National Angkor Museum 43–44
Netflix 59, 129
Nirenburg, S. 19
Nord, C. 78
Nuit Blanche 79–82, **81**, 93–94; AD evaluation on **92**, 92–93; comprehension issue with 90–91, **91**; emotional reception of **89**, 89–90; film language reception and 87–89, **88**; immersion and 90, **90**; narrative space and time of 84–86, **85**; narrative theme of 86–87, **87**

OFCOM 60
Olivier, L. 15
Orero, P. 3–4, 13, 55, 59, 64
outdoor areas, museum 41–44

people with sight loss (PSL) 33, 35–36; *see also* museum environments
Plantinga, C. 77
Poland, cinema accessibility in 136–137
Polish Film Institute (PISF) 136–137
Polish National Centre for Research and Innovations 135
presence 16–18, 98; people with sight loss (PSL) in museum environments and 36; systems of measurement of 22–24
Principal Axis Factoring (PAF) 18

QR codes 45, *47*, 137–138, *141–142*
QSoundLabs 128
quality, audio description 13–16; systems of measurement for 22–24

Rai, S. 67
Ramos Caro, M. 77–78
Rand, J. 35

reading and learning difficulties 6, 50, 56–57, 59
reception study 78–93, 100–101, 116
Reiss, K. 104, 106
Relevance Theory (RT) 162–163
Return of Mr Bean, The 105–110, 114–116, **115**
Rodríguez, A. 62

Samis, P. 34
Saving Mr Banks 186, **187**
Schmid, W. 76
Secchi, L. 45
Shakespeare, W. 15
Shardlow, M. 57–58, 67
Shlesinger, M. 14
Short, J. 16
simplification 50, 57–59, 68
Singer, M. J. 24
skopos 15–16, 108–110, **109**, 110
'skopostheorie' 103
Slater, M. 17, 20, 24
Snow White: The Fairest of Them All **111**, 111–112
Snyder, J. 60
social-emotional reciprocity 100
Spanish Association for Standardisation and Certification (AENOR) 58
Sperber, D. 164
Starr, K. L. 55, 189
story arcs 174–176, **175**, **176**
storytelling, linear 126–127
subjectivity 89, 106, 161
Szarkowska, A. 62

tactile tours 45–49, *48*
Tate Modern, London 33
telepresence 16
text elaboration 65
text simplification (TS) 57–59, *59*
text types 104, 106
theory of mind (ToM) 106
Tinker, M. A. 58
Travers, M. 186, 188

Udo, J. P. 55, 122
Uljarevic, M. 100
United Nations Convention on the Rights of Persons with Disabilities (UNCRPD) 13, 56, 123
Universal Design 56
university museums 44–49

user-centred design (UCD) 123–124; focus group on 124–129; within interactive aspects of 360-degree video 127–128; results on 126–129; spatial audio within 360-degree environment 128–129

user research/study 77–78, 82–83, 122, 124–126

Usoh, M. 17, 24

van Dijk, T. A. 63, 65
Vercauteren, G. 15
video description 169, 171–174, 176, 179
viewer experiences 130
Vilaró, A. 64
virtual art gallery 25–27
Virtual Barbershop 128
virtual reality (VR) 25–27
Visual Genome 168
visual impairments 1, 22, 78, 97, 153
visual storytelling: cognitive-pragmatic frameworks of 162–164; through cognitive-pragmatic lens 164–167, **165**, **167**; computer vision and automated description of audiovisual content and 167–170, **168**; conclusions and next steps in 189–191; data processing and annotation in *177*, 177–181; human understanding and description of audiovisual content and 161–167, **165**, **167**; initial observations on 181–189, **182–185**, **187–189**; introduction to 159–161, **161**; materials in 171–176, **173**, **175**, **176**; methodological approaches to 171–181; story arcs in 174–176, **175**, **176**

VocalEyes 25, 50
Volver 77

Walczak, A. 62, 78, 94, 122
WCAG 2.1 62, 64–65
What Happens While 143
Wilbur, S. 20
Wilken, N. 90
Williams, P. 34
Wilson, D. 164
Winnie the Pooh 186, **188**
Witmer, B. G. 24
World Health Organization (WHO) 123
World Wide Web Consortium (W3C) 64–65
WYSIWYS paradigm 79

YouTube 45, 124, 126

Zabalbeascoa, P. 76

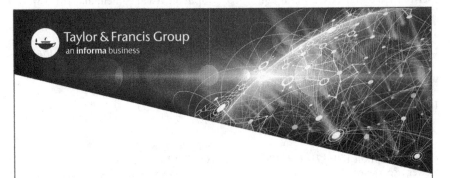

Printed in the United States
by Baker & Taylor Publisher Services